ID0929974

Lead Domination

Heather & Joyce

All the best in the care
and Nurturing of your sales
leads.

Jamie 5/09

The care and nurturing of a sales lead.

Lead Domination

21 Proven Strategies
for Effectively Generating Leads and Converting Leads into Sales

Jamie Klein

Lore Institute Publishing
SAN CLEMENTE, CALIFORNIA

ATTENTION CORPORATIONS, UNIVERSITIES, COLLEGES, AND PROFESSIONAL ORGANIZATIONS:

Quantity discounts are available on bulk purchases of this book for educational, gift purposes, or as premiums for increasing magazine subscriptions or renewals. The author is an accomplished keynote speaker and is available for educational training based on the content of his book. Special books or book excerpts and personnel presentations can also be created to fit specific needs.

For information, please contact
leaddomination@loreinstitute.com

Although the author and publisher have made every effort to ensure the accuracy and completeness of information contained in this book, we assume no responsibility for errors, inaccuracies, omissions, or any inconsistency herein. Any slighting of people, places, or organizations is unintentional.

First printing 2009

ISBN 978-0-9821630-5-4 (hardcover)
ISBN 978-0-9821630-6-1 (softcover)
LCCN 2008938317

Susan Klein

To my loving wife Susan, who was so supportive and allowed me to focus on countless days of planning, creating, writing, editing, and designing this book. She helped me in my search to find the right illustrator for the characters; she also helped produce the front cover of this book. My wife is a fashion designer; she hand made with loving care my tie and handkerchief for the picture on the front cover. Honey, thank you so much for your understanding, support, and for being my wife and my best friend. I love you very much.

And to all my marketing and sales friends who worked with me through the years. We experienced together the thrill of victory and the great lessons of defeat, which both made this book possible. Creating this book was a little like having a baby. It look thirty years to conceive and, once conceived, nine months to develop. As the nine months advanced, we could hardly wait to get it delivered. Thanks to Allan Burns, Deb Ellis, and Cathy Bowman of About Books for helping me deliver the book. A special thanks for the encouragement from Neil Freiberg, Doug Dykehouse, Carlos Hill, Eve Findling, and Mike Eckroat, who were there with their mental support as I gave birth to my first book. A high five to Neil Freiberg and Mike Eckroat for the countless humorous hours we spent on the phone completing the final edition of this book.

Preface

WHAT YOU ARE ABOUT to read will change your sales and marketing results forever. After thirty years of exceptional performance in sales and marketing for some of the most respected brands in the world, I have perfected a sales and marketing program called *lead domination* that works in today's complicated sales and marketing world. I will share in this book the vital 21 strategies that are the keys of success. The great news is that they're easy to learn and really will make a big difference in your sales and marketing economics. If your sales and marketing programs have anything to do with prospecting for a lead and then selling that lead your product, you are holding in your hands a sure way of substantially improving your business— guaranteed.

As with most things in life, you need to follow the right steps for success in sales and marketing; if you do, the results you will achieve can be quite astounding. The right steps and strategies you need for success are contained in this book. The presentation is simple, logical, understandable, and can produce powerful results, and the information applies to all sales and marketing programs that depend on generating leads and converting those leads into sales.

The formula for success consists of 21 proven strategies. The 21 chapters of this book examine each one of those strategies in detail. Essentially, the strategies can be grouped according to four very simple concepts you have used all your life for success: preparation, performance, revenue, and results. I will share with you what to prepare and practice, how best to perform what you are practicing, how most effectively to produce revenue, and how to measure your results so you can accelerate what is working best and forecast powerful results as you move ahead.

When you apply these 21 strategies and four concepts to your sales and marketing programs, everything will change. Your cost for each lead will be less, your leads will be more qualified, more leads will purchase your product, and more leads who purchase your product will purchase again and/or refer friends. It is that simple, and I promise you the most impressive results you have ever achieved in the realm of lead management.

With these 21 traits you can become a master at developing profitable sales and marketing enterprises, effectively managing growth, and converting challenges into opportunities. Your new-found lead management skills will allow you to craft meaningful new programs to meet the demands of today's changing sales and marketing realities.

Because of these 21 strategies I have become one of the premier real estate sales and marketing experts in North America. So can you. I am often asked by industry leaders to speak and/or consult throughout North America on sales, marketing, and lead management practices. *All the major developments I have led since 1980 have concluded as profitable enterprises in all scopes of review. This result was clearly achieved because of the 21 sales and marketing strategies fully explained in this book.*

I hope you enjoy this book but most of all your new-found success.

If you have comments or questions about the 21 proven lead strategies or anything else in *Lead Domination*, feel free to email me at

leaddomination@loreinstitute.com

Table of Contents

How to Manage Leads So You Dominate the Competition and Your Market

Part One: Introduction

Part Two: Marketing

Part Three: Innovation and Execution

Part Four: Sales

Part One
Introduction

Introduction

How to Manage Your Leads So You Dominate

I AM SO EXCITED about writing this book that I find I am having a hard time sleeping. Not that sleeping is something I do a great deal of anyway. In the words of my favorite rock band, Bon Jovi: "Until I am six feet under / I don't need a bed; / Gonna live while I am alive / I'll sleep when I am dead!" I'm sure many of you have been excited about projects and can relate to how I feel.

Now, how does someone get so excited about lead management? In my case I have been generating leads and/or converting leads into sales for over thirty years. It's what I do, what I do best, and what I love to do. Of course, I would rather be the drummer for Bon Jovi, but since that is probably not going to happen soon, I will continue to dedicate my life to lead management and now teaching lead domination. My real excitement comes from the fact that, by sharing with you my best practices on how to dominate in your lead performance, your sales and marketing enterprise will make a dramatic change for the better.

During the thirty years I have been managing different kinds of leads, part of that time has been devoted to consulting for other companies, which is still the case today. I have also had the privilege of working in executive leadership roles, helping with lead management programs for the real estate divisions of some of the finest companies in the world, such as Marriott, Four Seasons, and Starwood, to name a few.

Because of the results I achieved with my lead management programs, I was strongly encouraged to continue to perfect what I had been doing. I was trying new approaches in the hopes of continual improvement and had come to realize my lead management practices were a little different than most. That realization motivated me to do even more. When major brands started seeking my expertise to help them with their lead management, I became really energized and focused my energies not just on lead management but on lead domination. That led me to create the 21 proven strategies of lead management.

I am very excited through this book to bring to you in detail these 21 proven strategies of lead management. They will change the way you manage your leads. These 21 proven strategies divide into 12 for marketing, generating quality leads, and 9 for sales, converting quality leads into sales. These strategies are proven because they have been used for an extended period of time and yield exceptional results. Each of the chapters that follow explores one of these strategies in detail. If followed, they will bring you the same favorable results I had using them. You will soon not just be managing your lead process; you will be dominating your lead process with outstanding production.

Most of my lead management programs were geared to real estate and the shared ownership industry, but as I branched out to help other companies in other industries with lead management I found the principles I had developed crossed over quite well. The bottom line is if your company is generating leads and converting leads into sales, then the principles in this book will vastly improve your process. If lead generation that is converted to sales revenue is some part or a major part of your business plan, this book is a must for you.

You will find that there are two very different ways to excel in your enterprise with lead management, and you need to do them both well to dominate. The first is marketing, which is the pure generation of cost-effective qualified leads. The other is sales, which is converting these leads into purchases. I am very confident that if you follow what I have shared in this book, you can dominate your lead markets in both of these important areas.

Across the board, professional service and ownership product companies are looking to generate more leads than ever over the next few years. According to business publications, 62 percent of companies surveyed are looking to acquire new customers for their enterprises through lead generation. An overwhelming 84 percent said that they were planning a significant or moderate increase in their lead generation efforts. In other words, 84 percent of your competitors are going after your prospects with more lead generation plans, programs, people, energy, resources, and dollars than ever.

It's not just your competitors' investments in plans, programs, people, and resources that should concern you—although those things should be something of a concern. You need to be concerned with your relative standing with respect to how well you manage your leads compared to the competition. Your competitors do not have to be world-class in their lead management processes, just better than you are. Will you be out-managed in your lead processes by the competition? If competitors are investing more dollars and have superior lead management processes and a competitive product, you are going to have a very difficult time going head-to-head with them in lead performance and pro-duction.

Are your lead management plans and process up to par in light of the fact that 84 percent of your competitors are going after your same lead sources? Will your lead management process yield better results so you can diminish the effect of competition? Will your competitors out-manage you in their lead management process, leaving you with a smaller market share?

Look at this year's annual sales and marketing budgets and see what percentage of your sales and marketing dollars are going to be invested in lead generation. Write that number down, and then ask yourself whether you have a proven plan for a successful out-come for this investment? If you were to build a house, how detailed would the plans be to ensure that the end results were what you wanted? Would you look for an experienced contractor to ensure that the house you were going to build was built right and that the builder had the experience and track record to give you what you were looking for from your investment? Think of this book as your blueprint plan for getting positive end results from your significant investment in lead generation.

There is no better time than now to become the best of the best in lead management. I will share with you in this book 12 vital strategies for lead domination from a marketing standpoint, which are worth thousands of dollars of increased yield from your marketing enterprise if used properly. Then I share 9 vital sales strategies for converting leads into sales. These are pure revenue-producing guidelines to increase the effectiveness of your entire sales operation.

In Blackjack, 21 is a winner with a payoff. In lead manage-ment, these 21 sales and marketing lead strategies will also pay off when you put them into action. I have used these 21 strategies over and over again with great results, and they still have power-ful relevancy in the lead generation world today.

My present company is dedicated to bringing you the best practices when it comes to generating leads effectively and con-verting these leads into sales. For additional support beyond this book, you can become a member of our team and receive our monthly lead management newsletter and our quarterly video webcast. If you have comments, suggestions, or questions about the content of this book, you can send us an email. Feel free to establish a relationship with our team. Our email address for your comments and support is leaddomination@loreinstitute.com. We would love to hear from you.

Of course, I would be remiss if I did not mention that I cannot even count how many lead generation programs I have tried that did not work. I was told by my editor that it is not a good practice to review my failures. But they taught me as much about what not to do as my successes taught me about what to do. So I do not offer in this book lead ideas that do not work. If you want to try something new and want our opinion, feel free to email us what it is you are planning to do and let us comment. There will be a good chance that during our thirty years in the business we may have done what you are thinking about or something similar.

There are four basic ways to gain knowledge from this book. I tend to be more of a visual learner myself, and I think we visual learners are cheated in business education and improvement books. I find most of the books I have read are filled with words and charts. Now, words and charts are not usually what I love, but I love to learn, so I read these books anyway.

I designed this book for all the different styles of learning, includ-ing my personal favorite of not reading at all. Yes, fans of visual learning, this is the perfect book for you because all you have to do is go to the end of each chapter and look at the pictures.

That's right—at the end of each chapter I have included an action scene that depicts the essence of the entire chapter. Just look at the picture, and all the words in the chapters will come to you. How is that for a five-diamond experience? Imagine how much more you can absorb using a combination of all the learning opportunities this book offers.

Here are the four different ways to learn from this book:
1. Read the words.
2. Read just the paragraphs highlighted for you in the margins.
3. Just look at the pictures at the end of each chapter.
4. Use all three of these together for the best learning experience.

I have not just created visuals at the end of each chapter but have also created characters to guide you through this book and enhance your learning processes and experience. You will relate to each of these characters and their personalities, and I am sure you have people in your organization who are very similar to each of them. These characters are your personal guides through the book. So I think it is only appropriate that I introduce you to your personal guides.

This Book Comes Complete with Your Full Support Staff!

First, let me explain a little about why we picked the characters we did. The business world can be tough. At times, it's a lot like living in the jungle. Some enterprises will survive, and some will not. To ensure that you not only survive but prosper with your lead performance strategies, both from a sales and marketing standpoint, let me introduce your support staff.

I would like you to think of your business world as a jungle and your sales and marketing programs as your means of survival. In the jungle, as we all know, lions are the kings of survival. Always learn from the best, right? So, lions will be your personal guides to survival in this book.

A female lion hunts for food. That is her specialty and what she does best. Why have a male lion hunt for food when a female does it so well? When the female lion kills prey, she feeds it to the male lions. Like the female lion, in our business enterprise the marketing teams are the only ones who should hunt for leads. Why? Because they are the most effective and efficient at it. When the marketing teams hunt down the leads, they feed them to the sales team. So in this book you have a very knowledgeable and experienced female lion who will give you great tips on hunting for leads for the marketing side of your enterprise.

Male lions have big egos and are very self-assured and confident. They depend on the females to hunt and feed them, and in return they protect the pride. Likewise, most sales teams have big egos and are very self-assured and confident. Sales teams depend on marketing teams to feed them leads, but the survival of the sales and marketing enterprise is dependent on sales converting the leads marketing gives it into purchases. So in this book the male lion will provide tips, guidance, and support to your sales operation.

In the jungle there are hyenas that watch the lions, always looking for them to make a mistake. When the lions do make a mistake, the hyenas rush in and take their food away. In your sales and marketing world, your competition waits for you to make a mistake, and when you do, they rush in and take your leads and/ or sales away. Most of the time, sales and marketing teams are not aware of their losses to the competition in terms of prospective leads and leads that should have been converted to sales, but getting your share of leads is a very big part of survival in the jungle. The lions know that if they make too many mistakes, the hyenas will take enough of their food away that they will not survive.

The hyenas are in this book to teach you the problems frequently made in sales and marketing environments. They will share with you the problems you need to look out for and correct; otherwise, the competition will rush in and take your market share away from you. I have learned a great deal about what not to do, and the hyenas will share these lessons with you so you do not make the same mistakes. I expect you will fully understand the personality of the hyena because, unfortunately, every sales and marketing organization has hyenas. Hyena problems are both *external* with the competition as well as *internal* with your own teams as we will point out in this book.

In the jungle, lion prides support both female lions in their hunting and male lions in their defense. In the business jungle, sales and marketing receives support from the all-important administrative team. Its members are represented by lion cubs. You cannot survive in the sales and marketing jungles without skilled support from administrative teams.

The leaders or managers of your company must do the best they can to make sure there are not too many obstacles in the way of the sales and marketing team. These obstacles will reduce your effectiveness in hunting for leads and converting them into sales. Leadership is represented in the book by the safari leader, who provides great leadership tips.

Finally, there are the lead characters. Leads are the reason we are in business. They are what we invest in and what we prospect and work so hard to generate and convert into sales. These characters are qualified leads whom we want to have viewing our products. There is lots of competition vying for these leads and looking to capture their time, dollars, and interest. You really need to take care of these leads and give them your very best presentations before, during, and after you meet with them. The name of the game is converting leads to sales.

The Female Lion

The Female Lion represents the marketing team, which is responsible for hunting for leads—and not just any leads but the leads the Male Lion (or your sales team) likes to be fed. The Female Lion is very smart and does her homework to identify where leads are hiding so she can track them down without expending too much effort. Likewise, marketing teams have to understand how to generate the most cost-effective leads, the ones that meet budgeted cost per lead targets and are most likely to be converted into sales. These sales give marketing the ability to go out and hunt for more leads. Without the great lead hunting skills of this Female Lion, the pride cannot survive.

The Male Lion

The Male Lion represents the sales team. The Male Lion does not want just any old lead; he wants his favorite kind: qualified leads. When you feed the Male Lion the leads he likes, he turns them into sales. The more you feed the Male Lion what he likes, the more sales revenue he produces. The Male Lion takes care of the pride through his sales revenue production, which keeps the sales and marketing teams together and in business.

The Hyena

The Hyena represents potential problems the lion pride will need to confront in the sales and marketing jungle, both external and internal. Most sales and marketing teams have hyenas on them; they are the ones who are not the best team players and not very good at supporting a positive working environment. Like it or not, I am sure each of you can think of hyenas who work for your teams.

If you are lucky enough not to have hyenas on your teams, they will still be found among your competition.

The Hyena represents the problems that your own team represents as well as problems that your competition represents. You can be much more successful if you understand potential problems and avoid them. Millions of dollars are wasted in the sales and marketing world each year by companies that make mistakes that have been made for years. The Hyena will help you avoid these mistakes by giving voice to the attitudes and assumptions that lie behind them. Take what he says with a grain of salt, but learn to recognize his attitudes, in case you find them among your own employees. If you do, you'll need to take the appropriate steps. The Hyena is always trying to slack off and undermine the team and is not very positive in your work environments. When he represents the competition, he is trying to take your market share away. The better the pride deals with this situation, the better its existence within the jungle will be.

The Safari Leader

The Safari Leader represents your sales and marketing management. His job is to remove as many obstacles that may get in your way in the sales and marketing jungle as possible; that is why he carries a machete. The Safari Leader has maps close at hand, which are his strategic and written business plans, so he can keep your team on track. This leader also has a compass to determine where you are currently compared to where the maps say you

Hello, it's going to be nice working with you on leadership and management. Except for the hyena, we have a really good team.

need to be. Finally, the leader has binoculars to look out and forecast the future. All these tools are important so you can make necessary adjustments.

The Lion Cubs

The Lion Cubs represent your administrative support staff. They must support the work of the Female and Male Lions by doing things such as keeping track of how many leads

have been hunted down and how many have been given to sales. Without the great administrative skills of these Lion Cubs, the pride could not survive.

The Leads

Here are the stars of this book. They are the reason this book was written and probably the reason you are reading it. Your ability to generate quality leads in the correct amount to hit your revenue budgets and to convert them from leads to sales is what lead domination is all about.

Your book support team will provide you with valuable information about lead domination skills as you read this book. In the margins of the book you will see your book support team members holding their highlighters so you can go right to the most important paragraphs in the chapters, whether that is marketing, sales, leadership, or administration. If it has to do with marketing, you will see the Female Lion in the margins; for sales you will see the Male Lion in the margins, and so on. When appropriate, sometimes more than one figure will appear in the margin. This feature, again, is a way to help you pull the most relevant information out of this book easily.

In the future these characters will be featured in our monthly newsletter as well as in an animated training video we are producing based on this book. For information on our monthly sales and marketing newsletter or our up-and-coming animated training film, please contact us at leaddomination@loreinstitute.com.

Lastly in this introduction, I want to talk about *lead domination*. I did not just pick a title randomly for my book. Lead domination is a business lifestyle that companies either have or wish they had. It is a vital part of a sales and marketing culture that leadership must establish and nurture. If you are in the lead business today, your lead management enterprise while you read this book is either moving toward a dominating or diminishing lead lifestyle. If you do not pay attention to your lead management, it will usually get worse, and if you have a healthy direction with your lead lifestyle team, it will always get better. You must be proactive with respect to your lead management team lifestyle.

Also know that lead domination is a journey, not a destination. The journey never really ends as you continue to try to improve the sales and marketing sides of your enterprise. The best way you can do that is by following the 21 proven strategies presented in this book.

There are studies that have shown some sales and marketing teams that work for very impressive, branded *Fortune* five hundred **companies only follow up effectively on about 20 percent of the leads their companies provide. That is a shocking reality.** I am sure the leaders of these companies do not know of this situation, or they would do something about it. The problem is there is nothing to show these companies what poor lead lifestyles exist within their organizations.

With this book you can now score your lead domination process just like in a sporting event. By the end of this book you will know how to keep score and how effective your lead management lifestyle really is. Where does your company stack up today? What have you done to ensure you have a lead lifestyle that is moving toward domination and not diminishing?

I believe you have to know where you are in your current lead management program before you can decide where you want to go. After you have read this book, you can determine where your team is with its lead management process by completing the lead domination ratings explained at the end of this book. Then give yourself a clear path as to where you want to go by focusing on one or a few of the different 21 proven strategies you want to improve first. This process is a great way to move closer to lead domination, and it will bring the best practices in this book alive in your sales and marketing organizations.

For years my successes were tied to what was best described in the book *Good to Great* by Jim Collins as a "culture of discipline." The formula for a disciplined culture is disciplined people, disciplined thoughts, and disciplined action. First, though, you have to understand and commit yourself to what it is you want to be disciplined about. This book will give you specific areas in your lead process to be committed and disciplined about.

There is a great deal of material in each chapter. I would highly recommend that you read no more than one chapter at a time and reflect on what you can implement in your organization before you read on.

It look thirty years to develop the 21 proven strategies, and it is with great pleasure on behalf of your character support team and myself that we present this informative book, *Lead Domination*. Enjoy your learning.

Part Two
Marketing

The Building of Your 21 Proven Strategies

It has taken over thirty years to develop these 21 proven strategies. After years of testing, refining, performance enhancing, and reporting on actual results with a variety of products and brands, we offer these proven strategies as opportunities to effectively improve the sales and marketing of your products. The boxes below show you the marketing side of our proven strategies, which we will be covering in detail on the pages that follow.

Marketing

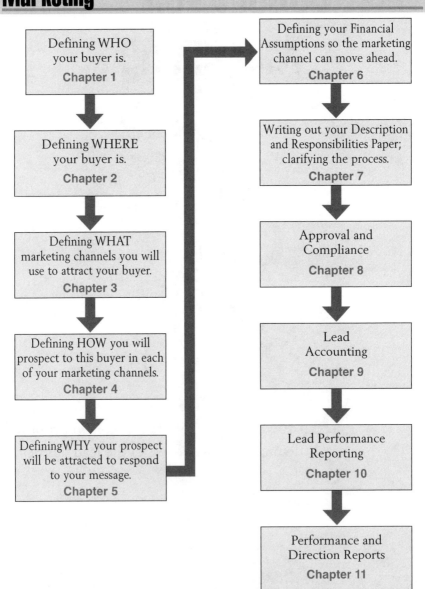

Defining WHO your buyer is.
Chapter 1

Defining WHERE your buyer is.
Chapter 2

Defining WHAT marketing channels you will use to attract your buyer.
Chapter 3

Defining HOW you will prospect to this buyer in each of your marketing channels.
Chapter 4

Defining WHY your prospect will be attracted to respond to your message.
Chapter 5

Defining your Financial Assumptions so the marketing channel can move ahead.
Chapter 6

Writing out your Description and Responsibilities Paper; clarifying the process.
Chapter 7

Approval and Compliance
Chapter 8

Lead Accounting
Chapter 9

Lead Performance Reporting
Chapter 10

Performance and Direction Reports
Chapter 11

Introduction

Lead Generation

Twelve proven strategies for effective lead generation

IF YOU WANT TO dominate in the world of leads, you need to be a lead expert. If you aren't, make sure someone on your team is. There is very little financial forgiveness in the lead business for inexperienced marketers trying to generate quality leads. Generating leads in the quantities and the quality you need to be competitive in today's sales and marketing world is the lifeline of your business. The leads you generate must also have an acceptable conversion ratio of presentations to sales. Generating these quality leads takes planning, discipline, commitment, sound processes, and experience.

So your lead generation process must target the most qualified potential buyers. Where are these buyers? How do you attract them? What will make them respond to your offering? If you are marketing a product, keep in mind that most of your customers' most valuable asset is time. How can you get customers to share their most valuable asset with you? Can you get them to invest enough time to become potential leads for your offering?

Before we get too far into this subject of lead generation I would like to establish some ground rules for the purpose of clarification. First, if you are going to develop marketing channels that produce leads, you must be able to track those channels. If you can't, they don't belong in your lead generation budget. Public relations (PR), brand building, and product awareness should not be items in your lead generation budget. Any money you spend to produce leads must be analyzed in terms of the number of leads produced, the cost per lead, and the volume per lead. If you cannot accurately calculate these three vital statistics (which we will discuss later in detail) for a given marketing channel, do not spend a single dime out of your lead generation budget. If you need brand awareness or product PR, then create another sub-section of your budget for these expenses.

Second, lead generation is the responsibility of marketing, not sales. Prospecting for leads takes very skilled marketing talent. Keep in mind that marketers should not just be looking for leads but for leads that convert to sales.

Who converts your leads to sales? The answer is your sales team, not your marketing team. Keep the sales team focused on converting leads to sales and the marketing team focused on generating quality leads.

In most sales and marketing enterprises you will find some overlap between sales and marketing responsibilities. Where there is overlap there is inefficiency. You find overlap especially in owner programs. Owner programs are marketing lead generation programs that center on the owners of your products, producing leads called referrals wherein sales people make sales and want to protect the owners' future lead generation for themselves. If you allow this to happen, you are letting salespeople undertake a marketing task. I promise it will not be as successfully executed as it could be if marketing was to work the owner base. Would you give a marketing person leads to convert to sales? If you did, the results would probably not be what you want. If you give sales people their owners to work for leads and expect that they are going to generate owner referral leads, they will, but not as successfully as trained marketing personnel.

Also, if you give marketing people the ability to pre-qualify leads before you turn them over to sales, you would be giving marketing people sales responsibilities, which would also be inefficient. Please look at all your programs and make sure you do not have sales creeping into marketing or marketing creeping into sales. This is an important principle to follow if you want to dominate in lead production in your field.

How will marketing professionals know when they are producing the level of quality leads needed for sales? The best way is through what I call *the quality leads formula*. Marketing must diversify, monitor marketing channels, redirect marketing dollars as is appropriate, and adjust lead production up and down to produce a sufficient number of leads. The quality leads formula has four parts: the number of leads produced compared to budget, the cost per lead, the volume per lead compared to budget, and the cost as a percentage of revenue, which is what I call the report card.

If you want to dominate through your lead management, you need to deliver the most qualified leads. Let's expect our marketing experts to know this formula very well. By the end of this section you should understand clearly what this formula is and how best to use it. If your marketing team can generate the number of quality leads you need in order to meet budgeted cost per lead (CPL) and volume per lead (VPL) per budget requirements, you will be on your way to success.

To generate leads you need a well-thought-out plan of action and a world-class process for producing and tracking quality leads. If you master the marketing lead generation sections of this book, you can acquire years' worth of marketing experience. I am confident you can use that knowledge to dominate your competitors and increase your market share of lead generation and sales.

Regardless of whether you are an experienced marketing executive who just wants to obtain better results from your lead production program or are new to the lead business and want to protect your investments, it is so important that you have a plan of action before you start to spend marketing dollars to generate leads. That plan of action should be a tried-and-true one. Most lead budgets have lots of dollars allocated for lead generation. If you are responsible for investing these dollars, make sure you have a plan that will support an "A" game. You have hundreds of thousands of dollars at risk if you don't formulate a sound plan.

Some managers think a very talented sales team can make up for marginal quality lead generation. Others are so enthusiastic about their product they imagine it will sell itself. Both of these are scenarios for disaster. What it really all comes down to is how effectively you can generate leads. These leads you generate must be convertible at target levels to sales. Get that right and your enterprise will be well on its way to success.

Concerning the theory that if you just build it the leads will come, let me share my experiences with you. I had the privilege of heading up the sales and marketing efforts at the St. Regis New York and the St. Regis Aspen. When you think of products that should sell themselves, these two might well be on your short list. They are world-class luxury products with great locations: 5th Avenue in New York City and the base of the famous Ajax Mountain in the center of Aspen, Colorado.

But guess what? When we opened both these St. Regis properties, no customers were simply standing in line waiting to hand their hard-earned dollars over to us. Instead, we spent thousands of hours focusing on lead-generation strategies. Both developing a lead plan and harvesting the leads were more than full-time jobs. Again, I cannot emphasize enough how important lead strategies are for your success, no matter what kind of product you are selling.

Through the course of this book I will share with you most of the lead plans I have developed and the strategies I have used. As you can imagine, over the thirty years I developed sales and marketing strategies I made many mistakes. But I learned from those mistakes, and they helped me produce more effective sales and marketing programs. I hope that the knowledge you gain from this book about tried-and-true successful strategies will allow you to profit from my experience and not to repeat the mistakes most sales and marketing teams make.

Before we start I would like to share with you some surprising information about lead management. It certainly shocked me when I learned about it. In *Lead Generation for the Complex Sale* author

Brian Carroll points out that only one in ten companies operates with a definition of a lead that both sales and marketing have agreed upon. Generating leads is what we do. How can we do it if we haven't defined what it is we are doing? To put it another way—how can we generate leads if we do not know what a lead is?

If you do not have a consistent definition of what a lead is, shared by both sales and marketing, now is the time to formulate one. There is no better catalyst for building bridges between sales and marketing and no better way to begin to generate a greater return on your investment than getting sales and marketing to agree to a definition of what a lead truly is.

Brian Carroll's book also points out that on average sales teams fail to act on upward of eighty percent of the leads they get—an astounding fact if it's anywhere near being accurate. More than likely the figure is high because many of the so-called leads being handed over to sales in many companies are not really leads. If you don't have a working definition of what a lead is, how can you even know? But I must also ask you how sure you are that your sales team is working all the leads you give it? Could you and your company be in the twenty-percent-or-less group with effective follow-up on leads? The real question is: How do you really know what percentage of the leads you give your sales team are followed up on effectively? I promise that any of you who study and use the next four parts of this book will know where they stand in sales and effectively follow up on their leads. This fact alone should make you sleep at night and feel much more in control of your success as far as your sales and marketing programs are concerned.

What you are about to read is what you need to know to have a successful, dominant lead generation team. What at this point could be more important?

Let's start with your two takeaways from this part of the book:

1. A clear image of what it's like to create a lead and capitalize on it.

2. The Dominating Dozen—your offensive and defensive playbook for running your lead generation team.

Below is a representation of what it looks like to generate a lead. There are four phases to this process:

1. The prospect—someone you have targeted as a good potential lead but have not marketed to yet

2. The inquiry—mostly third-party inquiries or maybe someone curious about the offering but not yet wanting any sales information

3. The lead—a qualified lead or just an inquiry who wants to know more about the offering and wants to talk to sales about it

4. The client—a lead who buys your product

So let's summarize the four phases: You start by focusing on the most qualified prospects you are going to invest your money in and market to. These are your prospects. When you begin your prospecting to these potential leads, you generate leads and inquiries, leads being interested in talking to sales and inquiries being not yet ready to talk to sales. Leads who actually talk to sales are converted at some percentage to a presentation, and a percentage of those presented to will purchase the product.

When you review the flow chart below, make sure you understand each step in the lead process and that you also have an administration lead team that understands and follows it. The administration team and what I call the lead bank team need to be fully responsible for reporting on each of the steps in the flow chart. Once reports have been submitted, you can adjust strategies or create new ones as is appropriate.

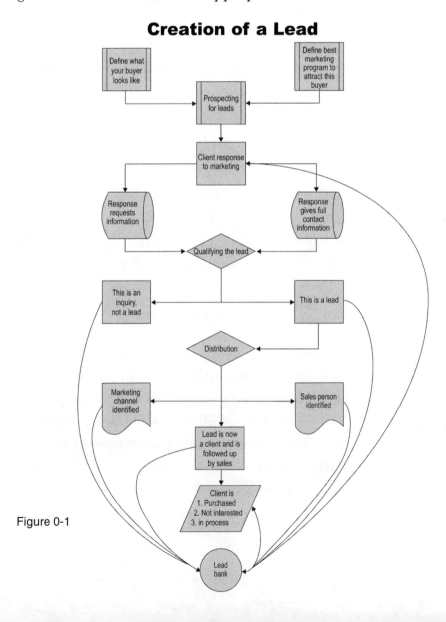

Creation of a Lead

Figure 0-1

If figure 0-1 is not completely clear to you at this point, do not be concerned. As you review the chapters in part two and beyond of this book, you will come to understand this flowchart. I recommend that at the end of the marketing section you come back and review this flowchart. At that point it should be very clear to you.

Take your time reviewing the marketing domination chart below. These are 12 of the 21 proven strategies that we will focus on in this book. These 12 are the proven marketing strategies. You really need to understand *who* is responsible on your team to execute each item, *why* these steps are important to your lead success, *what* they mean for the lead programs you implement, *when* they will be needed in the process, and *how* they are going to be done.

Marketing Domination

A Dozen Proven Lead Generation Marketing Success Strategies

1. **Defining Your Buyer**—Start by developing a clear definition of your best targeted leads. Make sure marketing and sales agree about what a lead is.

2. **Where Is Your Buyer Located?**—You need to determine where this buyer you have defined is located.

3. **Marketing Diversification**—Marketing channel diversification is essential for a balanced lead strategy.

4. **Prospecting for Leads**—You need to understand all the steps to turn your best potential prospects into quality leads.

5. **Messaging for Results**—Make sure your marketing message is in sync with your prospecting profile in order to attract the best potential leads.

6. **Marketing Financial Assumptions**—Develop your financial marketing briefs on each channel. Get key team players

(continued on next page)

to review and support your financial lead plans, assumptions, and strategies.

7. **Description and Responsibilities Paper**—Draft a description and responsibilities paper that details the people, process, accountability, and direction of each of your marketing channels.

8. **Approval and Compliance**—Get key team players to review and assess the image, quality, message to the customer, branding standards, and legal requirements of your lead marketing programs.

9. **Lead Accounting**—When a lead is generated, track the marketing channel responsible for the lead and to whom the lead is distributed for follow-up.

10. **Lead Performance**—Track vital performance statistics against targets on a daily, monthly, quarterly, and annual basis, and then redirect lead strategies appropriately as you move ahead. These vital statistics are lead counts, cost per lead, volume per lead, and percentage of cost compared to revenue produced on each channel compared to targets.

11. **Direction and Performance Vision**—This report reviews all vital statistics on each marketing channel and then presents a written executive summary on the future direction of the marketing team's strategies. This report should be completed after the lead performance reports have been deposed. It communicates to the team in writing the future lead strategies and the plan for achieving results.

12. **Marketing Innovation and Execution**—Every team needs to produce new ideas about more efficient ways of executing existing marketing strategies and about new lead strategies. Make sure you have a solid execution plan to put your innovations into practice.

Figure 0-2

Key Notes for Generating Leads

1. Make sure marketing teams are not taking on sales responsibilities and vice versa.

2. If a program cannot account for lead generation, it should not be in your lead generation marketing budget.

3. Make sure you understand all the different stages a lead goes through and that you can account for each step.

4. Know the twelve proven marketing strategies for achieving marketing lead domination. The more you use these strategies, both offensively and defensively, the more effective your lead generation will be.

Here are some comments from our characters on lead generation.

Introduction: Marketing Lead Generation

Here our characters are learning about the 12 important marketing traits.

Focus on the twelve proven strategies to achieve marketing lead domination.

Chapter 1

Defining Your Leads

Defining your leads and inquiries

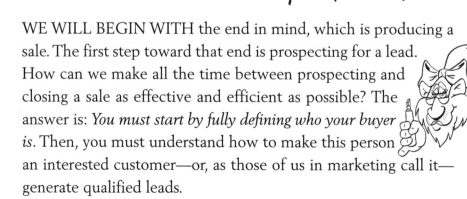

In this simple but very important chapter we will define our leads. This crucial first step will enhance the effectiveness of our marketing.

WE WILL BEGIN WITH the end in mind, which is producing a sale. The first step toward that end is prospecting for a lead. How can we make all the time between prospecting and closing a sale as effective and efficient as possible? The answer is: *You must start by fully defining who your buyer is.* Then, you must understand how to make this person an interested customer—or, as those of us in marketing call it— generate qualified leads.

Who are your best leads, and what are their principal characteristics? Don't stop there, though; define all your potential leads, even if they are not your most promising customers. There is no way to reach your full potential without doing this type of lead defining—and doing it well.

Only one out of every ten companies has a definition of a lead in writing that has been agreed upon between its marketing and sales branches. If you haven't defined who your best leads and potential leads are, then how can you possibly manage an effective lead process? It's like the old saying that if you don't know where you're going, any road will take you there—but you never know when you arrive! Let's make sure we know where we're going and which road to take. Let's also celebrate when we arrive at our destination. Simply put, you cannot manage leads until you have defined what a lead is and who your target customers are.

So what must you know about potential buyers—particularly your best leads—as well as all the leads you are looking to generate? You can start by targeting the customers you want in terms of age, income, lifestyles, life experiences, and family size.

You need to define target customers, from the most promising leads to more marginal possibilities. Sales, marketing, and management leadership teams should work together to create these definitions. This collaboration will help develop the teamwork between sales and marketing that is essential for success.

Think of the resulting definitions as constituting a kind of dart board. Leads will become more difficult to sell to as you move away from the center of your target, but talented sales people will have at least the potential to convert leads into sales from all areas on your lead target.

The key is to have marketing provide sales with quality leads. In other words, you do not just want to generate leads that are all bull's-eyes; there will be far too few, and that would slow down your lead count and your sales pace. You have to have the ability to generate leads and to sell to customers who don't match all the characteristics of your ideal client.

Let's take a look at how to define the different lead targets for your product. In my view, the potential exists to sell to all of these leads in the target except for the inquiries located in the outer rim of your target.

Figure 1-1

The sweet spot is the center, but the number of leads available there might be very small. The best strategy is to expand your base of potential leads as much as possible. Just recognize that leads who have fewer of your defined attributes and are further from your bull's-eye will probably require more effort and a little better sales presentation. In the search for new customers, though, don't try to expand too far. Consumers who do not have sufficient interest or do not have enough defined buyer characteristics, when you can control it, should not be counted as leads or be passed along to your sales team. Doing either of these things will prove counterproductive in the long run. Responses that do not meet your lead definitions are called inquiries, and these should, when possible, not be given to sales without further qualifications.

Defining your leads is a complex marketing process that should be done before you start prospecting. Prospecting is the pure marketing generation process of your leads through your marketing channels. When you start prospecting for leads, you will generate both inquiries and leads. Leads go to your sales teams. An inquiry is a response that does not meet the qualifications of a lead and therefore should not go to sales. I would recommend you define inquiries just as you have defined leads.

Inquiry follows prospecting. An inquiry is usually a response from a third party. Examples are referrals and brokers who can give you clients' names that they believe are interested. Because actual clients have not yet been contacted to determine whether they are interested, these referrals are considered inquiries rather than leads. Marketing still needs to contact these clients to determine whether there is an interest level and whether the client meets your lead definition before these inquiries can be regarded as leads. Once they are considered leads, they can be turned over to sales.

Once you have defined your leads, then you can generate leads, make presentations, and close sales. Note, though, that this process is much easier to discuss than to put into practice effectively. A lead process that produces actual sales revenue can take sometimes months to complete. One thing for sure is that this lead-to-sale process must be a team effort between sales and marketing. You cannot be successful without a talented, well-trained marketing team that is actively producing good to great leads; likewise, a talented, well-trained sales team must convert leads into sales.

Because each team member needs the other members to be successful, make sure to promote teamwork actively. Effective communication between sales and marketing is something you have to work on. It takes time, effort, and leadership to accomplish this goal, but it's well worth the investment. If you do not work at improving communication between these groups, your sales and marketing teams will separate from each other, and the result will be reduced efficiency. I have seen this happen time and again. The scenario plays out like this: Sales people tend to think marketing delivers unqualified leads, and marketing people tend to think sales cannot sell their qualified leads. Believe me, you do not want the kind of resentment that builds up from such assumptions to poison the relationship between your sales and marketing teams. Unless you adopt a proactive approach to good communication between these two important teams, though, that is precisely what is likely to happen.

The bottom line of our lead business is to make cost-effective sales. You need marketing to produce defined, targeted leads and then to hand them over to qualified sales people to convert these leads into sales. A tight-knit professional ethic is necessary for this process to unfold without a hitch. Make sure you have a respected leader in charge of the process so that meetings between teams are as productive and positive as possible.

How important is cooperation between marketing and sales? Well, imagine if a quarterback of a football team did not meet with receivers to tell them where he would be throwing the ball. It's that important. Winning teams have to work together.

That being said, though, each group has to understand its responsibilities. Make sure your sales team knows its job is to sell leads, not to produce leads or to determine whether a particular lead is qualified. Likewise, marketing's job is to produce the best leads, not to sell them. The principal responsibility of marketing is to develop a prospecting system that generates promising leads and meets the expectation of a well-trained sales team.

As you start to define your ideal lead or customer, you first need to set up a meeting with senior leadership, sales, marketing, and possibly IT, your administration lead distribution team, along with anyone else who has a role in the process, to help define your most qualified leads. Here are some activities and questions to consider at that meeting:

1. Have everyone at the meeting write down their definition of the most qualified leads. Then have everyone read what they wrote. This will make for an interesting and productive start.

2. What characteristics do the leads have?

3. What are the ideal sales opportunities?

4. What do we really need to know about the leads?

5. What would be nice to know about the leads?

6. Whom should we be focusing on, in particular?

7. What common needs are we addressing?

8. What is the likely income range of these customers?

9. What is the likely age range of these customers?

10. Where are these customers located?

11. How will this type of customer likely respond to the company's offerings?

12. What do these customers like to do that your product will enhance or encourage?

13. How big is the average family of these customers?

14. Why would these customers want to see your product?

15. Why would these customers want to buy your product?

16. How will these customers see your product?

17. Would they have to see it in order to purchase it?

Put together a draft from that initial meeting of what your best leads look like. Call another meeting to review the draft in detail with the team and get input, update it, and ensure that everyone is on the same page. From that meeting develop a completed document specifying what the buyers or qualified leads will look like. Get final input from the team. Establish and publish the definition of leads at every level, from your bull's-eyes to more peripheral targets. This is a great time to establish a definition of your inquiries and what distinguishes an inquiry from a lead. Also, this may be a good time to establish some standard operating policies that will guide how the team should deal with these inquiries and leads.

Here is an example of a lead definition that could come out of such meetings. Our leads will be customers who have been prescreened before the prospecting process has been started by marketing. Leads and inquiries should be determined by the marketing team using its definitions. If the prospecting turns up a lead or inquiry, it is defined by marketing, never by sales. Here is an example of a bull's-eye lead definition:

1. Average age: 55
2. Average family size: four
3. Average income: more than $200,000
4. Lifestyle fits your product
5. Good potential to use your product
6. History of already using your product

These important items will define a qualified lead. Some leads will have most all of these characteristics and some will have just a few. But if they have any one of 3–6, they are considered leads. All clients who want to talk to sales about additional product information, prescreened or not, will be counted as leads also.

Inquiries will be defined as any leads who have not been contacted about the product yet or meet none of the criteria above or have not called for information. Many of these leads will be given to marketing by a third party, a common situation with referral and broker marketing programs. In these cases inquiries are not aware they have been referred. They should not be passed on to sales until future prescreening is completed by marketing.

In this case the team did not stop when it had defined a lead and an inquiry but went on to define a presentation and then took it further to follow a lead through the entire lead accounting process, even identifying when an agent had a lead protected and not protected. This example represents an *outstanding* outcome to a meeting, with sales and marketing agreeing on the entire process.

Because a lead and an inquiry have been defined, you can stop here if you like and go to the key notes at the end of the chapter. Or if you like you can read on to learn about some other lead definitions. The following information is one account of a team putting together its lead definitions:

Lead Definition and Application

A lead is defined as anyone who has contacted your company and requested information about your product offerings or been prescreened by marketing. Leads are categorized as "assigned," "unassigned/DNC (do not call)," and "unregistered." If a lead has been assigned, you have the green light for sales to work it for a follow-up.

If a lead is unassigned, it has not been given to sales to work. Two examples of leads that are unassigned, regardless of qualifications, are do not call leads (customers who have registered themselves on the "do not call" state or national lists) and unregistered leads generated in a state you are not registered to sell your product in. Both of these are examples of leads that are unassignable.

Only assigned leads given to a sales person are included in the daily lead count and subsequent production/performance metric reports. Unassigned/DNC and unregistered leads are counted only for the purpose of building strategies to convert them into assignable leads.

Once a lead has been assigned, specific pieces of information must be collected about that lead. The marketing group needs to collect the lead's name with at least one of the following pieces of information: 1. telephone number (home, mobile, business); 2. email address; 3. home/business address; 4. room number if the lead is a hotel guest. The key is that the sales team must be able to contact the lead.

Presentation Definition

When you produce a lead, the only way it can be converted to a sale is if sales makes a presentation about your product. The percentage of leads converted to presentation is an important performance number. So let's define what constitutes a presentation.

A presentation is defined as a clear explanation, by a sales person, of a program's benefits and rewards in enough detail that a prospective purchaser can make a buying decision. A presentation may be made in person or over the phone. Simply giving a brochure to a client is not considered a presentation. In some applications marketing personnel may not be licensed and therefore are expressly forbidden to discuss any terms or conditions of the product offering. Only a sales person being assisted by your administrative team or lead bank can make a presentation and so change the status of the lead.

Leads either have or haven't been given a presentation. The percentage of leads who have seen presentations should be accounted for carefully and reviewed in the performance evaluations of sales agents. You want to make sure that sales and your administration team update and change lead status as is appropriate.

Lead Maintenance

To keep things as simple as possible, leads should only have three statuses: not interested, purchased, or in progress. All leads assigned to a sales person will count against his or her maximum until such a time as the sales person physically changes the status of the lead to "not interested" or "purchased" in the company database. At that point the "not interested" lead becomes unprotected, which will allow the company to remarket the lead and reassign it to other sales agents as necessary. The maximum number of leads that are protected and being operated by a sales agent in this example is 250.

Here are some definitions useful for categorizing leads:

1. **Protected leads** belong to a sales person with the entitlement of a commission or partial commission should the customers decide to purchase. These include both purchased and in-progress leads.

2. **Unprotected leads** have been given back to the company or been taken back because the sales person is no longer employed. They may be reassigned to another sales person or become company leads; either way, the sales person is no longer entitled to any commission should these customers purchase the company's products. If the lead is reassigned to the original sales person through normal rotation, all standard commissions will apply.

3. **New leads** have been assigned to a sales person by the sales administration coordinator or other authorized personnel. Once the sales person has made contact or attempted to make contact with the lead, an appropriate status change should be made. If a lead remains in the "new lead" status for more than 72 hours, it will become an unprotected lead.

4. **In-progress leads** have been assigned to sales people but have not purchased yet or have not yet said they are not interested. They are still protected.

5. **Site-visit leads** have been contacted and have scheduled a site inspection visit. The category of these leads will be reassessed after the site inspection visit. These leads are also protected.

6. **Purchased leads** have purchased products from a sales person. They are part of every sales person's owner base. Protection is provided as long as the sales person is employed in a sales role at the project site where the owner purchased the product. In addition, these owners are not counted against the maximum lead total of a sales person.

7. **Not-interested leads** have been contacted and have expressed a lack of interest in the product offering. Once a lead has been placed in "not-interested" status, it is considered unprotected and will be removed from the sales agent's maximum lead count. Should the lead call or make contact with the company in the future, the customer will be put back in rotation for assignment. The previous sales agent will not receive credit for volume or commission if a sale is produced from this lead unless by chance the customer is reassigned through rotation to the original sales agent.

8. **No-contact leads** have not been successfully contacted despite the efforts of sales agents. They are still considered leads in progress and are protected. A package may have been sent to the lead, or the lead may have been called and/or emailed, but the sales agent has not received a response. Therefore, the level of the potential client's interest cannot yet be determined. Once a lead is moved into this status and remains there for a period of time, management may reassign the lead. If interest is generated through a remarketing effort, the lead may be reassigned to a sales agent through the standard rotation process.

Key Notes for Defining Your Leads

1. Put time, money, and resources into defining your leads.

2. If you know what your lead target is, you can hit it. Make a clear target.

3. Defining your leads is one of the keys to your success as a sales and marketing enterprise.

4. Make it a team effort; bring in your best minds as you really want to get this right.

5. Initiate and maintain great communication between sales and marketing.

6. Define the best leads as a team so that marketing will know better where to market and sales will know better how to sell.

7. Put the criteria for all levels of leads in writing. Make sure all teams sign off on and agree about the criteria, especially your sales and marketing teams.

8. Continue as needed to update the definitions of your best leads on the basis of the best available information. Base your marketing strategies on these findings.

Let's hear from our characters about *defining leads.*

Chapter 1: Defining Your Leads

Here is an action scene with our characters, who have defined their leads and are starting to prospect for them.

You need to know what you are looking for before you can find it. So define who your qualified leads are before you start prospecting for them. This just makes financial sense.

Chapter 2

Locating Your Buyers

How to find the best potential leads

Once you know who your leads are, you need to know where to find them.

NOW THAT YOU HAVE defined who your buyers or best leads are, it's time to find where they are. You need to consider carefully the best locations in which to invest your marketing dollars. These locations need to have plenty of potential buyers who match the characteristics of your lead definition from last chapter.

Finding the correct demographics for your lead prospecting can require many different approaches. First, you need to identify where your defined buyer is, and then you need to understand why this buyer is interested in your offering. Before attempting to attract the buyer, you should make sure your potential buyer count in a particular location is relatively accurate. Think about the states you want to market in first and then the cities inside those states where you think your defined buyers are located in the largest quantities and greatest concentrations.

At first, this approach will not be very accurate because it is almost impossible to hit your defined buyer with any consistency when you are looking at really large population clusters. These clusters will include all kinds of people, both in your target group and outside it. Some of your initial locations will have areas with no potential interest, others with some potential interest, and others still with a lot of potential interest. The goal is to hone in on areas with lots of potential buyers.

Think of this process as being like running liquid through a filter. If there are a lot of locations where your potential buyers are, then as they go through the filter, what will come out at the end of the process will be worth the effort. Filtering your leads from different locations where you have identified potential buyers can be done in a variety of ways. For example, you may decide to do some kind of networking program that gives you a fair bit of control in your targeted areas. This marketing channel will produce highly filtered leads, assuming that you pick the right networking locations to target. You may decide, in addition or instead, to run an ad in local publications such as a newspaper, in which case you need to know which publications your target audience reads. This type of lead flow, however, will not be as precise.

Let's look at the five essential steps in the filtering process whereby you locate your buyers:

1. Determining the *location* of potential buyers
2. Estimating the *disposable income* of potential buyers
3. Characterizing the *lifestyle* of potential buyers
4. Listing *buyers who currently use your product*
5. Listing *buyers who are looking for your product.*

Location: First, identify where you think your potential buyers are, starting with the state your product and/or sales office is in and then adjacent states and cities. You are looking for the largest pool of potential buyers.

Disposable income: Within your location, you need to identify where potential customers with the disposable income to purchase your products are. This step seems quite obvious, but I have seen marketers pick a location and start marketing without having applied this additional filter.

Lifestyle: If you can filter your clients' lifestyle as well, you have just improved your marketing demographics significantly for prospecting leads. Here's an example of filtering for lifestyle: Let's say you are selling a ski or a golf property. Filtering for lifestyle would mean looking for leads who are skiing or playing golf now or have the potential to do so in the future. This is a really well-defined lead characteristic. Finding where these clients are really makes sense.

Buyers who currently use your product: If you can then filter leads who already use your product or a similar one, you will have really gotten down to qualified clients. A relatively small number of these potential buyers will be well worth the marketing investment it takes to locate them.

Buyers who are looking for your product: If you can filter leads who are looking for your product, you will really have an outstanding prospect. A broker/networking program can usually do a very good job of identifying these leads.

Depending on your goals and resources, you may want to apply all of these filters within your location. You would always start your marketing with the most filtered or qualified leads first. This graphic represents the application of your filters:

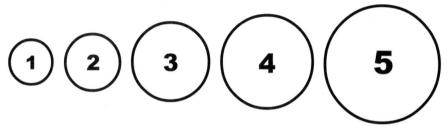

1. This smallest circle represents leads with the following characteristics:

   a. Age 55

   b. Family of four

   c. Income over $200,000

   d. Lifestyle that fits your product

   e. A history of using your product

   You need to market to these clients first.

2. This next circle represents leads with the following characteristics:

   a. Age 55

   b. Family of four

   c. Income over $200,000

   d. Lifestyle that fits your product

   Market to this group second.

3. This next circle represents leads with the following characteristics:

   a. Any age

   b. Income over $200,000

   c. Lifestyle that fits your product

This group would be next on the list you work.

4. This next circle represents leads with the following characteristics:

   a. Any age

   b. Lifestyle that fits your product

5. The last circle represents leads with the following characteristic:

   a. Income over $200,000

This last circle's scope has been limited by the application of
only one filter: disposable income of the buyers. This will be
the largest grouping of potential buyers but clearly the least
qualified. Depending on your lead count and the ability of
your sales team to convert leads like this into sales, you may
use a portion of these leads or all of them. So your least qualified leads/buyers still have had at least one of your qualifying
parameters applied to them.

These filters are very important when you are creating a variety of targeted marketing channels and less important when you
cannot target your marketing. Let's look at the differences:

Possible targeted marketing programs:

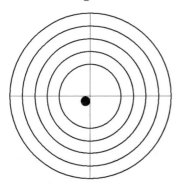

Current users—Direct targeted

Broker/networking—Direct targeted

Events—Direct targeted

Owners referrals—Direct targeted

Direct mail—Direct targeted

Possible non-target marketing programs:

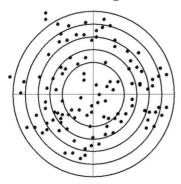

Local advertising—Shotgun targeted

National advertising—Shotgun
targeted

Web advertising—Shotgun targeted

Remember that many marketing programs have a big appetite for leads, so you may have to use all five of these circles. Keep in mind that the more potential customers you target, the more expensive the lead generation usually will be. This makes it all the more important to have your marketing filtered properly before you launch a marketing program and to have your sales team well prepared ahead of time to convert these expensive leads into sales.

Next you need to determine how many states in which you are going to be active with your different marketing channels. You should be aware that some states have registration laws for offering out-of-state products, which may impose cost and timing considerations on your marketing plan. Check with your legal team to determine how such laws might apply to your product. You cannot start marketing in these states until you have completed the registration process. The cost needs to be added to the budget of your marketing program, and the time it takes needs to be factored into your schedule.

If the state you are headquartered in has a large percentage of your potential buyers, that is great news. It will reduce your marketing cost and be a more efficient situation from a marketing standpoint. As you look to other states where you believe there are additional buyers as defined by your lead identification plan, make sure you prepare well in advance of the marketing launch dates to secure these locations and to complete any necessary registration processes. Keep in mind that registration approvals can be unpredictable sometimes and can take up to a year. Make sure you also understand the cost to complete this process. Unacceptable delays and costs can force you to look elsewhere.

If you plan to market internationally, you have much more homework to do. Get your legal team aboard early. You'll need to review tax laws governing sales of North American products in foreign countries. Sometimes these registration processes make no sense to a company based on accounting and/or tax considerations. International marketing can potentially add a great deal to your marketing base, but you must be fully aware of the additional costs, the tax laws, and accounting laws before you become too invested in foreign sales.

As you can see, it will take considerable time and resources to discover your ideal selling locations. The more you are able to prepare in advance, the better the quality and quantity of marketing lead generation will be.

Key Notes for Locating Your Buyers

1. Start by defining your locations and marketing demographics in terms of where you will invest time, money, and resources.

2. Determine the location of buyers, their age, family size, disposable income, and lifestyle, whether they are currently using your product or a similar one, and whether they have the potential to use your product.

3. Identify the states in which you want to market well in advance of your launch date. Ideally, one of these states will be where your product or sales center is already located.

4. Create a detailed chart showing what the legal requirements (if any) of registration are in each of the potential states where you would like to market your products. You should select enough states to cover the sellout of your products.

5. Make sure you understand the cost of registration and the timing of registration so you can plan accordingly in your marketing strategies.

6. For international registration you need to determine costs, tax consequences, timing, and revenue accounting issues before you proceed.

7. See what percentage of your total leads fall into your five filtering areas.

Let's hear from our characters about *locating your buyers.*

Chapter 2: Locating Your Buyers

Here is an action scene with our characters locating their leads.

You will be much more successful if you harvest leads in an area rich in your defined qualified leads. Determine where most of your buyers are before you start prospecting. I promise this will increase your effectiveness.

Chapter 3

Lead Diversification

Establishing a good mix of marketing channels for lead production

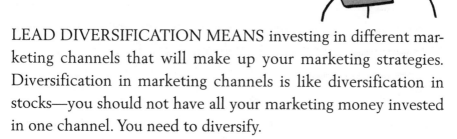

Let's think of marketing diversification as a way to hedge against risk. When one marketing channel is trending up, another may be trending down—so how do you have better control over your marketing performance? The answer is you have a number of productive marketing channels active.

LEAD DIVERSIFICATION MEANS investing in different marketing channels that will make up your marketing strategies. Diversification in marketing channels is like diversification in stocks—you should not have all your marketing money invested in one channel. You need to diversify.

You will find that top marketing professionals have invested in a strategic variety of channels. Each of these channels has different performance metrics based on the nature of the channel and its implementation. Examples of these differences include national advertising and web marketing. National advertising is usually very high in lead cost and lower in lead numbers whereas web marketing is usually very low in leads cost and high in lead numbers. By using these two marketing channels as part of your diversification approach, you can achieve better average lead counts at a predictable average cost per lead. Both will attract potential new leads that the other will not.

You will probably find that when some of your marketing channels perform well, others do not. Some channels may deliver face-to-face opportunities whereas others may involve communication by phone, email, text messaging, or business reply cards. A diversified approach will include a variety of strategies for making contact with potential customers.

Marketing should not only diversify but also monitor the vital indicators of each channel. You should look at your vital indicators then review, react, and redirect your marketing channels just like a mutual fund money manager would redirect money in or out of an investment fund in response to fluctuations in the marketplace. The more productive marketing channels you use, the more options you have to adjust, accelerate, or decelerate lead production. Overall diversification is the key to reducing risk in your marketing portfolio.

Marketing pros analyze their different channels and move marketing dollars in and out of those channels based on results. This is essential, because I can assure you that at any given time marketing sources are either in a positive or negative trend; they never simply remain neutral. You must be on top of these trends and react to them—or you could find yourself in a financial marketing tailspin.

Vital indicators of success include the number of leads produced, cost per lead (CPL), volume per lead (VPL), and cost as a percentage of sales revenue (report card).

Stop for just a minute and write down or highlight again the following:

Number of leads

Cost per lead (CPL)

Volume per lead (VPL)

Cost as a percentage of sales revenue (your report card)

Comparing these vital statistics with your budget and/or target numbers will indicate your dollar marketing channel distribution for the most effective marketing performance. Make sure that by the end of this chapter you fully understand these four vital statistics and how they relate to each other as well as to your lead generation process. This will be very important to your success.

Let's review a well-diversified marketing portfolio so we can actually see the diversification needed for success.

Below in figure 3-1 you will see an example of twelve different marketing channels that were invested in as part of a fractional project. These same channels or channels like these could be used to market any product. By applying the four vital indicators to each one, you can start to see the very different performance characteristics of these channels. By keeping your hands on the marketing dials, you can adjust them for success.

Figure 3-1 shows a six-year sellout of a large shared ownership/fractional ownership resort. The areas we will comment on in this marketing report are the ones we have highlighted. We will start by discussing leads.

Fractional Residence Club Marketing Programs Totals 2010–2015

PROGRAMS	LEADS	CONV.	PRES.	CLOSE	SALES	VOLUME	EXPENSE	CPL	VPL	%
Hotel Integration #1	2,856	60%	1714	9%	160	$56,800,000	$1,952,382	$684	$19,888	3.44%
Hotel Integration #2	377	60%	226	30%	68	$24,140,000	$831,440	$2,205	$64,012	3.44%
Broker Program SFV	1,200	30%	360	22%	80	$28,357,119	$3,195,217	$2,663	$23,631	11.27%
Broker Program LA	1,320	30%	396	28%	110	$39,050,000	$3,654,013	$2,768	$29,583	9.36%
Broker Program OC	1,080	30%	324	25%	80	$28,400,000	$3,196,093	$2,959	$26,296	11.25%
Broker Program SD	900	30%	270	22%	60	$21,300,000	$2,890,653	$3,212	$23,667	13.57%
Owner Programs	850	50%	425	28%	120	$42,600,000	$1,578,500	$1,857	$50,118	3.71%
Local Marketing	900	35%	315	13%	40	$14,200,000	$853,725	$949	$15,778	6.01%
Web Marketing	5,400	30%	1,620	6%	100	$35,500,000	$1,943,300	$360	$6,574	5.47%
Direct Mail	1,500	25%	310	13%	48	$17,040,000	$1,118,625	$746	$11,360	6.56%
National Advertising	3,250	40%	1,300	8%	100	$35,500,000	$4,162,000	$1,281	$10,923	11.72%
Event Marketing	600	40%	240	10%	24	$8,520,000	$513,600	$856	$14,200	6.03%
Total Marketing	**20,233**	**37%**	**7,500**	**13%**	**990**	**$351,407,119**	**$25,889,547**	**$1,280**	**$17,368**	**7.4%**

Figure 3-1

Leads—The lead production reported from the marketing programs above is 20,233 over six years, or 3,372 leads per year, or 281 per month, which is a pretty aggressive lead generation program. Each marketing channel should be reviewed on a daily basis against its targeted leads. Make sure you have a small team focused on daily reports accounting for all the leads by marketing channel. It also makes sense to have this same small team report on lead distribution by sales person as it is very important to track this lead information. We will talk more about the team that tracks these leads in the chapter on lead accounting.

Reviewing lead production should be done daily, but you should also be planning your future lead production at least one quarter in advance. You should not only be reviewing lead production, but you should also be making sure your marketing employees know you are conducting these reviews. It has always been my belief that *people may not do what is expected, but they will always do what is inspected.* Inspecting lead counts lets your responsible marketing employees know daily and weekly you are actively interested in their performance.

Ask questions of your marketing employees about hitting their monthly targets. How are they doing? Are they on target? Are they going to be over budget? How much over? What might the end of the month or the quarter look like? Why are we under or over in terms of lead count? Can we count on this performance trend to continue? What can we do to improve our lead performance trends?

If your marketing team is over in lead count compared to budget, make sure you congratulate its members. It is important that they understand how pleased you are when lead counts are over budget. It sounds simple and obvious, but I have been amazed at how many leaders say nothing positive to their marketing staff when lead counts exceed budget. Make them feel appreciated because you should appreciate them—they are exceeding expectations! Don't you wish all employees could do this for you?

If the marketing team isn't hitting targets, then you need to work with the marketing person in charge. He or she must understand how important it is to the company that the team hits its targets. Marketers must have a solid plan for how to increase lead performance cost effectively. You must review with them how the current slowdown in lead performance will affect sales. Provide support and a plan of action to engage them in increasing production.

In an ideal situation marketing people should be coming to you with ideas for increasing lead performance. But be prepared if they do not come to you. Also, make sure your expert marketing employees responsible for lead generation are compensated in some manner according to their lead production results.

When you review leads production, be sure to look at each channel and ask what you can do to drive more leads. Gauge the quality of leads, which is every bit as important as the quantity, as well. A well-run marketing lead performance program has the right quantity of leads targeted and meets the cost per lead (CPL) and volume per lead (VPL) tests. We will explain CPL and VPL in just a minute. You will soon understand how to review each of your marketing channels for both quantity and quality of lead performance.

If you have one marketing person on your team who wakes up every day thinking about what can be done now and in the future to increase the quantity of lead production, that is a good start. As that person puts a plan of action in play and lead production starts to increase, he or she also needs to monitor the quality of that increase in lead production. Obviously, producing extra leads can be counterproductive if the extra leads being generated are not quality leads. You need someone focused on this important balancing act on a full-time basis. That person can work carefully on your marketing channels and seek outside sources for new ideas as well as maintain a log on your competitors' lead programs, which may give you good ideas.

You should increase your marketing spending and try to increase your lead production beyond budgeted or targeted amounts whenever a marketing channel has exceeded lead targets or reached at least 65 percent of targets only if your cost per lead (CPL) is at or lower than budgeted while your volume per lead (VPL) is higher than budgeted. Try to drive as many leads as you possibly can as long as your CPL is at or below targets and your VPL is at or above targets.

The best way to look at quality lead production is to divide your cost per lead (CPL) by your volume per lead (VPL). The answer you get from this math is what we call your report card. Compare the resulting percentage to your budget or target. If the percentage is lower, crank up your lead machine and try to get as many leads as you can. If the percentage is higher than your budget or target, you should consider slowing your lead machine down. Also, if you should gear up your lead machine and start to generate more leads only to find that your volume per lead is declining and your percentage is increasing, jump on this right away and bring your lead flow back down.

Expense—On the report (figure 3-1), look at the dollars allocated to generate leads for the product: more than twenty-five million over the six-year period, or about four million each year. This lead expense is usually the largest variable expense in a sales and marketing budget. These dollars must be spent in the right channels at the right time to generate the most effective leads you can.

Always remember that just because marketing dollars are budgeted does not mean you can spend them. My view is that you must earn the right to spend marketing dollars. You earn this right by producing sales revenue.

Here is the way my marketing spending formula works—and the way you should look at earning marketing dollars. If you are at 100 percent of your budgeted sales revenue target, you have earned the right to spend 100 percent of your budgeted marketing dollars. If, though, you are at 75 percent of your budgeted sales revenue, you have earned the right to spend only 75 percent of your budgeted marketing dollars. Since, in reality, you must commit to spending marketing dollars well in advance of producing sales revenue, you should evaluate your earned marketing dollars to spend each quarter.

If you end the first quarter with 75 percent of budgeted sales revenue, then 75 percent of budgeted marketing spending should be your guideline for the second and third quarters, assuming that you are forecasting accurately and are comfortable, based on recent trends, that you will produce at least 75 percent of sales revenue in upcoming quarters.

Let's take a look at some examples:

What happens in the first quarter if you spend 100 percent of your budgeted dollars and are at 50 percent of the budgeted revenue at the end of the quarter? First, your margins—or what we call your report card—have doubled from 7.4 percent budgeted to 14.8 percent actual. In other words, you have lost 7.4 percent in your margins. (See the chart below in figure 3-2.) What do you spend in the next quarter? Using my formula, your guideline would be to spend 50 percent of your allocated budgeted marketing dollars. If you are only planning to spend 50 percent of your allocated budget, make sure you invest your dollars in the most productive lead channels. Look for channels with the highest VPLs first.

Let's look at what it will take to get back on track with your margins if you spend 50 percent of the budgeted marketing dollars in the second quarter. Sometimes, under these circumstances, you may want to spend more than 50 percent, but only after careful review and prudent strategic planning.

Figure 3-2 shows where you are at the end of this hypothetical first quarter, with 50 percent of revenue and 100 percent of marketing dollars spent. Look at your percentage of dollars spent versus revenue produced: 14.8 percent.

	EXPENSE	REVENUE	%
QT 1 Budgeted	$1,200,000	$16,200,000	7.4%
QT 1 Actual	$1,200,000	$8,100,000	14.8%

Figure 3-2

Figure 3-3 shows what will happen if you spend, according to the formula, 50 percent of your budgeted marketing dollars and have a great second quarter, producing 98 percent of your targeted revenue. Your budget will again be 7.4 percent, but you will come in at 3.7 percent, a gain in margins of 3.7 percent.

Figure 3-3 shows the end of the hypothetical second quarter, with revenue at 98 percent and only 50 percent of marketing dollars spent. In terms of dollars spent versus revenue produced, you will be at 3.7 percent.

	EXPENSE	REVENUE	%
QT 2 Budgeted	$1,200,000	$16,200,000	7.4%
QT 2 Actual	$600,000	$16,075,000	3.7%

Figure 3-3

So, at the end of the second quarter, on a year-to-date basis, you are now on target for your cost as a percentage of sales revenue as well as on budget in terms of your margins.

In figure 3-4, at the end of the second quarter, your year-to-date numbers are at 75 percent of budgeted revenues, and you're also at 75 percent of the budgeted marketing dollars spent. You are back on budget as far as the percentage of dollars spent versus revenue produced: 7.4 percent.

	EXPENSE	REVENUE	%
Total Budget	$2,400,000	$32,400,000	7.4%
Total Actual	$1,800,000	$24,175,000	7.4%

Figure 3-4

This is an important example. Here, you are only at 75 percent of your revenue targets year-to-date, but your marketing margins are on budget because you've controlled your spending at the same level while you've been producing sales revenue. You spent 75 percent of your budgeted marketing dollars and produced 75 percent of the sales revenue.

The key is that if you are going to miss your revenue production, try to save your margins. You never want to be, if you can control it, in a situation where at the end of two quarters you are at 75 percent of revenue produced and have spent 100 percent of your marketing dollars. The adjustment shown above controlled your marketing spending. You would probably make this kind of adjustment in the second quarter by investing more in your most productive marketing programs in terms of VPL. The key is to keep your margins, or percentage of marketing dollars spent versus revenue produced (your report card), at least at your budget levels. This is easier said than done, but the fact that you will be controlling your marketing spending based on sales results is very prudent.

Lead diversification gives you more flexibility in this area as you can use different marketing channels that are performing well to offset channels that are not. There are exceptions to this rule, such as in a launch startup and other special circumstances requiring unusual strategies.

Marketing Spending Formula = The actual sales revenue as a percentage of the budget is the percentage of marketing dollars earned you can spend.

CPL—CPL stands for cost per lead. You calculate this number by dividing the number of leads generated in a marketing channel by the amount you have spent to generate those leads. For example, maybe you've spent $100,000 in advertising and generated 100 leads. Divide the $100,000 you have spent by the 100 leads you've generated, and you get $1,000 per lead as your cost. The $1,000 is the cost per lead (CPL), one of the vital statistics that marketing pros need to monitor carefully.

Just as you earn the right to spend marketing dollars based on the percentage of budgeted sales revenue you produce, so the CPL will also give you direction when it comes to marketing channel spending. Based on CPL statistics, you may accelerate your earned marketing dollars or reduce them. Pay careful attention to your actual CPL versus your budgeted CPL or last year's performance. (Be sure to keep these statistics.) Then ask what this CPL comparison tells you about marketing channel trends. React to your answer through your marketing strategies. Remember that marketing channels are always trending either up or down. Look for trends that relate to the CPL. Then react accordingly.

Here's an example: Let's say your CPL on national advertising was $600 last year but $1,000 this year—an increase of 40 percent. You should probably check the ad you are running. Maybe it has run its productive course. A new ad could bring this cost per lead number back down by generating more leads.

The only time you can afford to the have your CPL consistently over budget is if the VPL (volume per lead) is also over budget. We'll talk more about VPL and the relationship between CPL and VPL in a minute. The bottom line is simply that diversification gives you more flexibility for improving your CPL.

VPL—VPL stands for volume per lead. The way you calculate your VPL is to take all the sales revenue you have produced in a marketing channel and divide it by the total leads that channel has produced. For example: If a marketing channel has produced $1,600,000 in sales revenue and 100 leads, your VPL would be $16,000 dollars. As with CPL, diversification will give you a wider range of possibilities for correcting under-performing channels.

Marketing Percentages—This is what we've been calling your report card. This percentage is calculated by taking the number of dollars spent divided by the sales revenue produced. It shows what the percentage of expenses was in relation to the sales revenue you generated. If you divide your total expenses by your total revenue, you will get the percentage of your revenue that has been consumed by expenses. You can also divide your CPL by your VPL to get the same result. A diversified marketing portfolio will most likely improve this percentage.

In our hypothetical example you have twelve different marketing channels. As you can see in figure 3-1, every channel is different, but your targeted overall average is 7.4 percent. The key is to hit or be under this overall percentage.

In figure 3-5 a few variables can produce this result of 7.4 percent. Just by reaching different CPL and VPL values, you can hit your targeted 7.4 percent.

LEADS	CPL	VPL	%
100	$1,280	$17,368	7.4%
100	$1,500	$20,388	7.4%
100	$1,700	$23,058	7.4%
100	$2,000	$26,943	7.4%
100	$1,000	$13,546	7.4%
100	$800	$10,818	7.4%
100	$600	$8,097	7.4%

Figure 3-5

Finally, you need to know whether you are successful in your lead generation by assessing both the *quantity* and *quality* levels of your production.

If the pure count or number of leads is at or above your targeted or budgeted amounts, your quantity levels are in good shape. Always drive quantity of lead performance by your quality performance levels. If your quality performance falls below standards, that usually means you need to reduce your lead flow. If your quality exceeds performance standards, you should try to increase the quantity of your lead production.

The more talented a sales team is, the better it will be at converting leads to sales and the better your quality of lead rating will be. Marketing cannot control the ability of the sales team, so marketers have to assume you have the best sales people available handling your leads.

Figure 3-6 presents the review process that should be used by marketing in its evaluation of the quantity and quality of lead production. If you want to dominate in your lead performance, then diversification and these performance metrics are clearly the way to get there.

Quantity and Quality Lead Performance Ratings

First: Compare the actual quantity of leads with what you've budgeted or targeted. Are you positive or negative in this first review?

Second: Gauge the quality of your leads in terms of your CPL and VPL. Are you over or under budget?

Third: Divide your CPL by your VPL to obtain the percentage (your report card). If this percentage is at or below your budget, you have a successful lead campaign.

Figure 3-6

Key Notes for Lead Diversification

1. Diversification is a key to flexibility in marketing performance. It also provides some insurance of risk due to market fluctuations.

2. To dominate your lead production, you need flexibility.

3. You earn marketing dollars by producing sales revenue. The percentage of sales revenue you produce compared to budget is the percentage of budgeted marketing dollars you should spend.

4. Review, understand, and use the quantity and quality lead performance ratings.

5. Adjust your spending of marketing dollars based on what the vital performance statistics are telling you.

6. Always be thinking about how you can drive more quality leads into the sales system.

Let's hear from our characters about *lead diversification.*

Chapter 3: Lead Diversification

Here is an action scene with our characters reviewing their diversification.

Marketing diversification gives you more choices, which means less risk. Manage your marketing channel diversification, and you will increase your effectiveness by keeping multiple adjusting options available.

#### Chapter 4

Prospecting for Leads

How you should prepare to prospect for leads using different marketing channels

> Marketing team, let's discuss our prospecting plans for each channel so we can achieve true *lead domination*.

NOW THAT YOU HAVE determined who and where your buyer is and have planned a diversified set of marketing channels to reach your buyer, you are ready to create your prospecting plan. Diversification is the *what* of marketing, as in what marketing channels you are going to use. Prospecting is the *how* of marketing, as in how you are going to prospect for leads through each marketing channel.

The right prospecting strategy will drive quality leads and give you the best chance of meeting your quantity and quality leads formula. Prospecting is your strategy for attracting leads. Leads are the end results of your prospecting strategy. Understand that not all prospecting will turn into leads.

How important is your prospecting strategy? You cannot be successful without a good one. If the prospecting you do does not produce good leads, you will not convert leads into sales. So prospecting is everything.

Prospect marketing is not just about looking for leads. You will be looking specifically for leads that have or could have an interest in your product offering. So you need to take some preparation time before you start prospecting.

I liken prospecting to fishing. If you are fishing just for recreation, that is one thing, but if you are fishing to eat because you are hungry, you will require a well-thought-out strategy that identifies what kind of fish you want to catch, where in the water fish are, and what kinds of baits and lures will attract them. All of these things will help you succeed long before you drop your line in the water. Knowing what kind of fish you want to catch is like knowing who your buyers are, and using a variety of baits and lures is like implementing diversified marketing strategies.

Targeting the correct customers is very important. For example, just because customers are wealthy does not mean they are the right customers for your product. There are exceptions to this rule; however, most of the time you will want to generate leads from qualified clients whose lifestyles your product represents or supports. These clients may already use or have a reason to use the product you are offering. If you want the best chance to hit your quantity and quality leads formula, you need to look for clients who use or have the potential to use your product already and/or have the disposable income and lifestyle you've targeted. If you start with these prospects, you will be in a better position to hit your quantity and quality goals. (See chapter 2.)

Let's look at each of our diversified channels with a new focus on prospecting. How do you prospect for potential leads? What is the best approach for turning prospects into qualified leads? Where do you find the leads? What indicators tell you that these are qualified leads? What vital statistics let you know you're on the right track? Figure 4-1 shows a plan with the different marketing channels you might use over the next five years to generate more than twenty thousand leads.

The example is of a fractional ownership marketing plan, but this type of plan can work no matter what your business or product is. As long as you are investing money in leads, you can use the same approach, processes, reviews, and reports. There may be different marketing channels and metrics, but the concept is the same.

In order to attain the goal of twenty thousand leads over the life of this property, there will need to be a well-thought-out prospecting plan that will be different for each of your marketing channels. Think about spending more than $25 million over a five-year period for prospecting leads. That is a lot of money! Make sure you spend it wisely.

On average you will spend approximately $1,200 per lead. You will need a strategy that ensures your prospecting converts into enough leads, presentations, and sales to produce a volume per lead of more than $17,000. Again, it all starts with a well-thought-out prospecting strategy.

The report card on your prospecting effectiveness comes down to marketing percentages, which determine your sales and marketing margins. You can see once again in figure 4-1 that this number is just over seven percent. You will never attain that percentage unless you have a marketing strategy that is solid in prospecting for leads.

If you want to achieve *lead domination*, you will have to create a world-class prospecting process for each marketing channel in which you want to invest. Whenever you modify your prospecting plans, you affect the cost per lead. Generally, the lower the cost per lead the better. If you bring in more targeted leads and sales has more success, you will increase the volume per lead. Each variation on the cost per lead and the volume per lead will have an impact on your marketing percentages, which are your report card on your sales and marketing performance efforts.

Fractional Residence Club Marketing Programs Totals 2010–2014

PROGRAMS	LEADS	PRES.	SALES	VOLUME	EXPENSE	CPL	VPL	%
Hotel Integration #1	2,856	1714	160	$56,800,000	$1,952,382	$684	$19,888	3.44%
Hotel Integration #2	377	226	68	$24,140,000	$831,440	$2,205	$64,012	3.44%
Broker Program SFV	1,200	360	80	$28,357,119	$3,195,217	$2,663	$23,631	11.27%
Broker Program LA	1,320	396	110	$39,050,000	$3,654,013	$2,768	$29,583	9.36%
Broker Program OC	1,080	324	80	$28,400,000	$3,196,093	$2,959	$26,296	11.25%
Broker Program SD	900	270	60	$21,300,000	$2,890,653	$3,212	$23,667	13.57%
Owner Programs	850	425	120	$42,600,000	$1,578,500	$1,857	$50,118	3.71%
Local Marketing	900	315	40	$14,200,000	$853,725	$949	$15,778	6.01%
Web Marketing	5,400	1,620	100	$35,500,000	$1,943,300	$360	$6,574	5.47%
Direct Mail	1,500	310	48	$17,040,000	$1,118,625	$746	$11,360	6.56%
National Advertising	3,250	1,300	100	$35,500,000	$4,162,000	$1,281	$10,923	11.72%
Event Marketing	600	240	24	$8,520,000	$513,600	$856	$14,200	6.03%
Total Marketing	20,233	7,500	990	$351,407,119	$25,889,547	$1,280	$17,368	7.37%

Figure 4-1

If you want to dominate in your lead performance, it is important to understand the planning that goes into each of the marketing channels listed in figure 4-1.

On the following pages, I would like to introduce you to your first detailed prospect marketing strategy sheet for the owner referral program. This will give you a good idea of what goes on before starting to prospect for leads. Also see the additional prospect marketing strategy pages at the end of the marketing section for your review. I would highly recomment that you review these sections and see how they can help you in the prospecting of your product.

The following prospecting addendum to chapter 4 will give you an idea of how a specific marketing channel works strategically. This is what I call a detailed prospect marketing strategy, which is essential if you want to achieve your best lead performance potential. Also see the additional detailed examples of prospecting at the end of the marketing section.

Owners Program Prospecting

I AM EXCITED TO review this prospecting channel with you and introduce you to my question five program. This one is so exciting it will keep you up at night thinking about the possibilities.

The prospecting of your owner base is the single most overlooked marketing opportunity. Why are these owner programs overlooked? I am not completely sure, but sometimes I think that sales and marketing companies believe that they have completed their goal when they convert a lead into a presentation and a purchase. The natural thought, which is a good one, is that creating a sale is the goal of prospecting. So once that is accomplished, teams will naturally move on to other prospects. If this sounds a little like how your operation works, let's see if we can improve on this process.

Think about it for a minute. What if you go out and look for more prospects to purchase and at the same time create stand-alone marketing channels for each individual owner you have already acquired. *Yes—each owner you acquire should be a separate stand-alone marketing channel.*

I belong to a charity organization called Life Forward, which raises money for the homeless in Orange County, California. Once a person contributes to this organization, he or she is asked to go out and support the cause. There are no better people to support this cause than the ones who are already contributing to it. Members may be asked to contribute time, money, or expertise or to bring in other contributors. This type of prospecting generates large amounts of time, money, and expertise, expands the base, and produces great results for the charity.

Why not do the same thing with your own owners? The plan is simple. Each owner should first be considered a separate marketing channel. If you have two hundred owners, then you now have two hundred new marketing channels—that is how the question five program begins.

The question five program will be the most productive prospecting program you have if you follow it. Implement question five in your prospecting and see what happens to the success of your owner prospecting from a sales and marketing standpoint. I know you will be impressed with the outcome if you use the power of question five as your owner prospecting strategy. Just as with the charity I mentioned above, your owners will contribute time and expertise and will help expand your owner base.

Like a charity donor, your owners have already contributed their money, and soon your owners will also invest their time in your product if you give them the opportunity to do so.

The core of the question five program consists of making sure you complete and update the following information each year. Be sure to set up a separate file on each owner to record their owner status. Here are the five important questions in the question five program:

1. Why did owners purchase?

2. What expectation do owners have now that they have purchased?

3. What has their experience been compared to their expectations?

4. Now that they have experienced their ownership, do they have new or different expectations?

5. Would they recommend this product to someone else? If so, whom?

Here's how you can update the separate files on each owner to increase your prospecting potential:

Why did owners purchase? You need to understand what your clients' motivation was to invest their time and money in your offering. Then make sure the reason they purchased is or has been fulfilled in their eyes. Be proactive with this, not reactive. Think of what else extra you can do that might exceed the expectations they indicated to you. You will find this is very easy to do because your owners won't expect it. For example, let's say your owner purchased so they could ski with the family once a year. Now that you understand this, you could research skiing in the area and send the client a personal hand-written letter with a special bonus:

Dear Mary and Bill,

I know how important skiing is to you and your family, so on your next visit to the resort I have arranged for complimentary ski tickets for you and your family to the Sugar Blow ski area. Most people who visit are not even aware of this mountain, but the locals think it is one of the best kept secrets in the area. I have also outlined some specific runs on this mountain that are especially beautiful. These are intermediate runs that I am sure your family will enjoy. If you let me know what day you would like to ski this mountain, I will make arrangements and have the ski tickets ready when you arrive. I will call you later in the week to tell you more about this outstanding ski area.

If you decide you do not want to purchase ski tickets for the client, that is okay—just adjust the letter and give them the information about the new ski area. As long as you understand why they purchased, this becomes an easy thing to do and something that the owners will not be expecting. It is all about helping your owners exceed their expectations. That will allow you to be on track to ask question number five and get a positive response and a list of prospects.

What expectation do owners have now that they have purchased? Now that you understand why clients have purchased, you need to understand what their expectations are for this purchase. The reason they have purchased will be the main motivation for the purchase, but the expectations involve the experiences owners believe will come with ownership.

For example, clients may have purchased because they like to ski with their families, but their expectation is that with this ownership they will have a great second home to stay in when they want to ski. What happens if it's not easy to book their second home? Your team, especially operations, needs to stay abreast of the times when they want to book so that it proves to be a simple process. If you know that these are your clients' expectations in advance, you can help ensure they have outstanding experiences. Think also of what else you can do to make this process a little better than planned. Meet or exceed their expectation and you have earned the right to ask question number five and to get a positive response.

What has their experience been compared to their expectations? As soon as clients use your product, you need to know about it and record it in your files. This becomes your report card on your owners' satisfaction levels. If they have great experiences, then your team has either met or exceeded their expectations, and you will have earned the right to ask question five and to get a positive response. If you have not met their expectations, then you need to be proactive in closing the gap. The owners will appreciate the effort, and it will increase their positive experience levels.

Now that they have experienced their ownership, do they have new or different expectations? This question keeps you in the loop if your clients' experience levels or expectation levels have changed at all. If their satisfaction level remains high, then you have earned the right to ask question number five and can again anticipate a positive response. If not, then you have some work to do. Put these responses in your owner file.

Would they recommend this product to someone else? If so, whom? This in my view is the most powerful question you can ask an owner. No other question will drive referrals more than getting a positive response from this question because you and your product will have earned that right. This is the prospecting question you earn the right to ask in return for all your efforts of keeping and updating your individual owner files to ensure expectations have been met. How many companies will work with their owner bases so diligently to earn client satisfaction? Not many—but the ones that do will definitely attain *lead domination* in their owners programs.

Some clients will refer people before they experience owner-ship, but most will not. Earn the right with your proactive efforts to ask and receive a positive response to question five, and the owner prospecting program will flourish. For an offering with a high satisfaction rate, do not be surprised if five to ten percent of your owner base decides to purchase another product for themselves.

One additional opportunity you should consider is to offer an incentive to owners to refer friends who purchase or, if the owner purchases, another interest. I have seen offers such as paying fifty percent of the owner's maintenance fees for the year if the owner refers and the referral purchases and closes escrow. These are good incentive programs but will not yield as many prospects and sales as a program that focuses on the owner's expectations and experiences. Both together can make a powerful combination.

I am always surprised to find that there are some sales people who do not like to call their owners—or at least some of their owners. The reason is that the sales people are concerned the conversation with owners may be negative, which is not a good thing for sales people to have to worry about. Keep in mind that the question five program needn't be done completely or perhaps at all by your sales teams. Sales people sell whereas marketing people prospect. If you have any questions about this important point, please contact me at leaddomination@loreinstitute.com. Giving this program to someone else other than the sales team is often a key to success in my experience. But you must receive cooperation from sales people, and their commission structure should not change.

It has been my experience that if you leave a program like this one solely to the sales team, it will not work. There are way too many details and follow-up activities that have very little to do with selling but a lot to do with servicing. These things can be handled by an outstanding marketing prospecting person, who will be perfectly suited for this type of work and should be compensated accordingly. By all means, though, let the sales team continue to earn commissions on owner activity. Sales people just need to understand that they have an administrative assistant to help and work with them on owners. Sales teams will usually like this. If you give owner referral and owner repurchasing to your sales team alone, you will leave millions of dollars of cost-effective sales revenue on the table. Let's help our sales teams earn more commission by setting up these programs accordingly.

This program represents prospecting at its finest. Think of question number five: *Would they recommend this product to someone else? If so, who?* If the answer is no, I would recommend that you look at questions one through four. Keep in mind that this program is supposed to provide a fair exchange. If the owners have a great experience, they will tell you about other prospects. You just need to stay proactive if you want this prospecting program to be highly successful.

Question three, concerning whether expectations are being met, lets you know if there is a gap between what your clients expect and what you are delivering. If you find such a gap, you need to make a full-time effort to fix it. This is usually done with full support from your operations team. But if you do not know there is a problem and your operations team does not know it, it is highly unlikely you will have an owner with a great experience. And if owners do not have great experiences, there is a great chance that you will not get a positive response to question number five.

Make it your responsibility as a marketer doing professional prospecting to try to get as many owners participating as possible by providing you with referral prospects. If you keep your owners satisfied, then you will earn the right again to ask question number five with the expectation of positive results. The key to the power of question five is always to know by updating and reviewing every six months why your owners purchased, what their expectations were when they purchased, and whether those expectations were met. Have a separate file on each of your owners and work them to increase satisfaction levels, so that you earn the right to prospect for referral leads and create great cost-effective owner revenues.

You need a team of people tied closely to your owner operations department to make this program work. As mentioned earlier, the responsibilities should not be left to your sales team. The owner operations department has a lot to do with the ownership experience, but your marketing team needs to stay in the loop. Do you think this operations group can influence the answers to question one though four without your support and help? The answer is no—you need a strong marketing person with client satisfaction goals close at hand to work with your operations team to get the job done.

Here is a million-dollar tip, as far as I am concerned: Your operations people should be part of the sales and marketing team when they are dealing with your owners. Operations and the sales and marketing teams should be trained together about how the product is sold and how the product works. When your sales team is trained about product knowledge by your sales leadership, have the operations team and the marketing owner specialist present as well. If what the sales team is selling is in line with what the operations team is delivering, you will be well positioned on question five. If what the sales people are selling and what the operations people deliver becomes a better experience than the sales presentation promised, you will have just hit gold!

How many people should be part of your owner prospecting team? Who does the calling and updating of the owner files and makes good on expectations is up to you and your teams. Just don't assign these responsibilities to the sales team.

Figure A-1 provides a sample of the potential results of this program. These are owners program numbers on a fractional resort for which we did the sales and marketing. But this type of program will work no matter what product you are selling.

Power of Five Prospecting Program for One Year

200 Owners

On-site prospect lead generation

Talk to 50 percent of your owners on-site and 25 percent give you 1 lead = 25 leads

Off-site prospect lead generation

Work with all your owner base and 50 percent give you 1 lead = 100 leads

On-site Reloads = 5 percent reload or purchase a second ownership

Off-site Reloads = 5 percent reload or purchase a second ownership

125 leads at a VPL of $50,118 = $6,264,750

10 percent reload @ $355,000 average price = $7,100,000.

Total POWER OF FIVE annual revenue production is $13,364,750.

Figure A-1

Prospecting owners should be the most cost-effective and efficient program you have among all your marketing channels. Can you think of a better source to prospect than one that has reviewed your offering and decided to purchase it? We spend a lot of time and energy trying to focus on the right clients to prospect—and we should in most all other marketing channels. But the owners program channel is the only marketing channel in which we start out with the perfect prospect.

This power of question number five is also your report card on how well you are really doing as a sales and marketing organization in delivering the owner experience. If you have a site in which owners have used the product and forty percent are not participating in one of your owner prospecting programs, then you are probably not delivering the experience to the owners that you should. Your sales and marketing experts must take the time to understand why less than sixty percent of your owners are not willing to refer a potential buyer to your resort. The careful records you keep will show you that owner participation is an important part of your prospecting program. Find out how to increase participation through satisfied owners, and you will be well on your way to one of the most cost-effective prospecting programs you could imagine. As your owner base becomes larger, the program will become more and more successful. The key to success in this program is tied directly to owner expectations and experience. Always target a minimum of forty percent of your owner base to participate in this owner prospecting program.

There are three areas of owner prospecting you should focus on: owner expectations and satisfaction levels, owner referral prospecting, and owner reload prospecting. We have covered owner expectations and satisfaction levels with the power of question five. Let's talk a little about owner reloads programs.

An owner reload is a current owner who decides to purchase more. The reasons owners buy more include:

1. They believe that what they have purchased has great value and want more.

2. They have had great experiences with your product and want more.

3. Whatever their expectations were, you were able to meet or exceed them.

4. They can afford to purchase more if they want.

5. They were asked to purchase more.

So if owners believe in the product that they purchased, that has a lot to do with the location of the product and/or the way the product looks but most of all with the way the product makes them feel. Get these important concepts to line up, and these owners will become outstanding prospects to purchase more.

If owners have been having not just good but great experiences with your product and feel special when they use your product, their family experiences will be outstanding, and their family members will want to spend more time with your product. These are all good signs that the owners may be good prospects to purchase more.

If they have the financial ability to purchase more and are satisfied with your product a percentage will purchase more.

The most important thing is that they are asked to purchase more in a way that they see benefiting them. It is a fact that the owners who purchase more are the ones who have been asked to purchase more and had a compelling reason for why they should.

If you are using this program for any kind of shared ownership program, I would highly recommend when you are working your owners that you split them into two very different categories: owners who are staying at your resort and owners who are not.

Owners staying at the resort need to be contacted during their pre-arrival confirmations and asked to stop by the sales office where they get a chance to discover the best and most popular opportunities and values of their ownership. You should have some type of on-site owners program in play that encourages them to come to the office. Let me share with you a great idea about how to get owners to drop by the sales office.

When owners arrive for their stay, a beautiful light blue Tiffany® bag should be waiting for them in their residences. The color of these Tiffany® bags seems to attract your owners, especially the women. Inside the bag will be a beautiful invitation for the owner to go to the sales office to pick up a special Tiffany® gift from their sales person. This strategy seems to get them interested in seeing what we have for them. The gift is Tiffany® sterling silver luggage tags with their names engraved on them, one for the husband and one for the wife. They only get the gift if they come to the sales office to meet their sales person or your owners program marketing person. These Tiffany® gifts cost about one hundred and fifty dollars each. I have found these gifts to be very special in the eyes of the high-end consumer.

It is well worth the cost to have just a few minutes with each of your owners to talk about their experiences and satisfaction levels and to update their files. Let's assume you have worked hard to ensure their satisfaction levels are high when they arrive. Then you have earned the right when they get their Tiffany® gift to ask them whether they are interested in purchasing more or have a friend who may be interested in looking at the offering. If you run this program, approximately forty percent will leave you with a referral name or will purchase another share. This is the most effective prospecting program I know of.

If you have two hundred owners, the Tiffany® gift will cost you about $60,000 for all your owners. If through these efforts you get to meet most of your owners, update their owner files, and only get through referrals and reloads three sales a year at $300,000 a sale, then this program will prove to be very cost-effective. Most of the time you should do even better than that. The key is to first earn the right to ask for referrals and reloads by having the owner's experiences and expectation met or exceeded.

Owners who are at their homes need to be informed of activities that interest them in and around the areas where they own their products. Be sure you take the opportunity to review and update your question five owners program files as needed. The way each of these owners is serviced and communicated with is the key to an off-site referral business.

Keep in mind that owners belong to the company, not the sales people who sold them their products. That may be a difficult message to send to your sales teams, but I promise if you want the owner business to excel, you need to have two separate operations that work the owner, one on-site when the owners arrive and one that works the owners when they are at home. Sales agents are not the best people to work either of these programs. You can turn over the reloads and referrals for the sales people to complete documentation and earn commissions, but the marketing team should generate the owner prospects.

Owner Referral

The owner referral program is based on satisfied owners. If you work your question five owners program well, you will receive referrals from your owners who will be interested in purchasing. These leads should be turned over to sales for processing.

Key Notes for
Owners Program Prospecting

1. Assemble the marketing team to run the question five program.

2. Have separate files on each owner with all five questions current and updated.

3. You only earn the right to ask for referrals and reloads when owners' satisfaction, experience, and expectation levels are met or exceeded.

4. When you have earned the right to ask for a referrals and/ or reloads, make sure your team asks.

5. Keep track of the percentage of owners who participate in your owners program with reloads and/or referrals. This number has to do with owner satisfaction and how well you work the program.

6. After the first year, owners should participate at least at twenty percent of the total revenues level if you have a satisfied owner base.

7. Do not leave this prospecting to sales. Sales should be focused on selling, and marketing should be focused on prospecting.

8. Have separate prospecting strategies for owners on-site and owners at home.

9. Obtain full support and cooperation from your owner operations department, which will help increase owner satisfaction, experience, and expectation levels.

10. Have owner performance reports to update progress on a monthly basis.

Key Notes for Prospecting for Leads

1. You have established *who* the buyer is, *where* the buyer is, and *what* marketing channels you will use; now it's time to determine *how you will prospect for the leads you need.*

2. Prospecting for leads requires a different focus and plan of action for each marketing channel you use.

3. How you prospect for leads in each of your marketing channels will affect your cost per lead (CPL). Usually, the lower this is, the better you have done.

4. Take a look at your volume per lead (VPL) as you begin prospecting in each channel. Even though this is a sales function, marketing will play a big role in the VPL by ensuring the quality of the prospecting generation.

5. Marketing percentages are your true report card on prospecting effectiveness.

6. There is much more to review on this subject in the pages that follow. Be sure to review the addendas to this chapter at the end of the marketing section. There are ten additional prospect marketing strategies detailed for your reference.

Let's hear from our characters about *prospecting for leads.*

Chapter 4: Prospecting for Leads

Here is an action scene with our characters working on their preparation before prospecting.

The more you plan, review, and study before you start prospecting, the better your end results in generating qualified leads will be.

Be sure to review the 10 additional detailed marketing strategy sheets at the end of this marketing section.

#### Chapter 5

Messaging for Results

How to stay on track while delivering your message

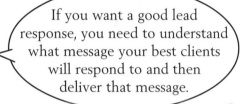

> If you want a good lead response, you need to understand what message your best clients will respond to and then deliver that message.

DEVELOPING A BROCHURE, direct mail piece, newsletter, website, script for face-to-face presentations, or collateral of any kind is really a matter of crafting a message. Even if your brochure is highly informative, there is still a pithy central message it will convey about your product. Marketing your product is all about understanding who the specific prospect for your product is and making sure your message is compelling to that targeted customer.

We all understand how important this is. How do we get the correct message on our marketing materials, one that speaks to our clients in such a way that they will be motivated to inquire about our offering? This is crucial, because most of these inquiries will become leads.

I have seen otherwise great marketing programs that had poor messages and did not connect or communicate with the potential prospect. This alone was the difference between success and failure. It was all about the message. Be careful that your message is not compromised by non-marketing minds so that the program will not be effective. Work with your legal, brand, and imaging teams and whoever else has a stake in the messaging process, but remember that the final responsibility for crafting an effective message belongs with your marketing experts.

How do we get through legal disclosures, branding opinions, outside influences, and different views and still have a compelling message to our targeted clients. The message should offer a combination of copy and imagery that really piques curiosity. Messaging means creating collateral that will support all the diversification of marketing channels and programs to help drive cost-effective lead generation.

Let me share with you my view on the top ten things you need to know before you start creating your message to support your marketing and produce leads:

1. **What is the objective of your message?** Take the time with your marketing team to list the objective of your collateral. Stay focused on the message more than just the look.

2. **What's the current situation?** There are situations when you have to finesse your message. New laws and changes in the image or branding of your company, for instance, can make it advantageous or even necessary to alter the message. Timing and costs are critical in these situations.

3. **Whom will you be trying to reach?** Identifying your audience is a two-step process. First, take time with your team to understand who is the ideal prospect you're targeting. Then, determine how you can motivate this prospect to respond.

4. **How much do you have to invest in your message?** Before you proceed too far with your plans, create a budget for your message. Don't push to develop a message that is too expensive for the program you are creating.

5. **How soon is the message needed?** Timing is everything when you are delivering your message. If you have a seasonal offering and your message needs to go out before the season starts, you obviously need to be able to work on that timeframe. The key is planning far in advance and trying to get your message finalized well in advance of when it will be needed.

6. **Who needs to approve the message?** It is always best to know whom you will need to have approve the message in advance. Get these people on board early so the process will move quicker. If you do not give your legal and branding team ample time for review, it can affect your revenue production. Establish a timeframe for the approval process and stick to it.

7. **Have you done this before?** I am always amazed at how many programs are recreated over and over again. If you have someone on your marketing team who has done this before, take the time to review what went well in the past, what needs to be improved, and what lessons have been learned. You should always learn from experience and improve your program.

8. **What is the vision?** The person in charge of a marketing program about to be launched needs to ensure the vision stays on track. The focus needs to be on the targeted customers and why this particular vision and message will be compelling to them. This marketing leader in charge of the vision needs to

stay focused on the number of leads, cost per lead, and volume per lead and needs to make sure the piece does not stray away in any of these areas. The marketing leader should keep all parties on track to help ensure success.

9. **What elements of the message are key?** The key elements of a message could include pitches such as: "Come see our exclusive, newly designed, limited product" and/or "Learn how this product will enhance your lifestyle." The marketing leader needs to keep the key elements in play as getting off track with any of them can ruin the marketing program. The marketing leader needs to understand what all your team's requirements are to move the project forward and whether these requirements interfere in any way with the key marketing messaging elements.

10. **What is the one most important message you want to send?** Stick to one message that is most important. This message needs to be in the forefront of the project and cannot be compromised in the review or production processes.

Messaging is a bit different in every company and also in every program and piece you develop. So it is hard to specify guidelines for messaging. The most important thing to understand is how important messaging and the approval process are.

I have seen marketing messages go from a great vision that would have been highly successful to a watered-down version that has no chance to succeed because of modifications by legal, branding, or other people involved. Your marketing leader must stop this from happening, because when messaging is compromised, lead generation production is also. Make sure that the targeted client you are going after with your message is still in play when you are done with your review process. If your key message cannot be run, you may want to re-consider the marketing program.

Also, keep the cost of the program in line with the assumptions you have made about leads and revenue production and keep an eye on forecasted cost per leads and volume per leads. The messaging in the marketing area is vitally important to the results you need from your investment. Follow these guidelines and you will always be positioned for success.

The remainder of this chapter presents some examples of pieces that need to be created to help support lead generation by different marketing channels. We will attach one important message we are trying to convey in each piece that supports the marketing channel. Keep in mind that, ideally, marketing programs, pieces developed, and key messages are done for one very important reason: to produce quality lead flow.

Let's take a look at the different messaging opportunities you will have in these various marketing channels:

Hotel Integration

PROGRAMS	PIECE TO DEVELOP	KEY MESSAGE
Confirmation	Confirmation letter	Lifestyle—be aware of our product
Pre-arrival	Message on pre-arrival price	Added value—of our product
In-room information	Brochure	Lifestyle—come see our models
Turn down	Card designed for the bed	Urgency—come see our models
Hotel outlets	Information about our product	Added value—come see our model
Marketing coordinators desks	Signage about the product	Lifestyle—the benefits of our program
Wine parties	Collectible wines	Lifestyle—the benefits of our program
Owners parties	Learn about new options in ownership	Urgency—about our product
Hotel awareness	PowerPoint for education	Learn the benefits about our program
Post-arrival letter	Letter and return brochure	Lifestyle—revisit our product

In the marketing programs above, designed to support lead production in a hotel integration program, you can see the message goes from raising your clients' awareness about your offering to getting clients to come see your models. Always try to make your messages urgent and provide added value whenever possible. Keep these message themes consistent and enticing from a visual and written standpoint, depending on where you are in the relationship, and this program will excel in lead production for you.

Broker Programs

PROGRAMS	PIECE TO DEVELOP	KEY MESSAGE
Icebreaker	Phone script	Review the business benefits
Managers presentation	PowerPoint	Review the business benefits
Invitation to presentation	Invitation piece	Come learn about our program
Office presentation	PowerPoint	Benefits of giving a lead
Take-away brochure	Information on benefits to the agents	Benefits of giving a lead
Registration form	Form developed	Simple to earn commissions
Broker referral contract	Contract developed	Simple to earn commissions
Follow-up program	Script and follow-up pieces	Simple to earn commissions

When you are dealing with outside high-end broker offices, the key message needs to be in line with the "radio station" WIIFM: What's in It for Me. You need to make sure these outside broker offices are earning commissions when they send qualified leads your way. Make sure also to give your new clients a warm introduction. This program does not interfere with any of their general real estate activities; it is easy to do; it protects you and your client; and you earn commissions while you continue with your normal work activities. The key message to deliver concerns the great benefits you're offering and how simple it is to earn commissions.

Owner Programs

PROGRAMS	PIECE TO DEVELOP	KEY MESSAGE
The Power of Question Five	Folders on each owner	Lifestyle—satisfaction levels
Referral program	Referral brochure	Added value—HOA paid,friends join
In-house program	Tiffany® bags	Added value—HOA paid,friends join
At home program	Direct mail	Added value—HOA paid,friends join
Newsletter program	Newsletter	Lifestyle—HOA paid,friends join

Three messages must be sent with an owner referral and reload program. First, you can create your own network of friends. Second, you can have your fees paid for. Most importantly, you need to convey that you are very interested in maintaining owner satisfaction levels. If your owners are satisfied, you have earned the right to receive referrals from them. Once you have earned that right, the owners can share with friends and build their custom neighborhoods as well as earn HOA fees (homeowner's association fees). Your messaging should start with owner satisfaction levels and then proceed to the benefits of referring friends to the development and earning fees.

Web Programs

PROGRAMS	PIECE TO DEVELOP	KEY MESSAGE
Develop your website	Website	Lifestyle on benefits of ownership
Banner ads in key media	Ads	Urgency—benefits of ownership
Key words buys	Key words purchased	Added value—benefits of ownership
URL sites	All media can use your web and URLs can identify where the lead came from	Tracking—benefits of ownership

Your website is one of the fastest growing media exposure programs you have. You need to get this message right. The message needs to be all about the benefits of your ownership program. Also be sure to monitor the competition's web messages.

Local Advertising

PROGRAMS	PIECE TO DEVELOP	KEY MESSAGE
Newspaper ad campaigns	Ads	Urgency—discover more about this
Magazine ad campaigns	Ads	Lifestyle—discover more about this
Other local ads	Ads	Added value—discover more

Ad campaigns can be expensive and complex. The key is that your message needs to be compelling enough that prospects will want to call in for more information. Completing messages need to be about some form of urgency, lifestyle enhancements, and added value to the clients. The great thing about your local advertising is that you usually have the opportunity for face-to-face contact with clients.

National Advertising

PROGRAMS	PIECE TO DEVELOP	KEY MESSAGE
Newspaper ad campaigns	Ads	Urgency—discover more about this
Magazine ad campaigns	Ads	Added value—discover more
Other national ads	Ads	Lifestyle—discover more about this

The same considerations apply to the message as in local advertising.

International Advertising

PROGRAMS	PIECE TO DEVELOP	KEY MESSAGE
Newspaper ad campaigns	Ads	Lifestyle—discover more about this
Magazine ad campaigns	Ads	Urgency—discover more about this
Other international ads	Ads	Added value—discover more

Again, the same considerations apply to the message as in local and national advertising. You want the client to inquire about more information.

Direct Mail Programs

PROGRAMS	PIECE TO DEVELOP	KEY MESSAGE
Direct mail	Letter and brochure	Lifestyle—discover more about this
Owner new letters	Newsletters	Added value—tell friends

This is a very direct message to a very specific customer. Again, the message is to respond to the offering, which will bring in potential new lead opportunities.

Event Marketing

PROGRAMS	PIECE TO DEVELOP	KEY MESSAGE
Event presentations	Face-to-face scripted presentation	Urgency—meet sales for more information
Event brochures	Brochure	Lifestyle—come learn more
Event lead harvest programs	Give-away program	Added value—win, then learn more

The event marketing program offers some interesting options. First, you get to talk casually to potential clients face to face before they become leads. Second, you can hand out brochures providing more information. Third, you can deliver actual marketing presentations, which is an outstanding opportunity to produce qualified leads.

Exit Programs

PROGRAMS	PIECE TO DEVELOP	KEY MESSAGE
Exit presentations—phone	Phone scripted	Added value—come back to experience
Exit presentations—face-to-face	Face-to-face script	Added value—come back to experience
Exit collateral brochure	Brochure	Lifestyle—come back and experience

An exit program gives you face-to-face contact with clients as well as phone contact and brochures to support your efforts. The message to clients is to come back and get a sense of what it's like to be an owner of the product.

As you can see, the message you send has to be cost effective and has to produce quality leads. I would highly recommend that when you get a piece of collateral approved you protect the message so the major drivers of response from the message are kept in place. Messages that concern urgency, added value, lifestyle enhancements, and whatever else you believe will drive performance need to be reaching your customers. If you cannot keep these things in place, then you need to reconsider doing the program. As you go through the process, ask: Is what we are going to get after this piece is approved enhancing, detracting, or not changing the important message we want to send?

Key Notes for Messaging for Results

1. Make sure you know what the important message is that you need to make your program work. Do not compromise this message.
2. The message combines imagery and written copy that will affect your response rates and return on investments.
3. Each marketing process within a marketing program should have at least one main message you would like to deliver.
4. Each marketing channel will have a slightly different message that needs to be delivered.
5. As you review the statistics on your marketing programs, look at the message as part of the performance of the program. If you do similar marketing programs in similar areas with different messages, be sure to track how these messages have affected performance.

Let's hear from our characters about the importance of *messaging for results.*

Chapter 5: Messaging for Results

Here is an action scene with our characters reviewing their marketing messages.

The message you send is critical for attracting the right consumer, and attracting the right consumer is the only way to achieve lead domination.

#### Chapter 6

Marketing Financial Assumptions

Forecasting marketing performance using history and knowledge

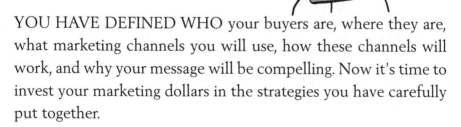

Marketing team, if you deal well with numbers and details, follow along. If not, find someone on your team to take the responsibility. Every program needs a brief detailing all your performance assumptions.

YOU HAVE DEFINED WHO your buyers are, where they are, what marketing channels you will use, how these channels will work, and why your message will be compelling. Now it's time to invest your marketing dollars in the strategies you have carefully put together.

There are usually more variable dollars spent in marketing programs than in any other line item in the budget. The marketing teams that can innovate and execute the best are the teams that produce the best results. If you are going to start spending hundreds of thousands of dollars, you need a process to govern all your financial assumptions and performance levels. We call this a marketing brief. A marketing brief will show you what you expect to invest and what you expect to get in return for that investment. That is the purpose of the dominating dozen we shared back in figure 0-2. The dominating dozen are twelve guidelines for creating an effective marketing lead campaign. Now we are going to focus on number six out of twelve on your financial planning.

If you are going to invest, you need to make a return on your investment. This process speaks to the return on investment that can be reviewed and signed off on by the parties that release the monies. These financial return assumptions will be used to monitor the results of the marketing investment through the life of the program.

When you put together your marketing expenses and the return you expect from your lead generation programs, there are three things you need to complete before you start spending. They are:

1. Financial marketing assumptions (sometimes called a marketing brief)

2. Description and responsibilities paper (see chapter 7)

3. Approval and compliance form (see chapter 8)

We will review all these important documents as we complete the section on marketing.

In this chapter we will focus only on the financial marketing assumptions, which from here on out we will call our marketing briefs.

Below in figure 6-1 is the entire marketing brief you need to complete for each of the major programs you will be funding.

Marketing Brief

Marketing Breif - The Residence Club - Broker Network - 2009

Date:	2/1/2009			
Prepared By:	Jamie Klein		Program Description:	Orange Country - Broker Program
Director of Finance:	Bill Jones		Source Code:	36001
Project Director:	Todd Smith			

Key Assumptions:

Broker Offices Targeted	120	% of leads turned HOT	15%	
# of Agents in Target (75 per)	9,000	Number of HOT leads	243	
Ice Breakers Performed (80%)	96	Hot Leads Per Month	20	
Ice Breakers Converted (75%)	72			
Presentations Performed (90%)	65			
# of Agents per presentation 20	1,296			
# of Leads per presentation 25	1,620	Promotion of Program		
		1 . Developer Piece		
		2 . Product Piece		
Total HOT Leads	243	3 . Broker information Piece		
Leads to Presentations	100%	4 . Powrpoint on program		
Contract Close	18.0%	5 . Broker Legal Agreement		
Average Net Price	$355,000			
Amortized Over	12	Months		

Location Expense		Location Expense		Per Lead	Monthly	Total
		Office Set Up	$14,000	$58	$1,167	$14,000
Total Cost	$614,500	Office rent	$42,000	$173	$3,500	$42,000
		Broker Newsletter (2 times per yr)	$7,000	$29	$583	$7,000
# of Leads	243	Broker Promotional Program	$8,000	$33	$667	$8,000
		Presentation expense	$30,000	$123	$2,500	$30,000
Cost Per Lead	$2,529	Other		$0	$0	$0
		Other		$0	$0	$0
		Other		$0	$0	$0
		Total Location Costs		$2,529	$51,208	$614,500

Employee Expense		Employee Expense Broker Commissions			Per Tour	Monthly	Total
		Office Commissions		4%	$2,556	$51,759	$621,108
Total Cost	$902,858	Broker Manager @ 85K	1	$85,000	$350	$7,083	$85,000
		BM Bonus Vol/HOT 85K	1	$85,000	$350	$7,083	$85,000
# of Leads	243	Broker Assistant	1	$50,000	$206	$4,167	$50,000
		BA Bonus Vol/Hot	1	$25,000	$103	$2,083	$25,000
Cost Per Lead	$3,715	Leader Benefits @18%		15%	$151	$3,063	$36,750
		Other			$0	$0	$0
		Other			$0	$0	$0
		Total Fixed Costs			$3,715	$75,238	$902,858

Overhead Expense		Overhead Expense		Per Tour	Monthly	Total
		Broker Brochures @ $5 per lead	$5	$33	$675	$8,100
Total Cost	$23,030	Broker Brochures @ $10 per Pres	$10	$10	$203	$2,430
		Supplies @ $100 per month	$1,200	$5	$100	$1,200
# of Leads	243	Printing @ $500 per month	$6,000	$25	$500	$6,000
		Postage @ 250 per month	$3,000	$12	$250	$3,000
Cost Per Lead	$95	Licenses @ $500	$500	$2	$42	$500
		Training $ 150 per month	$1,800	$7	$150	$1,800

Premium Expense		Other		$0	$0	$0
Total Cost	$40,500	Other		$0	$0	$0
		Other		$0	$0	$0
# of Leads	243	Other		$0	$0	$0
		Other		$0	$0	$0
Cost Per Lead	$167	Other		$0	$0	$0
		Other		$0	$0	$0

Total Cost Summary						Other		$0	$0	$0
	Per Lead	Total				Other		$0	$0	$0
Location Expense	$2,529	$614,500				Other		$0	$0	$0
Employee Expense	$3,715	$902,858				Other		$0	$0	$0
Overhead Expense	$95	$23,030				Other		$0	$0	$0
Premium Expense	$167	$40,500				Other		$0	$0	$0
Total	$6,506	$1,580,888				Other		$0	$0	$0

Anticipated Performance	Month	Totals	Other	Other	Other	Other		$0	$0	$0
Total Broker Leads	135	1,620				Other		$0	$0	$0
% Lead to HOT		15%				Other		$0	$0	$0
Total HOT Leads	20	243				Other		$0	$0	$0
% of Leads to Presentation		100%				Other		$0	$0	$0
Total Presentations	20	243				Other		$0	$0	$0
Contract Close Percent		18%				Other		$0	$0	$0
Multiple Contract Factor		1				Total Overhead Expense		$95	$1,919	$23,030
Total Fractional Sold	4	44				Premium Expense		Per Tour	Monthly	Total
Average Net Price		$355,000				Site Visits paid for owners @50%	27	$167	$3,375	$40,500
Net Volume		$15,527,700				Room Nights (three)	81	$0	$0	$0
VPL		$63,900				Other	$500	$0	$0	$0
Cost Per Lead		$6,506				Other		$0	$0	$0
Cost as % of Volume		10.18%				Total		$167	$3,375	$40,500

Figure 6-1

This brief records two major details of each marketing program: what you are going to spend and what you are assuming you will produce in net sales revenue. You need to focus on and fully understand all four sections to develop a good marketing brief:

1. Cover page

2. Key assumptions page

3. Expense section

4. Anticipated performance section

On the previous page is a broker program marketing brief that covers one year.

Let's start breaking this marketing brief down. We will begin with the cover page of the brief in figure 6-2.

You need to fill out the following:

1. Date the brief was completed

2. Who prepared the brief

3. Who approves spending

4. Who the project leader is

5. Program title

6. Source code for tracking this program in its marketing channel

Marketing Brief – The Residence Club – Broker Network 2009			
Date	2/1/2009		
Prepared by	Jamie Klein	**Program description:**	Orange County
Director of Finance	Bill Jones		Broker program
Project Director:	Todd Smith	**Source code:**	36001

Figure 6-2

Next are the key assumptions (figure 6-3). In the key assumptions area you will complete the following: your lead production assumptions, your sales production assumptions, and what you are going to need in promotional support to meet these assumptions. Each lead assumption brief will be a little different, but you can use the same format to explain how leads will be produced for the year. You also need to make your assumptions about what sales will produce from these leads. For promotional support you need to list what you need from a marketing collateral standpoint to hit these assumptions.

In the key assumptions section of this brief, we will review:

1. Broker office targeted—offices you will work in the year

2. Agents targeted—the number of agents on average that represent the offices you will be working

3. Icebreakers—at how many offices do you assume you will present icebreakers

4. Icebreaker converted—how many offices will accept and allow you to present an icebreaker

5. Presentations performed—at how many offices will you perform full presentations

6. Number of agents per presentation—how many agents you will deliver your presentation to over the year

7. Number of leads per presentation—how many leads will you harvest per presentation

8. Percentage of leads turned HOT—of the leads you harvest, what percentage will turn HOT

9. Number of HOT leads—number of leads turned HOT that can be given to a sales person to work

10. Hot leads per month—the average number of HOT leads you will produce from your broker program

Sales Assumptions

1. Leads to presentations—the percentage of leads who see a full presentation made by your sales team

2. Contract close—the percentage of clients who close or purchase after the presentation

3. Average price—the average price of the sales that have closed

4. Amortized over—the length of time that the marketing program will run

Promotion Items That Need to Be Approved for This Program

1. Developer piece—something that explains the credibility of the company developing the offering

2. Product piece—something that represents the product you are selling

3. Broker information piece—something that your brokers can take away from the presentation you deliver that reminds them of how the program benefits them

4. PowerPoint—an approved PowerPoint presentation that you use to deliver your message to brokers and their agents

5. Broker legal agreement—the broker referral agreement, which must be signed by each broker, explaining what they are contracted to do, what you are contracted to do, the commissions you will pay them, how they earn commissions, and when they will be paid

Figure 6-3 shows some assumptions about how lead production is supposed to occur. The nice thing about these lead production numbers is they can be tracked as the program rolls out. The sales assumptions really look at the percentage of the leads harvested that will take a presentation and will purchase the offering. It is also worthwhile on these briefs to list all collateral that needs to be approved to achieve these numbers. It's great to have all assumptions reviewed and signed off on. Below you will see the number of leads, sales, and brochures that are needed to hit these projected numbers.

Key Assumptions:			
Broker Offices Targeted	120	% of Leads Turned HOT	15%
# of Agents in Target (75 per)	9,000	Number of HOT Leads	243
Icebreakers Performed (80%)	96	Hot Leads per Month	20
Icebreakers Converted (75%)	72		
Presentations Performed (90%)	65		
# of Agents per Presentation 20	1,296	**Promotion of program**	
# of Leads per Presentation 25	1,620	1. Developer Piece	
		2. Product Piece	
Total HOT Leads	243	3. Broker Information Piece	
Leads to Presentations	100%	4. Powerpoint on Program	
Contract Close	18.0%	5. Broker Legal Agreement	
Average Net Price	$355,000		
Amortized Over	12 months		

Figure 6-3

Next we will review expenses, which are divided into four sections for allocating money for location, employees, overhead, and premiums. These will vary in content depending on the marketing channel you are briefing. (The example provided is for broker programs.)

Location Expenses

1. Office setup—$14,000 (this covers everything you will need to set up the 1,500-square-foot satellite office)

2. Office rent—estimated at $3,500 per month for your 1,500-square-foot office or $42,000 per year

3. Broker newsletter—$7,000 (published twice annually)

4. Broker promotional programs—$8,000 per year

5. Broker presentation expense—$30,000 per year

Employee Expenses

1. Office commission on all sales at 4 percent (Keep in mind that this is a marketing expense for operating a broker network program. It is not a sales commission expense.)

2. Broker manager, both base and bonus

3. Broker assistant, both base and bonus

4. Benefits on both at 15 percent

Overhead Expenses

1. Broker brochures that are given out at the presentation at $5 per brochure

2. Brochures that are given out after a presentation is delivered at $10 a brochure

3. Supplies, printing, postage, licenses, and training relating specifically to the broker program

Premium Expense

This is an expense of $40,500 to cover the broker leads who stay in your accommodations and purchase. At the close of these escrows you can reimburse them up to $1,500 per visit. This example assumes that fifty percent of the broker sales will come down to see the offering on our program.

Below in figure 6-4 are the details as recorded in the brief itself:

Location Expense

Total Cost	$614,500
# of Leads	243
Cost Per Lead	$2,529

Employee Expense

Total Cost	$902,858
# of Leads	243
Cost Per Lead	$3,715

Overhead Expense

Total Cost	$23,030
# of Leads	243
Cost Per Lead	$95

Premium Expense

Total Cost	$40,500
# of Leads	243
Cost Per Lead	$167

Total Cost Summary

	Per Lead	Total
Location Expense	$2,529	$614,500
Employee Expense	$3,715	$902,858
Overhead Expense	$95	$23,030
Premium Expense	$167	$40,500
Total	$6,506	$1,580,888

Anticipated Performance

	Month	Totals	Other	Other	Other
Total Broker Leads	135	1,620			
% Lead to HOT		15%			
Total HOT Leads	20	243			
% of Leads to Presentation		100%			
Total Presentations	20	243			
Contract Close Percent		18%			
Multiple Contract Factor		1			
Total Fractional Sold	4	44			
Average Net Price		$355,000			
Net Volume		$15,527,700			
VPL		$63,900			
Cost Per Lead		$6,506			
Cost as % of Volume		10.18%			

Location Expense

		Per Lead	Monthly	Total
Office Set Up	$14,000	$58	$1,167	$14,000
Office rent	$42,000	$173	$3,500	$42,000
Broker Newsletter (2 times per yr)	$7,000	$29	$583	$7,000
Broker Promotional Program	$8,000	$33	$667	$8,000
Presentation expense	$30,000	$123	$2,500	$30,000
Other		$0	$0	$0
Other		$0	$0	$0
Other		$0	$0	$0
Total Location Costs		$2,529	$51,208	$614,500

Employee Expense Broker Commissions

			Per Tour	Monthly	Total
Office Commissions		4%	$2,556	$51,759	$621,108
Broker Manager @ 85K	1	$85,000	$350	$7,083	$85,000
BM Bonus Vol/HOT 85K	1	$85,000	$350	$7,083	$85,000
Broker Assistant	1	$50,000	$206	$4,167	$50,000
BA Bonus Vol/Hot	1	$25,000	$103	$2,083	$25,000
Leader Benefits @18%		15%	$151	$3,063	$36,750
Other			$0	$0	$0
Other			$0	$0	$0
Total Fixed Costs			$3,715	$75,238	$902,858

Overhead Expense

		Per Tour	Monthly	Total
Broker Brochures @ $5 per lead	$5	$33	$675	$8,100
Broker Brochures @ $10 per Pres	$10	$10	$203	$2,430
Supplies @ $100 per month	$1,200	$5	$100	$1,200
Printing @ $500 per month	$6,000	$25	$500	$6,000
Postage @ 250 per month	$3,000	$12	$250	$3,000
Licenses @ $500	$500	$2	$42	$500
Training $ 150 per month	$1,800	$7	$150	$1,800
Other		$0	$0	$0
Other		$0	$0	$0
Other		$0	$0	$0
Other		$0	$0	$0
Other		$0	$0	$0
Other		$0	$0	$0
Other		$0	$0	$0
Other		$0	$0	$0
Other		$0	$0	$0
Other		$0	$0	$0
Other		$0	$0	$0
Other		$0	$0	$0
Other		$0	$0	$0
Other		$0	$0	$0
Other		$0	$0	$0
Other		$0	$0	$0
Other		$0	$0	$0
Other		$0	$0	$0
Other		$0	$0	$0
Other		$0	$0	$0
Other		$0	$0	$0
Other		$0	$0	$0
Total Overhead Expense		$95	$1,919	$23,030

Premium Expense

		Per Tour	Monthly	Total
Site Visits paid for owners @50%	27	$167	$3,375	$40,500
Room Nights (three)	81	$0	$0	$0
Other		$500	$0	$0	$0
Other		$0	$0	$0
Total		$167	$3,375	$40,500

Figure 6-4

The last section is the anticipated performance. This section takes all the assumptions in the brief and summarizes them.

Here are the numbers covered in this section of the brief:

Anticipated Performance

1. Total broker leads
2. Percentage of HOT leads
3. Total HOT leads
4. Percentage of leads to presentations
5. Total presentations
6. Contract close percentage
7. Multiple contract factor
8. Total fraction sold
9. Average price
10. Net volume
11. Volume per lead
12. Cost per lead
13. Cost as a percent of volume

Below in figure 6-5 is the section of the marketing brief that shows these numbers:

ANTICIPATED PERFORMANCE	MONTH	TOTALS	OTHER	OTHER	OTHER
Total Broker Leads	135	1,620			
Percentage of Leads to HOT		15%			
Total HOT Leads	20	243			
Percentage of Leads to Presentation		100%			
Total Presentations	20	243			
Contract Close Percentage		18%			
Multiple Contract Factor		1			
Total Fractional Sold	4	44			
Average Net Price		$355,000			
Net Volume		$15,527,700			
Volume per Lead		$63,900			
Cost per Lead		$6,506			
Cost as Percentage of Volume		10.18%			

Figure 6-5

This is a marketing brief from a shared ownership resort. However, you can (and should) create a marketing brief on any marketing program you are investing money in and want to have a return on the investment. A return is made by producing qualified leads and converting them to sales. These briefs set the anticipated performance levels of each marketing channel you will want to track.

Like everything else, once you work with these marketing briefs, they become much easier to put together. If you have questions about these briefs, please let us know as we would be happy to walk you through the sheets.

Key Notes for
Marketing Financial Assumptions

1. Financial briefs anticipate your performance with specific marketing channels. They estimate cost and revenue as well as leads and sales performance.

2. Make sure you understand each section of the brief and how it relates to the other sections.

3. We use these briefs to compare projected performance to actual performance.

4. Briefs should be well-thought-out and supportable. Draw upon your past history whenever you can. Briefs need to be signed off on by the leaders approving spending. Briefs should make these leaders comfortable knowing that you have done your homework and have workable assumptions for your investment.

Let's hear from our characters about tips on how to make your *marketing assumptions*.

Chapter 6: Marketing Financial Assumptions

Here is an action scene with our characters preparing their marketing performance assumptions before starting to prospect.

Make your assumptions carefully, drawing on all the history and experience you have. These assumptions will create realistic targets for performance expectations.

Chapter 7

Description and Responsibilities Paper

Creating clear direction for the people, processes and action steps

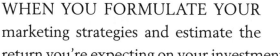

The description and responsibilities paper covers nine key aspects of a marketing campaign.

WHEN YOU FORMULATE YOUR marketing strategies and estimate the return you're expecting on your investments, there are three things you need to complete before you start spending:

1. Financial marketing assumptions (sometimes called a marketing brief)—in the last chapter

2. Description and responsibilities paper—this chapter

3. Approval and compliance form—next chapter

127

You should start with your financial marketing assumptions, which we reviewed in the previous chapter. You need to complete the financial marketing assumptions first because you need to make sure the marketing program you are about to invest in has sufficient return potential. Once it has been completed and shows a positive outcome, you should draft a description and responsibilities paper. In order to make your marketing programs work, you need people, processes and action steps in place so that everyone on your marketing team thoroughly understands what needs to be done. The description and responsibilities paper outlines these important processes and steps.

Very few marketing teams actually put these papers together. I believe, though, that you will not perform to you highest potential without drafting this paper, which identifies your processes, targets, a clear description of the program, and guidelines about who is responsible for what and when. If you start using these papers, you will see how they help increase your efficiency, most of all by identifying clearly what everyone will do and what processes will need to be in place when the program is launched.

Just as different metrics are essential for measuring the performance of marketing channels, so the description and responsibilities paper is equally essential for reviewing the objectives, processes, and responsibilities entailed by each marketing channel. I have seen companies do great jobs evaluating and preparing the financial metrics of a marketing channel only to complete nothing concerning the description and responsibilities of the channel. You will soon see that if you want to be a first-class operator you cannot do one without doing the other. It's great to forecast all your financial numbers; however, if you do not spell out descriptions, objectives, processes, lessons learned, and responsibilities, you do not have a complete program. I have seen many marketing programs fail or at least not meet their full potential because the marketing team was not ready to execute the program's details.

Marketing experts who read through these papers will probably be surprised by how many areas they can improve. When your objectives, processes, and responsibilities are written down, they can be reviewed by many different talents who can provide significant feedback that improves a program. Team members sometimes think they know how a program is supposed to function, but when they actually sit down together, they may discover everyone has a slightly different notion about how things should be done. As you create this document, you may discover better ways to run a particular process in a marketing program. Always challenge this document and look for more effective and efficient ways to process a marketing program. You will soon discover that this type of discipline will create better cost per lead production, better conversions to presentations, and eventually better volume per lead statistics.

This description and responsibilities paper should be completed and reviewed thoroughly before a marketing program is approved. The paper should detail nine aspects of a marketing program. Each of these needs to be well thought out before you implement your program. Here are the nine descriptions and responsibilities for each marketing program:

1. Program description
2. Who and where the buyer is
3. Objectives
4. Benefits
5. Processes
6. Offer
7. Assumptions
8. Lessons learned
9. Action items

Below is a brief overview of each of the nine key aspects of your marketing campaigns you need to complete for a description and responsibilities paper. Also, at the end of this chapter you'll find an example of a completed direction and responsibilities paper that you can reference.

Program Description

You need to start with a description of what you are about to do in a marketing channel to generate leads. This very important section consists of a two or three paragraph description of the program you are about to fund. Anyone who reads this description, whether he or she is directly involved with marketing, will fully understand how the program operates.

Who and Where the Buyer Is

This subject has been covered in prior chapters, but you need to get in writing your ideas about who qualified leads are and where you are going to find them. This section is especially important for your legal and branding team leaders and for sales people so they can prepare to help generate leads and convert those leads into sales.

Objectives

The objective of all programs is to generate quality leads, but if there are also other objectives that must be accomplished, state them in this section. You should also state clearly how you expect this marketing program to perform in terms of vital statistics. Record the number of leads you want to generate, the expected cost of each of those leads, the volume per lead you are forecasting, and your assumptions concerning the percentage of cost compared to revenue produced for this program.

Benefits

You will find that many people benefit when you launch a marketing program. Take the time to list them and briefly state why they will benefit if that is not obvious. There are many opportunities for a marketing channel to benefit the local community, a business partner, economies, your property, employees, charities, your company, and other companies.

Processes

Without well-defined processes you cannot be very effective. Write down the entire process that is in place when a lead responds to your marketing—who receives the response, how is it tracked, who does the performance reporting, who counts inquiries and what happens next, who counts and distributes leads to sales and what happens next, what your follow-up process is, and so forth. These are important steps, and there is no better way to have efficient programs than to write down in detail and have them reviewed by all key players. Thousands of dollars can be saved in lead costs and effectiveness can be greatly improved if this step is done correctly.

Offer

If your marketing program includes an offer, describe it in this section. It is important to share this information with everyone in your company.

Assumptions

Financial assumptions should be transcribed from your marketing briefs. To realize these returns, you must have your people, processes, and action steps all in place. The people in the program must understand what is expected from them and the program.

Lessons Learned

If you have run this program before or something similar, what have you learned? What went well, and what would you not want to repeat again? "Lessons Learned" should be a straightforward and very useful section of your paper, but many times it is overlooked. It helps you not repeat past mistakes and can give your program a big head start.

Action Items

This section should record what needs to be done, who is going to do it, when it will be done, and how often it will be reviewed. This section is very important because it ties everything together in a neat action plan that can be executed efficiently. It is crucial if you want to dominate in lead management.

I have always found these description and responsibilities papers to be outstanding communication tools for all players involved in marketing your product. These papers clarify what it takes to deliver an effective lead generation marketing program.

Key Notes for the Description and Responsibilities Paper

1. The description and responsibilities paper should be completed after you assess the financial viability of your marketing program.

2. Complete all nine areas of your description and responsibilities paper. This document establishes expectations about people, processes, and responsibilities, just as your marketing brief does about your financial performance.

3. Take time to review each of the nine areas with all people directly or indirectly involved in the marketing program.

4. Use this paper as a way to ensure that everyone who is part of the approval process understands the urgency of timing, messages, image, and cost to the success of this marketing program.

5. The paper should be completed and signed off on by everyone involved in the project before you start spending marketing dollars.

6. The devil is in the details. Take care of the details, and many of your potential problems go away.

Let's hear from our characters about the important *description and responsibilities paper*.

Chapter 7: Description and Responsibilities Paper

Here we have our characters in action working on their description and responsibilities paper.

The most overlooked strategy for securing lead domination is establishing and reviewing your processes. People, processes, the individual responsibilities of each marketing channel, and teams are the focus. The devil is in the details. Addressing these marketing details will bring you big success.

Example of a Description and Responsibilities Paper

Santa Barbara Residence Club
Description and Responsibilities Paper
Hotel Integration
Prepared 2/1/2008

Program Description

This Hotel Integration program is designed to create awareness about The Santa Barbara Residence Club offering for all guests staying and visiting the hotel. This marketing process must be crafted so as to provide a warm introduction to and a good first impression of The Residence Club in a way that is advantageous to the company brand, The Residence Club itself, and our high-end guests. It is important for this marketing channel that customers staying in the hotel be made aware of the offering through an agreed-upon introduction process. The marketing and sales team and the hotel staff must work together to create a seamless process that can deliver an effective introduction to The Residence Club. Guests will then determine whether they are interested in pursuing more information. The way the hotel staff and the residence team cooperate will be the difference between a poor, mediocre, or highly successful program for all.

This program will be driven at a Residence Club gallery location in the hotel lobby area. A small team of high-end marketing coordinators will staff the gallery location; in addition, there will be an in-room awareness campaign. The gallery, in-room awareness campaign, and the marketing coordinators need to function as extensions of the hotel and The Santa Barbara Residence Club.

Residence Club employees should go through the same training and orientation as a concierge hotel employee. This training will be helpful in making The Residence Club marketing coordinator adept at informing guests about the hotel, its amenities, available activities, and The Residence Club itself. The hotel gallery and in-room awareness program will be reviewed and signed off on by a select group representing the hotel team, the branding team, and The Residence Club. We will call this group The Committee. The coordination and cooperation between members of The Committee to create a seamless experience will be very important to the success of this marketing channel. The Residence Club employees will respond to in-bound calls generated by the in-room materials and talk with interested guests who walk into the lobby gallery.

The performance of marketing coordinators and their teams will be reviewed on a monthly basis, with particular emphasis on how well they interact with the hotel team, the way they handle the guests they service, the cost per lead they produce, and their percentage of leads converted to presentations.

We will review our hotel performance based on the percentage of interest from arriving guests in two categories, FIT (frequent independent travelers) and group guests. This performance matrix will be reviewed by The Committee to ensure all teams are meeting expectations.

Who and Where the Buyer Is

Buyers are between the ages of 45 and 60, have an income of $250,000 or more, live in a house with a value of $1 million plus, and have a second home or an interest in a second home. They are currently spending time in the Santa Barbara area on a regular basis. Buyers who do not spend time in Santa Barbara enjoy and have a history of spending time at beach locations. They spend time in the water or like to be by the water in beach locations. They also enjoy golf, fishing, surfing, or just the weather that beach locations like Santa Barbara offer.

Buyers live in the Los Angeles area and are looking for a second home close by where they can get away from the hustle and bustle of the city and enjoy the relaxing environment of a small beach town like Santa Barbara.

Even though this marketing channel will focus on buyers who usually stay in the hotel, other marketing programs will drive additional people to the hotel. Make sure they understand the marketing dollars you are investing to make people aware of the resort—usually a larger number than the entire hotel marketing budget for a year.

They should also know that many of the clients the Residence Clubs markets to will respond directly to the hotel as paying customers, which will increase occupancy rates.

Objectives

There are two objectives of this hotel integration program: First, to help market and sell the Residence Club in Santa Barbara. Second, to provide additional advertising and a heightened profile for the hotel, thereby increasing hotel room occupancies. Most of the dollars invested in this program will provide direct and indirect benefits for the hotel. The marketing and selling of The Residence Club will be fully funded by the Club itself.

The primary objective is to introduce at least 3 percent of arrivals to The Residence Club. These guests will be considered leads. Our experience shows that 60 percent of these leads will be intrigued enough after an introduction to want more information and accept a presentation opportunity. Our next target will be the 9 percent of those taking advantage of the presentation opportunity who will purchase a Residence Club ownership interest. We will manage the cost of this hotel lead at or below $684 per lead. Targeting only 3 percent of arriving guests allows us to provide a warm, non-evasive, professional introduction driven completely by the guest's own interest. With effective professional cooperation between the hotel and The Residence Club, along with a strategic marketing approach, we could possibly double this interest level among hotel guests.

We have divided hotel guests into two categories: FIT guests (frequent independent travelers) and group guests. We have three potential opportunities to create a lead, a presentation, or a sale with these guests: pre-arrival opportunities, in-house opportunities, and post-stay opportunities. Each of these marketing objectives is described under the "Processes" section. Walk-by guests not staying in the hotel afford additional opportunities. All pre-arrival, in-house, and post-stay opportunities will be agreed upon by The Committee in advance and can be modified as we move forward to meet our goals. Marketing strategy meetings with The Committee will be very important for the creation of a seamless, successful hotel integration program.

Benefits

Over a six-year marketing period, $1.9 million will be invested in this program, with most of this money being used to promote the developer, the hotel, and The Residence Club. Six different marketing introduction pieces will be proposed to The Committee for this program. The benefit for The Residence Club of this marketing source will be to capitalize on guests who have committed to come to Santa Barbara. We are looking for guests who are possibly considering purchasing a second home. The price of entry in the second home market in Santa Barbara is several million dollars, and the clients we are looking for will not be able to justify that investment versus usage. Our Residence Club may be the perfect match for their lifestyle.

The Santa Barbara Residence Club offering is one more additional service offered to the hotel guests.

Process

The following is a short summary of our suggested process efforts focused on FIT and group guests staying in the hotel. All items will be reviewed and approved by The Committee.

1. The hotel concierge, who sends pre-arrival information and may even call incoming FIT guests, can share information about The Residence Club. A message could be sent on all confirmations as well as communicated upon the FIT guest's pre-arrival. If the guest elects to request some information on The Residence Club, he or she will be turned over to our marketing coordinators for follow-up.

2. A brochure providing information about The Residence Club, placed strategically in guest rooms.

3. Turn-down cards, placed next to chocolates by room service, for guests on the first night of their stay.

4. Special amenity gifts for a few select FIT guests each month, with a welcome card introducing The Residence Club.

5. Wine tasting events in The Residence Club sales gallery once a week for select hotel guests.

6. A hotel employee awareness program so that all employees who interface with guests are aware of The Residence Club offering and can answer questions and direct guests to the lobby gallery.

7. Post-stay letter sent to select prime candidates based on their visiting patterns to Santa Barbara. We will send them a revisit package to return to the hotel and take an opportunity to pre-view The Residence Club offering.

The following is a short summary of our efforts focused on group guests:

1. Review in advance each group profile. When a group is iden-tified as matching our profile customer, we will work with the hotel's group planning coordinator on ways of reaching that specific group.

2. A brochure providing information about The Residence Club, placed strategically in guest rooms.

3. Turn-down cards, placed next to chocolates by room service, for guests on the first night of their stay.

Offer

The offer is to have guests who wish to learn more about The Residence Club return to the hotel for a tour. It would consist of a special three-night package based on occupancy and rate coor-dinated by the hotel team and The Committee.

Assumptions

CATEGORY	BUDGETED PERFORMANCE	ACTUAL PERFORMANCE	VARIANCE
Leads	2,856	0	2,856
Presentations	1,714	0	1,714
Conversion Percentage	60%	0%	60%
Close Percentage	9.3%	0%	9.3%
Net Sales	160	0	160
Average Price	$355,000	$0	$355,000
Net Volume	$56,800,000	$0	$56,800,000
Total Expense	$1,952,382	$0	$1,952,382
Cost Per Lead	$684	$0	$684
Cost Per Presentation	$1,139	$0	$1,139
Volume per Lead	$19,888	$0	$19,888
Volume per Presentation	$33,139	$0	$33,139
Cost Percentage of Program	3.44%	0.%	3.44%

Lessons Learned

1. The Committee must work together well and keep in mind the brand, the customers, the cost, and the timing.

2. Make as many guests as possible aware of The Residence Club offering and let them choose the next step for information.

3. Multiple marketing steps are the key to success.

Action Items

KEY PRODUCTION ITEMS	RESPONSIBILITY	REVIEW OR COMPLETION DATE
Develop the in-room, turn-down, wine invitations, SB Residence Club brochures, and collateral.	The Committee	Monthly/Quarterly/YTD
Set marketing coordinator hours to 8:00 A.M. to 9:00 P.M.	Santa Barbara Director of Marketing	Monthly/ Quarterly/YTD
Extend membership executives hours to 8:00 A.M. to 9:00 P.M.	Santa Barbara Director of Sales	Monthly/ Quarterly/YTD

Insure that the membership executives and marketing coordinators are working together for a seamless guest experience. We would have a membership executive able to accept appointments at the guests' request.	Santa Barbara Director of Marketing Santa Barbara Director of Sales	Monthly/ Quarterly/YTD
Work with the hotel on in-room brochures and second-night turn-down pieces.	Santa Barbara Director of Marketing	Weekly
Select with hotel the guest that should receive an invitation to the wine-tasting parties in the gallery.	Santa Barbara Director of Marketing	Weekly
Marketing coordinators performance reviews	Santa Barbara Director of Marketing	Monthly/ Quarterly/YTD
Hotel penetration reports that review penetration on leads and presentations based on arrivals	Santa Barbara Director of Marketing	Monthly/ Quarterly/YTD
Check-in activators, if used from time to time, making sure of supply at the front desk	Santa Barbara Director of Marketing	Weekly/ Monthly
Work with hotel leadership to ensure all aspects of this program are producing favorable results for all.	Santa Barbara Director of Marketing	Weekly/ Monthly
One hundred best FIT guests per month get an amenity gift with invite to see the models.	Santa Barbara Director of Marketing	Weekly/ Monthly
Develop a high-end once a week collectible wine party offering aficionado wines in the lobby gallery through special invitation to hotel guests.	Santa Barbara Director of Marketing	Weekly
Pre-arrival marketing work with hotel and get direction so The Residence Club could be part of the pre-arrival process.	Santa Barbara Director of Marketing	Weekly/ Monthly
We feel it is important that The Residence Club is treated like a hotel extension and is respected as such.	Santa Barbara Director of Marketing	Weekly/ Monthly
Review reports to see how each of these programs is performing.	Santa Barbara Director of Marketing	Weekly/ Monthly/ Quarterly/YTD

Chapter 8

Approval and Compliance Form

Good current communication on all marketing programs can bring future success

> It's important to get the people you need to approve or participate in your marketing programs on board early, so no delays or misunderstandings hinder your progress.

AN APPROVAL AND COMPLIANCE form will help ensure that everything necessary has been completed from a financial and processing standpoint. The approval and compliance form should not be confused with any other documents. The approval and compliance form has the marketing brief and the description and responsibilities paper attached to it. The approval and compliance form is used to make sure everyone who needs to review the marketing program before any spending occurs has done so. When all parties sign off on this approval and compliance form, you are ready to fund the program. Then, you'll be ready to move ahead as a united team.

This form is very important because sometimes marketing programs are funded and started only to be delayed or stopped because one or more of the key players turns out not to have been on board, which can be embarrassing for the marketing team, poor from a lead generation standpoint, debilitating for team cooperation, and a disaster in financial terms. When this approval and compliance form is signed off on, your marketing team should not experience any internal delays or surprises as it rolls out your program. Everyone, including the people directly responsible for the results, will have been briefed, and they will understand what they need to accomplish. You can all move ahead as one united team, which is how you want to start all your major marketing programs.

The bottom line is that this form is great for getting started on the right foot and ensuring all your ducks are in a row. You can move ahead with expectations of great success and a focus on lead domination.

Below is a sample approval and compliance form (figure 8-1). You will note that you should attach two supplemental documents, the marketing brief and the description and responsibilities paper (covered in the two previous chapters). This package should be reviewed by your legal, branding, and leadership teams and signed by all, including the person who approves funding for your programs.

Approval and Compliance Form

Property _____

Marketing channel _____

Tracking number _____

Name requesting _____

Marketing dollars needed _____

[ ] Please attach your Financial Assumptions

[ ] Please attach your Description and Responsibilities Paper

Approvals Needed

[ ] Legal _____

[ ] Branding _____

[ ] Leadership _____

Marketing Compliance

What needs to be completed before the marketing of this program begins?

1. _____

2. _____

3. _____

Who needs to complete the above items?

1. _____

2. _____

3. _____

Sales Compliance

What needs to be completed before the sales of this program begin?
1. _____
2. _____
Who needs to complete the above items?
1. _____
2. _____

SIGNATURES for APPROVAL: _____
Legal

_____
Branding

_____
Financials

_____
Sales

_____
Marketing

_____
Figure 8-1   Leadership

Key Notes for the
Approval and Compliance Form

1. Have your marketing program authorized with an approval and compliance form.

2. Get all decision makers from all disciplines on the same page so the approval process will be complete.

3. This form will help prevent embarrassing situations after the program has already started.

Let's hear from our characters about the *approval and compliance form.*

Chapter 8: Approval and Compliance Form

Here is an action scene with our characters showing how they handle the marketing expense approval process.

Lead domination is all about teamwork. If you get your teams to work together to approve marketing expenses and programs, you will accomplish more in a much shorter time and build great momentum.

#### Chapter 9

Lead Accounting

If you can't account for the performance of a lead, don't spend your money generating one

> If you want to achieve lead domination, you must have a lead bank!

LEAD SUPPORT

LEAD REPORTS

LEAD TRAINING

A LEAD BANK IS the heartbeat of any lead accounting operation. Its job is to communicate to marketing leaders about lead production and to sales leaders about the conversion of leads to presentations and presentations to sales. After a presentation has been made, the lead bank will track a lead in progress and report back to sales leaders. The lead bank should track all leads until they are either not interested or make a purchase.

Your ability to track leads has everything to do with the potential success of your marketing programs. If you cannot account for the leads you are generating, then it's not really a marketing program and you should not invest marketing dollars in it. It might better be described as a PR program or something like that, so find another area besides marketing for budgeting this expense.

Let's assume you have established accountability for all marketing dollars and all programs in which you are going to invest. You invest marketing dollars to produce sales, but you cannot produce sales without a sales presentation, and you cannot have a sales presentation without having a lead. The dollars you invest in your marketing channels are for generating quality leads, ones that will meet the targeted percentages of conversions to presentations and then to sales. To be effective, you must account for the leads you generate through each marketing channel.

So lead accounting means not just tracking leads but tracking presentations and sales. The number of leads you generate, the number you convert to presentations, and the number of presentations that convert to sales are what you are tracking and investing in. Your lead accounting is every bit as important as the marketing campaigns you produce and will give you the vital statistics you need to run your marketing programs wisely. It will tell you what it has cost you to produce leads, presentations, and sales.

In the chart below, showing the cost of a lead, the cost of a presentation, and the cost of a sale, you can start to see how these expenses add up. It is important to track these costs and to keep them as low as possible. Lead costs become lower with better responses; presentation costs become lower with a higher conversion rate from a lead to a presentation; and sales costs become lower with a higher conversion rate from presentation to sales. The lower these costs are, the more effective and efficient your sales and marketing operation is.

The local marketing program in figure 7-1 shows the following:

Cost per Lead	$949
Cost per Presentation	$2,710
Cost per Sale	$21,343

Figure 7-1

The Lead Bank

It is best to put one central operation in charge of all your lead accounting and reporting. That keeps your lead reporting consistent if you have multiple sites or products and, even if you cannot operate a lead bank, you should keep a small team focused full-time on this important component of your marketing team and programs. The lead bank is responsible for all the daily, weekly, monthly, quarterly, and annual reports on lead production. It coordinates its activities with administrative teams at company headquarters or any other locations that may receive leads. Most of the leads will be initiated at the site or other locations where the administrative teams work. These teams will account for the leads initially, but at the end of each day all of them will report to the lead bank, which functions as the keeper of all the reports. There needs to be a well-defined process whereby administrative teams report to the lead bank, and reports should be made each and every day. There needs to be a lead reconciliation process between the lead bank and administrative teams daily to ensure counts and accuracy.

The lead bank also coordinates lead production with the director of sales, who must track all leads that convert to a presentation. This important information must be communicated back to the lead bank on a daily basis.

The lead bank must also take the sales volume generated by each marketing channel and divide it by the total number of leads to produce the volume per lead. Volume per lead is one of the statistics used to determine the quality level of the leads you are producing.

From a sales standpoint, the lead bank must keep leads in three categories: purchased, not interested, and in progress. Not interested and purchased leads definitely require follow-up, but it is the lead bank's role to account for these two categories so they can be followed up on. The lead bank should work closely with sales on leads in progress to make sure that the thirteen levels of a lead in progress are followed and that leads can be accounted for as such. These important thirteen levels of leads in progress will be covered later in the sales section of this book. The lead bank has the important role of accounting for these statistics.

The last accounting process the lead bank must perform is coordinating all costs to the correct marketing channels to determine the cost per lead. The cost per lead is the number of dollars spent in a particular marketing channel divided by the number of leads the channel has generated. You should look at the cost per lead on a monthly, quarterly, and annual basis. Marketing teams need to focus on cost per lead trends.

This is a vital statistic as well as part of the quantity and quality level formula. The quantity and quality formula gauges whether a marketing channel meets, exceeds, or falls below the number of leads targeted and whether the channel is at or under the cost per lead and volume per lead. You can look back at chapter three to review the quality and quantity lead formulas.

Here are our lead guidelines:

Leads

1. Formulate a definition of what a lead is.

2. This definition may vary slightly from one marketing channel to the next.

3. You must have a process that accounts for all leads by marketing channel.

4. Some marketing channels will produce inquiries that do not qualify for leads. You must also account for these inquiries.

5. You should account for inquiries that convert to leads and the conversion percentage.

6. Lead quantity accounting reports should be completed and reconciled daily.

7. Lead quantity performance should be compared to budgets or targets daily.

8. Lead quantity performance reports by marketing channel should be completed on a monthly, quarterly, and annual basis.

9. Keep track of lead generation dollar investments for each marketing channel.

10. You must be able to determine the cost per lead and volume per lead by marketing channel at the end of each month.

11. You should calculate cost per lead and volume per lead performance reports on a monthly, quarterly, and year-to-dates basis for each marketing channel.

The flowchart below (figure 9-1) shows five different individuals or groups you must track: the client, the leads distribution specialist, the sales person, the director of sales, and the lead bank.

Lead Accounting Flowchart

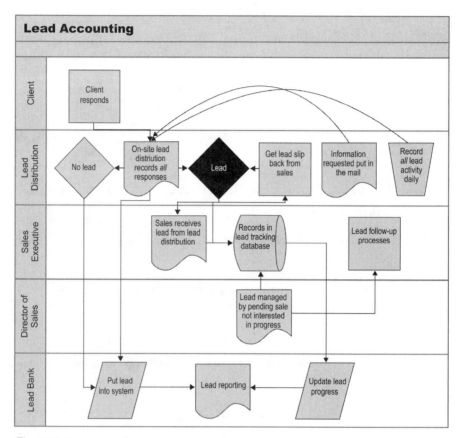

Figure 9-1

Here are our presentation guidelines:

Leads Converted to Presentation

1. You should have a company definition of what a sales presentation is.

2. Conversions from leads to sales presentations are usually done by sales, so you need a well-defined process and effective cooperation between the lead bank, marketing, and sales.

3. Sales people tend to do what is inspected rather than what is merely expected. I highly recommend you inspect this process so you can track conversion statistics accurately.

4. You must have a process whereby all leads converted to presentations are accounted for—by marketing channel—through the lead bank.

5. Leads converted to presentations should be completed and reconciled daily.

6. Compare these conversions against your budget or targets on a daily basis.

7. Leads converted to presentations performance reports by marketing channel should be completed and reviewed on a monthly, quarterly, and annual basis.

8. You should be able to calculate the cost per presentation by marketing channel at the end of each month.

9. You should generate cost per presentation performance reports for each marketing channel and review them on a monthly, quarterly, and year-to-date basis.

When you track conversion of leads to sales presentations and the accounting process in the flowchart below, you will need to be able to trace the activities of three key players: salespeople, the director of sales, and the lead bank. Here's what this looks like on a presentation flowchart in figure 9-2:

Presentation Accounting Flowchart

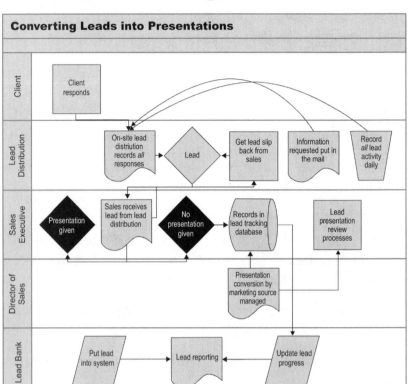

Figure 9-2

Here are our sales guidelines:

Presentations That Convert to Sales

1. You should have a company definition of what a sale is.

2. Conversions from presentations to sales are usually done by sales, so a process should be in place whereby sales communicates the number of these conversions to marketing.

3. Track sales for each site or product and where they occur.

4. Sales produced and the lead bank should have a process for accounting for sales and tracking them back to leads and marketing channels.

5. Presentations converted to sales should be completed and rec-onciled daily.

6. Presentations converted to sales performance should be com-pared to your budget or targets and reviewed monthly, quarterly, and annually.

7. You should be able to calculate the volume per lead by mar-keting channel at the end of each month.

8. Volume per lead performance reports for each marketing chan-nel should be reviewed on a monthly, quarterly, and year-to-date basis.

When you track conversion of presentations to sales and the accounting process in the flowchart below, you will need to be able to trace the activities of three key players: salespeople, the director of sales, and the lead bank. Let's see what this looks like on a presentation flowchart in figure 9-3.

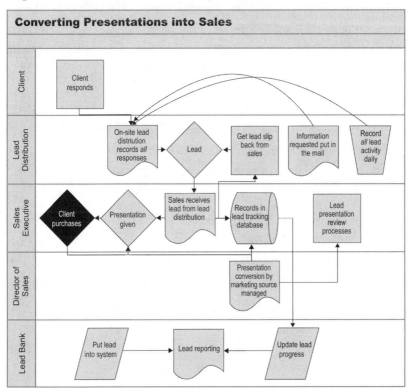

Figure 9-3

Your lead bank operation keeps track of many major performance statistics that will drive the number of dollars you invest in marketing channels:

1. Number of leads by marketing channel

2. Percentage of leads converted to presentations

3. Leads not interested

4. Leads who purchased

5. Leads in progress

6. All leads in progress (update on a weekly basis)

All of these statistics above are tracked by marketing channel and by sales agent. That means there will be two different reports provided by the lead bank, both of which are very important for running a lead domination sales and marketing process.

This information must be communicated from each site's administrative and sales teams to the lead bank. Each marketing channel will probably have a slightly different lead flow, depending upon how responsibilities have been assigned.

I would highly recommend that you create a lead flowchart and have all parties review it so they understand who's responsible, how leads will flow through your system, and how each marketing channel will be tracked. That is one important way you can ensure lead accounting has been set up on each of your different marketing channels. I believe a flowchart on each marketing channel should be required. It will really help you visualize how leads will flow through your established systems. Keep in mind that each marketing source may be a little different. In the following pages we will review how this should be done.

Hotel Integration

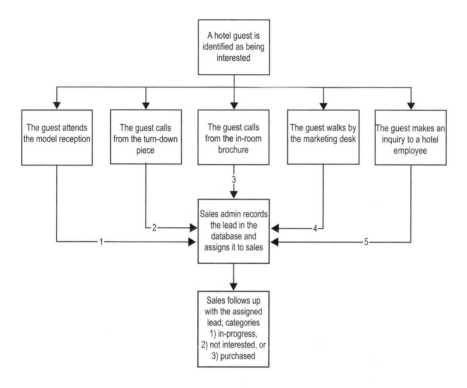

In a hotel integration marketing process, you need to track lead generation in terms of five areas of prospect contact: meeting guests in the models, turn-down pieces put on the guests' beds each night promoting your product, in-room pieces promoting your product, making contact with walk-bys, and providing incentives to hotel employees for referring guests to your offering. Then the leads should be qualified for interest and turned over to sales as soon as possible. These guests will have a high conversion from lead to presentation because of the large percentage of face-to-face presentations.

Be sure your lead accounting support is set up advantageously for both marketing and sales in terms of both performance and compensation.

Broker Network

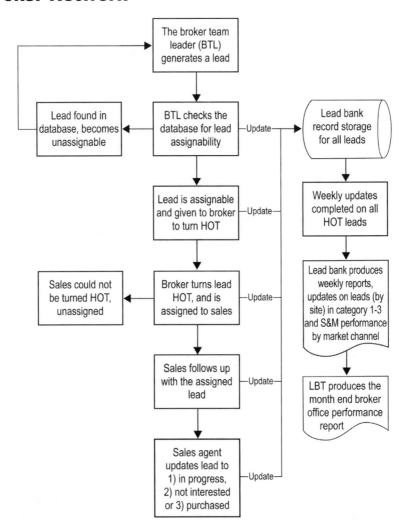

The flow of lead generation through a broker network includes many critical steps that must be followed to ensure success. First, you need to account for all leads generated by this program. Second, you must check for lead duplication in your database. Third, you need to protect the brokers' leads that are not in your database. Fourth, work with brokers on turning leads HOT, even though only about thirty percent will. Only HOT leads should be counted in the broker stats and given to the sales team to work. Fifth, turn HOT leads over to the sales team for follow-up. Sixth, get back to the brokers on how their leads are progressing.

Be sure that your lead accounting support is set up well. This lead accounting is for broker agents who have referred the lead, the broker team leaders who run the program, the marketing team for the appropriate channel, and the sales team that follows up on all leads.

Owners Program

In an owners program lead generation needs to be tracked for all owners participating and even ones who are not. This process is important for the expansion of the program. You can expand this effective program if you know what owners are not participating in your referral program and why. Then take appropriate action to see whether you can comfortably get them involved. These are some of the best leads you will obtain, so the system must be in place to turn these leads over to sales for follow-up processes.

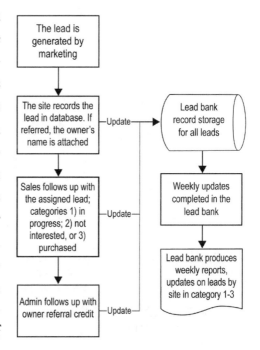

Be sure your lead accounting support is set up well. The lead accounting for owner programs needs to be seperated by referral leads and reload leads. Performance reports need to be completed and reviewed carefully on a monthly basis. If this marketing chan-nel is tracked correctly by the lead bank and managed properly by sales and marketing leaders, it can account for a large percentage of your sales volume.

Web Advertising

Tracking lead genera-tion through a web program starts with a hit on your site. Some of these hits are then transferred to your database for account-ing as leads. After that a web concierge should make contact with the lead for some pre-qualification. The lead should then be sent to sales for a follow-up. For web lead accounting you need to ensure you have the proper URLs set up so you can separate true web lead generation from web leads driven to your site by other marketing channels.

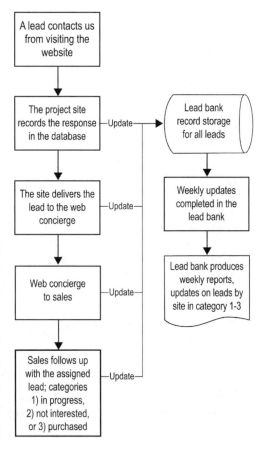

There will be many hits on your website, and it could well be one of your top lead generators. Daily, weekly, and monthly re-porting of these leads in essential to the success of this program, which may be your least expensive in terms of cost per lead. Pro-cess your leads from the web concierge to sales and the follow-up in a highly professional manner. Keep in mind these leads require more follow-up than most. This channel's economic success can be second to none if you have a decent performance in terms of volume per lead by sales.

Local Advertising

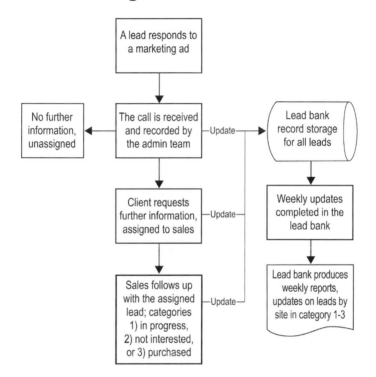

The flow of lead generation through your local marketing advertising is pretty straightforward also. It's all about accounting for the leads coming in and making sure your leads are corectly sourced. Then turn them over to the sales team for follow-up and have your lead bank track the results.

Make sure you review performance on this source as it tends to be expensive. As you review your cost per lead on this program, you will want to keep an eye on the volume per lead to make sure this marketing channel is really worth the investment.

National Advertising

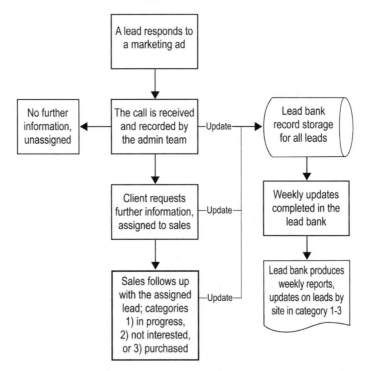

The flow of lead generation through a national advertising campaign is also pretty straightforward. It involves accounting for leads coming in and sourcing them correctly. This marketing channel will drive leads to your website, so you need to make sure you have URLs set up correctly to give credit to national advertising and not to your website, when appropriate. These leads need to be turned over to the sales team. Make sure all systems are in place for follow-up, and have your lead bank track the results. Follow-up performance should be reviewed on a monthly basis as these leads could be among your most expensive.

Be sure you keep track of the vital performance statistics on this program: the number of leads, cost per lead, volume per lead, and percentage of cost versus revenue (your report card). All these statistics need to be compared against what was budgeted. This source has to be watched closely as it tends to have an expensive cost per lead. A single ad in national advertising can run between $25,000 to $50,000.

Direct Mail

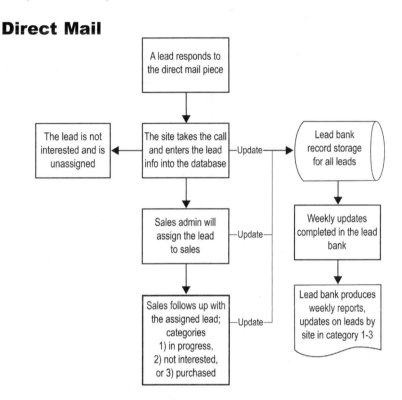

Keeping track of lead generation produced by your direct mail programs is pretty simple. It starts with the percentage of response you get from your mail piece, which is your lead count. Leads coming in need to be accounted for and correctly sourced, then turned over to the sales team for follow-ups. The lead bank should track the results of sales presentations.

Make sure you review the performance of this source as it tends to be expensive in terms of cost per lead. Also make sure the volume per lead indicates this marketing channel is cost effective.

Event Marketing

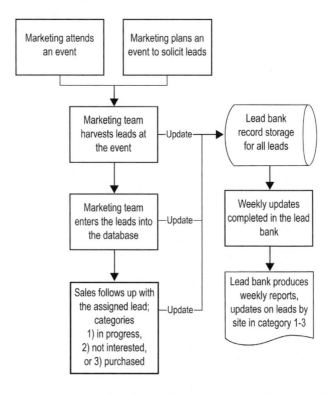

Marketing at events takes lots of time to coordinate and to get to the point where you are actually generating leads. This marketing source takes the most preparation for booking the event and getting ready for the event. It could take three months to plan for an event, and you will not receive any leads until the event happens. These events may happen once a quarter, so the leads you do generate are precious. Account for incoming leads and turn them over to the sales team. Sales needs to follow up, and your lead bank should track the results.

Make sure you review performance on this source as it tends to be an expensive one. You also want to make sure the volume per lead is acceptable.

The lead bank must have very clear guidelines about accounting for leads, presentations, and sales as well as for tracking the status of a lead through the accounting process. Below is a typical set of guidelines used for lead accounting. Yours could be a little different depending on the type of lead and the product you are selling, but I think this example will give you a good idea of what you need to have in place before you start accounting for your leads.

Lead Definition and Application

A lead is anyone who meets your lead definition established by marketing and sales or has contacted your company and requested to talk with sales about your product offerings. Leads are categorized as assigned, unassigned/DNC (do not call), and unregistered. Only assigned leads may be given to a sales agent and are included in the daily lead count and subsequent production/performance metric reports. Unassigned/DNC and unregistered leads are counted only for the purpose of building strategies to convert them to assignable leads.

Once a lead has been assigned, specific information about the lead must be collected for both the marketing and sales groups. Marketing will require the lead's name with at least one of the following pieces of information: telephone number (home, mobile, business), email address, home or business address (and room number if the lead is a hotel guest). The key is that a sales agent must be able to contact the lead.

Sales can create an assignable lead with only a name, but we prefer to obtain the same kind of information marketing collects.

Presentation Definition and Application

A presentation is defined as a clear explanation, by a sales agent, of a program's benefits and rewards in enough detail that a prospective purchaser can make an informed buying decision. A presentation may be given in person or over the phone. This presentation can last fifteen minutes or three hours. If the lead gets enough information to make a buying decision, it is a presentation. Simply giving a brochure to a client is not considered a presentation. Only a sales agent can give a presentation. Marketing personnel are expressly forbidden to discuss any terms or conditions of a product offering.

As you can clearly see, the responsibilities of the lead bank are absolutely critical to the success of any marketing team. Because of our extensive experience in operating lead banks, should you have any question about your lead bank operation, feel free to contact us at leaddomination@loreinstitute.com.

Key Notes for Lead Accounting

1. You should have one team that accounts for all lead accounting and performance, known as a lead bank.

2. Lead reporting needs to be done on a daily, weekly, monthly, quarterly, and annual basis.

3. Lead reporting needs to be done for each marketing channel and reconciled each day to ensure accuracy.

4. All lead performance reporting needs to be done by the lead bank. The performance reports generated will be critical to future marketing strategies for your product.

5. Make sure you can accurately account for leads, presentations, and sales produced.

6. When leads are in the progressing stage, the lead bank needs to be able to report on the status of each one weekly.

7. The lead bank should have clear definitions for each level of a lead in progress. There are thirteen different definitions (we will define these in an upcoming chapter), and each one should be clearly understood by your marketing and sales teams.

8. The lead bank should true-up on all lead production the prior day with the site by the beginning of each day. This means all lead accounting must match between the people receiving and counting the leads and the lead bank daily.

9. Lead flowcharts for each marketing channel should be completed and understood by all. That is the only way to be certain leads are being accounted for accurately and the flow of the lead has been established.

Let's hear from our characters about *lead accounting.*

If you cannot account for every one of your leads, their cost, and the sales volume they produce by marketing channel, do not invest a single marketing dime.

Chapter 10

Lead Performance Reporting

People may not do what's expected, but they tend to do what's inspected

Here is one of the most valuable contributions to the team—performance reports that are accurate, are on time, and will shape future strategies.

LEAD SUPPORT

LEAD REPORTS

LEAD TRAINING

THIS CHAPTER FOCUSES ON marketing channels and lead performance reporting from a marketing standpoint. Keep in mind that if you cannot account for the number of leads by marketing channel and the performance of these leads produced, you should not spend any money from your marketing budgets. I recommend setting up a lead bank operation that accounts for all your lead production and performance.

Even if you don't have a lead bank, some team must be assigned the responsibility for reporting back to you on the number of leads and how they are performing. This team would have to interface with many disciplines to create the reports you need to operate your marketing enterprise. Given your investments in marketing, I strongly recommend that you prepare your lead bank or report team to report back on all levels of performance. You need to have accurate and timely reports to dominate in lead management.

In this chapter I will share what I call my top eleven reports. I use as many as twenty-three different reports, but these eleven are the main drivers of productivity and should prove the most helpful to you. These vital reports will function as report cards, allowing you to gauge how well your marketing operation is performing. When I introduce you to these reports in this chapter, I will do the following:

1. First, show you the report

2. Second, tell you a little about the report and point out some key marketing areas that should be reviewed

3. Third, let you know how often this report should be produced and reviewed

4. Fourth, let you know who is responsible for the accuracy of the reports as well as the timing and delivery of the reports

Lead Bank Performance Reports

Quarterly Team Culture Performance Report—Report #1

I feel this employee is a positive influence in the business environment.

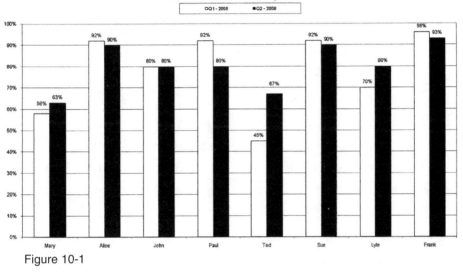

Sales and Marketing Engagement Survey
Question 23 Comparison

Figure 10-1

The Report—This is one of the most overlooked reports in sales and marketing operations. It will help you be more successful and will also help you and your leadership teams understand who to and how to manage on an individual basis. This report provides feedback on your team culture. I have found it to be extremely helpful for creating awareness about how other people on the team view the business environment. Remember that people may not do what is expected but do tend to focus on what is inspected.

How important do you think it is to be able to report on team members and their influence on the business environment? Do you think if you could get good information on this subject it would help you create a more positive working environment for your team? Do you think a more positive working environment leads to better production overall? If your answers are "yes," you'll want to use this report.

All employees, including leaders, rate each other at the end of each quarter on the following statement: *I feel this employee is a positive influence in the business environment.*

The rating scale is from one to five, with one being the lowest score and five being the highest. Ratings should be conducted in a private manner. No names should appear on the scoring sheet, and the sheet should be sent off-site to a neutral party for tallying the results. Employees must be reassured that their scores are private and that no one will know who scored whom what. At the end of the process employees will get to know only their own individual overall scores and how they compare to the scores for the overall team.

How important is it that each team member works hard to create a positive work environment? I say it is essential, and like everything else, it will not just happen on its own. You must work at it.

The results will be compiled, and leadership only will get something back like what you see in figure 10-1. I recommend that only management should receive this report and that it not be shown or distributed to the rest of the team. You should only go through the individual scores with the individual team members, letting each know how he or she did compared to everyone else as a whole. They should not see anyone else's score but their own and whether that score was above our below performance standards. You should also put together a plan of action for everyone to try to improve their scores no matter how good or bad they were.

The people who receive high scores need to be rewarded. You need to figure out how best to do that. If you reward those with high marks, everyone on the team will strive for top scores. The people on the bottom need to be coached and counseled on how to increase their positive influence on the team. Give them support and direction and really have them work on improving their scores for the next quarter. You will be surprised at how many people who receive low scores will have no idea that they were not perceived as positive influences on the team. Just the fact that they know how others see them will make a big difference. I would definitely suggest making this report part of their performance review.

Do you really want someone on your team who is not a positive influence, even if he or she can perform well? These people may be your hyenas today, but they do not need to continue to be hyenas on your team in the future. It's up to management to correct the situation. You and I know that eventually people who are not positive will affect the overall efficiencies of the team. Do this report once a quarter, and I promise you will see progress in your team morale, which is so essential to your results.

When Received—The report should be completed at the end of each quarter. As you can see, scores are compared to scores from prior quarterly reviews so everyone can gauge positive or negative trends.

Who's Responsible—I would engage a third party that is distant from the team. The employees rating others need to know their scoring will be kept confidential and that no one will know who scored whom what. That is the way it must be done to work. Ask employees to be as honest and accurate as possible and remind them each time how important it is that they complete the survey questions for everyone else on your team.

Quarterly Team Culture Performance Report—Report #2

I feel this employee is a good team player.

Sales and Marketing Engagement Survey
Question 24 Comparison

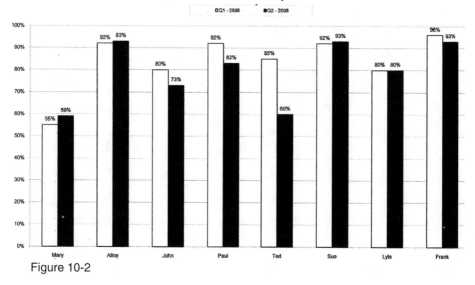

Figure 10-2

The Report—The same process applies for this second question. Ideally, you really want people who are team players and have a positive influence on your business environment. These are your outstanding employees in terms of culture and should be recognized as such. We score and rate performance on everything else: sales, number of leads, and so on. Rating employees' influence on the culture is every bit as important as having a successful results-driven sales and marketing team.

Look at Mary's score. What should you do? How about Ted's score? Better yet, what are you going to do to support the three employees who scored over 90 percent? All of these things, if followed up on effectively, can produce big results for your marketing and overall performance.

When Received—The report should be completed at the end of each quarter. As you can see, scores are compared to those from the prior quarterly review.

Who's Responsible—I would engage a third party who is distant from the team. The people who rate you and other members of the team need to know their scoring is strictly confidential and that no one will know who scores whom what. This is the way it must be done to work. You should ask employees to be as accurate as possible and remind them each time how important it is that they complete this survey.

Daily Marketing Lead Log—Report #3

Daily Marketing Lead Log 12/28/07

MARKETING CHANNELS	12/28 LEADS	12/29 LEADS	12/30 LEADS	12/23 –12/29 LEADS	DEC LEADS	DEC BUDGET	% OF BUDGET
Hotel Integration	2	1	2	12	56	48	117%
Broker Program	1	1	2	6	27	25	108%
Owner Referral	1	0	1	3	14	15	93%
National Advertising	1	2	2	13	48	55	87%
Local Advertising	1	0	0	3	18	15	120%
Web Marketing	3	3	2	18	57	65	88%
Direct Mail	1	0	0	3	15	10	150%
Self Generated	0	0	0	0	0	2	0%
Event Marketing	0	1	0	2	15	10	150%
Total	10	8	9	60	250	245	102%

Figure 10-3

The Report—The report in figure 10-3 should be completed daily so you can stay focused on your pure lead generation. This report is all about quantity, which is an important consideration from a performance standpoint. The key to this report is that you should receive it the next morning, and it should show you your lead performance for the prior day. Not only can you review what you did the previous day, but the report will also document trends in the last three days and the last full week as well as lead performance for the month compared to budget.

When Received—The report should be completed the day after the activity so that all numbers can be reconciled before distribution. This report should be delivered daily.

Who's Responsible—The lead bank is responsible for producing the report in an accurate and timely fashion. It will probably need support from the on-site team to make this happen.

Database Lead Performance—Report #4

Database Lead Performance

Updated 12/28/2008

UNREGISTERED STATES	JAN	FEB	MAR	APR	MAY	JUN	JUL	AUG	SEP	OCT	NOV	DEC	TOTAL
Hotel Integration	0	0	0	0	0	0	0	0	0	0	0	0	0
Broker Program	3	5	2	6	27	25	5	1	1	2	6	27	110
Owner Referral	1	0	1	3	2	2	0	1	0	1	3	1	15
National Advertising	1	2	0	1	0	3	0	1	2	2	3	3	18
Local Advertising	1	0	0	3	2	2	0	1	0	0	0	0	9
Web Marketing	4	2	0	0	2	2	0	2	0	0	0	2	14
Direct Mail	0	0	0	0	0	0	0	0	0	0	0	0	0
Self-Generated	0	0	0	0	0	0	0	0	0	0	0	0	0
Event Marketing	0	0	0	0	0	0	0	0	0	0	0	0	0
Total	10	9	3	13	33	34	6	6	3	5	12	33	167

(Continued on next page)

UNASSIGNED/DNC	JAN	FEB	MAR	APR	MAY	JUN	JUL	AUG	SEP	OCT	NOV	DEC	TOTAL
Hotel Integration	0	1	2	0	0	0	0	2	1	2	1	1	10
Broker Program	10	6	12	116	130	4	8	42	87	43	32	1	491
Owner Referral	0	0	0	0	0	0	0	0	0	0	0	0	0
National Advertising	0	0	1	0	0	2	0	0	2	0	0	0	5
Local Advertising	1	0	0	2	1	2	0	1	0	0	2	1	10
Web Marketing	1	0	0	4	1	2	1	2	1	0	0	0	12
Direct Mail	0	0	0	0	0	0	0	0	0	0	0	0	0
Self-Generated	0	0	0	0	0	0	0	0	0	0	0	0	0
Event Marketing	0	0	0	2	0	0	0	0	1	0	2	0	5
Total	**12**	**7**	**15**	**124**	**132**	**10**	**10**	**47**	**92**	**45**	**37**	**3**	**534**

ASSIGNED LEADS	JAN	FEB	MAR	APR	MAY	JUN	JUL	AUG	SEP	OCT	NOV	DEC	TOTAL
Hotel Integration	43	16	32	35	36	32	35	19	19	30	34	24	355
Broker Program	23	24	21	29	31	22	16	11	18	17	17	8	237
Owner Referral	4	3	7	9	2	8	6	21	10	12	13	10	105
National Advertising	111	52	65	82	74	71	50	36	54	109	85	65	854
Local Advertising	2	3	6	7	1	2	4	2	1	9	10	3	50
Web Marketing	65	36	68	126	63	72	53	64	61	87	91	124	910
Direct Mail	2	3	1	1	1	5	6	3	3	2	2	2	31
Self-Generated	1	0	2	0	0	2	0	1	0	1	1	0	8
Event Marketing	0	0	15	0	0	10	0	0	8	0	0	15	48
Total	**251**	**137**	**217**	**289**	**208**	**224**	**170**	**157**	**174**	**267**	**253**	**251**	**2,598**

Figure 10-4

The Report—The report in figure 10-4 should be done monthly and is an important one in my view. Keep in mind that all the prospecting being done does not always produce a lead. It depends on how the team defines a lead, which was reviewed in chapter 1.

Assigned Leads are ones that have been turned over to the sales team for follow-up, including the inquiries that have been converted to leads. These leads are counted on all performance reports. There are, though, other inquiries and prospects you produce that never become leads. Each business may be a little different.

Unassigned/DNC are inquiries you have received that are on the "do-not-call" list. These inquiries do not count as leads and should not be given to sales. A large number of these prospects can be generated by a broker program. Let's review these broker prospects because they have nothing to do with the "do-not-call" issue. These are simply leads you received that did not turn HOT. (You can review the broker prospecting addendum to part two, which explains what a HOT lead is.) If a prospect does not turn HOT in the broker program, it should not be considered a lead and should not be given to sales, but you will still want to account for it. Many more unassigned inquiries will be generated by the broker program than leads.

The reason to track these prospects is to see how many of them your marketing team can turn into leads and assign to sales for follow-up. This exercise can make a big difference in terms of performance. If you elect to give these prospects to the sales team before they become leads, you will be making a big mistake that will hurt your performance.

Unregistered States—These inquiries come from states where you are not registered and therefore cannot follow up on them (if your product requires state registration before you can sell in a particular state). The reason to track these leads is that if you are getting a lot of inquiries from a certain state, then maybe it will make sense to spend the time and money to get that state registered.

When Received—This report should be completed at the end of each month. But you can get it sooner if you need it and request it.

Who's Responsible—The lead bank is responsible for producing the report in an accurate and timely fashion.

Monthly Key Metrics Report—Report #5

Key Metrics: January
Residence Club

	ACTUAL	BUDGET	VARIANCE	YTD	PTD
Leads	275	253	22	955	3,500
Leads % to Presentations	43%	40%	3%	37%	35%
Presentations	118	101	17	353	1225
Gross Sales	11	8	3	28	105
Sales Canceled	0	0	0.0	3	10
Percentage Canceled	0%	0%	0%	11%	10%
Net Sales	10	8	2	28	100
Net Closing Percentage	8.5%	8.0%	0.5%	7.9%	8.2%
Average Price	$380,000	$375,000	$5,000	$389,000	$385,000
Net Volume	$3,819,475	$3,036,000	$783,475	$10,858,799	$38,673,250
Volume per Lead	$13,889	$12,000	$1,889	$11,370	$11,050
Total Marketing Dollars	$247,500	$230,000	$17,500	$764,000	$3,100,000
Cost per Lead	$900	$909	(9)	$800	$886
Total Cost As % of Volume	6.5%	7.6%	-1.1%	7.0%	8.0%

Figure 10-5

The Report—The monthly key metrics report in figure 10-5 gives you a very simple summary of how the month performed compared to budgeted goals. It also gives you a chance to review the month's performance compared to the year-to-date and project-to-date performance. You can see in this report all vital statistics are accounted for. It is an overall performance report, not an individual marketing channel report.

From the standpoint of marketing quantity and quality of lead performance, let's take a look at this month to see how we have done. Let's first review the formula for a quantity and quality lead production program in figure 10-6:

Quantity and Quality Lead Performance Ratings

Remember the formula for quantity and quality of leads.

First—Look at your quantity of leads versus budget and/or target. Are you positive or negative in this first review?

Second—Look at the quality of your leads, which is indicated by your CPL and VPL. Are you over or under budget?

Third—Divide your CPL by your VPL to calculate a percentage. If this percentage is at or below your budget, you have a successful lead campaign.

Figure 10-6

First—We produced 275 leads against a budget calling for 253 and so exceeded our target by 22 leads. Production was 108 percent of what had been budgeted. Great performance here!

Second—We produced a $900 average cost per lead (CPL) for the month and had budgeted to produce $909 per lead. We were $9 under for the month with all channels combined. Very nicely done!

In terms of volume per lead (VPL), we produced $13,889 whereas the budget was $12,000, so we were $1,889 over budget on our VPL. This shows the quality of the leads was very high.

Third—Our report card, which is the percentage of cost compared to revenue, shows we were 1.1 percent under budget. This is the best news of all—indicating a very successful marketing month! Well done.

Still, the next set of reports we will review, which break performance down by separate marketing channels, show some great opportunities for improvement remain.

When Received—This report should be received at the end of each month. You need it no later than seven business days after month's end.

Who's Responsible—The lead bank is again responsible for the timing and accuracy of this report and must coordinate with the site and your financial team as costs need to be included.

Monthly Key Metrics by Marketing Channel Actual—Report #6

Monthly Key Metrics by Marketing Channel
Residence Club

ACTUAL	HOTEL	BROKER	OWNER	LOCAL	WEBSITE	D. MAIL	NATIONAL	EVENT	TOTALS
Leads	70	63	27	20	19	13	45	18	275
Leads % Pres.	60%	33%	44%	55%	16%	46%	38%	33%	43%
Presentations	42	21	12	11	3	6	17	6	118
Gross Sales	3.0	2.0	2.0	0.0	1.0	0.0	2.0	1.0	11
Canceled	0	0	0	0	0	0	1	0	1
% Canceled	0%	0%	0%	0%	0%	0%	50%	0%	0%
Net Sales	3	2	1.98	0	1	0	1	1	10
Net Closing	5%	20%	17%	10%	7%	0%	25%	25%	8.5%
Average Price	$366,667	$432,238	$383,838	$0	$380,000	$0	$355,000	$360,000	$382,713
Net Volume	$1,100,000	$864,475	$760,000	$0	$380,000	$0	$355,000	$360,000	$3,819,475
VPL	$15,714	$13,722	$28,148	$0	$20,000	$0	$7,889	$20,000	$13,889
Total Marketing	$38,700	$66,961	$28,756	$19,865	$7,350	$12,765	$47,665	$25,438	$247,500
Cost per Lead	$553	$1,063	$1,065	$993	$387	$982	$1,059	$1,413	$900
Cost As %	3.5%	7.7%	3.8%	0.0%	1.9%	0.0%	0.0%	0.0%	6.5%

Figure 10-7

The Report—The monthly key metrics by marketing channel *actual* report in figure 10-7 gives you all the vital statistics, but now you can see them by marketing channel. This way you can really drill down into which marketing channels are working and which need improvement. This report is done once a month and gives you an excellent overview of your marketing performance. In fact, it is probably your most informative report because it allows you to evaluate all your marketing channels individually. You can review the quantity and quality of each channel and all other vital statistics that will help you invest your marketing dollars wisely in these different channels.

When Received—This report is reviewed at the end of each month. You need it no later than seven business days after month's end.

Who's Responsible—The lead bank is again responsible for the timing and accuracy of this report and must coordinate with the site and your financial team as costs need to be included and separated by marketing channel.

Monthly Key Metrics by Marketing Channel Budget—Report #7

Monthly Key Metrics by Marketing Channel
Residence Club

BUDGET	HOTEL	BROKER	OWNER	LOCAL	WEBSITE	D. MAIL	NATIONAL	EVENT	TOTALS
Leads	67	55	24	17	17	18	42	13	253
Leads % Pres.	51%	38%	33%	59%	24%	28%	36%	31%	40%
Presentations	34	21	8	10	4	5	15	4	101
Gross Sales	3.0	2.0	1.1	0.0	1.0	0.0	1.0	0.0	8
Canceled	0	0	0	0	0	0	0	0	0
% Canceled	0%	0%	0%	0%	0%	0%	0%	0%	0%
Net Sales	3	2	1.1	0	1	0	1	0	8
Net Closing	5%	20%	17%	10%	7%	0%	25%	25%	8.0%
Average Price	$366,667	$384,000	$338,182	$0	$380,000	$0	$416,000	$0	$374,815
Net Volume	$1,100,000	$768,000	$372,000	$0	$380,000	$0	$416,000	$0	$3,036,000
VPL	$16,418	$13,964	$15,500	$0	$22,353	$0	$9,905	$0	$12,000
Total Marketing	$41,461	$46,700	$28,756	$19,865	$7,350	$12,765	$47,665	$25,438	$230,000
Cost per Lead	$619	$849	$1,198	$1,169	$432	$709	$1,135	$1,957	$909

igure 10-8

The Report—The monthly key metrics by marketing channel budget (figure 10-8) gives you the same information as the monthly key metrics actual, only these are your targeted budget numbers, to which your actual performance will be compared. This is a very conservative report taken early in the year. Most reports like these have much more variance on the last line, cost as a percent of volume. Most of the time you can scan across this bottom line and see the current status of each marketing channel, which will give you a great starting point for the future direction of each channel.

When Received—This report is received at the end of each month. You need it no later than seven business days after month's end.

Who's Responsible—The lead bank is again responsible for the timing and accuracy of this report and must coordinate with the site and your financial team as costs need to be included and separated by marketing channel.

Monthly Key Metrics by Marketing Channel Variance—Report #8

Monthly Key Metrics by Marketing Channel
Residence Club

VARIANCE	HOTEL	BROKER	OWNER	LOCAL	WEBSITE	D. MAIL	NATIONAL	EVENT	TOTALS
Leads	3	8	3	3	2	-5	3	5	22
Leads % Pres.	9%	-5%	11%	-4%	-8%	18%	2%	3%	3%
Presentations	8	0	4	1	-1	1	2	2	17
Gross Sales	0	0	1	0	0	0	1	1	3
Canceled	0	0	0	0	0	0	1	0	1
% Canceled	0	0	0	0	0	0	0.5	0	0
Net Sales	0	0	1	0	0	0	0	1	2
Net Closing	0.00%	0.00%	0.00%	0.00%	0.00%	0.00%	0.00%	0.00%	0.44%
Average Price	$0	$48,238	$45,657	$0	$0	$0	($61,000)	$360,000	$7,898
Net Volume	$0	$96,475	$388,000	$0	$0	$0	-$61,000	$360,000	$783,475
VPL	-$704	-$242	$12,648	$0	-$2,353	$0	-$2,016	$20,000	$1,889
Total Marketing	-$2,761	$20,261	$0	$0	$0	$0	$0	$0	$17,500
Cost per Lead	-$66	$214	-$133	-$175	-$46	$273	-$76	-$544	-$9
Cost as %	-0.3%	1.7%	-3.9%	0.0%	0.0%	0.0%	0.0%	0.0%	-1.1%

Figure 10-9

The Report—The monthly key metrics by marketing channel variance report (figure 10-9) documents the variances you had in each of the channels and all of the statistics. Since budget is usually your target, this report is a quick way to review your actual compared to budget on a simple report.

When Received—This report is received at the end of each month. You need it no later than seven business days after month's end.

Who's Responsible—The lead bank is again responsible for the timing and accuracy of this report and must coordinate with the site and your financial team as costs need to be included and separated by marketing channel.

Monthly Sales Details—Report #9

Monthly Sales Details—February 2008

#	SITE	FIRST	LAST	DATE	PLAN	SIZE	GROSS	INCENTIVES	NET	SOURCE	AGENT	MARK
40067	NY	Paul	Klein	1-Feb	2 Bed	1,630	$345,000	$5,000	$340,000	Hotel	Susan	Linda
40052	NY	John	Teed	4-Feb	2 Bed	1,630	$365,000	$5,000	$360,000	Broker	Randy	
40036	NY	Bill	Smith	7-Feb	3 Bed	1,950	$435,000	$5,000	$430,000	National	John	
40053	NY	Peter	Sevel	9-Feb	2 Bed	1,630	$355,000	$5,000	$350,000	Owner	Susan	
40053	NY	Randy	Gram	9-Feb	3 Bed	1,950	$440,000	$5,000	$435,000	Web	John	
40075	NY	Hal	May	11-Feb	3 Bed	1,950	$495,000	$5,000	$490,000	Event	John	
40068	NY	Ron	Hensel	14-Feb	2 Bed	1,630	$310,000	$5,000	$305,000	Hotel	Shara	Linda
40071	NY	Gary	Hughes	18-Feb	3 Bed	1,950	$464,475	$5,000	$459,475	Hotel	Susan	Linda
40050	NY	Greg	Hague	25-Feb	2 Bed	1,630	$320,000	$5,000	$315,000	Broker	Shara	
40057	NY	Janet	Reed	27-Feb	2 Bed	1,630	$340,000	$5,000	$335,000	Owner	Bill	
Totals	10					17,580	$3,869,475	$50,000	$3,819,475			

Sales Agent Performance

	VOLUME	SALES
Susan	$1,149,475	3
Randy	$360,000	1
John	$1,355,000	3
Shara	$620,000	2
Bill	$335,000	1
	$3,819,475	10

Figure 10-10

The Report—The monthly sales detail report (figure 10-10) is produced by the site but reviewed and reconciled by the lead bank. It is really a sales report, not a marketing report, but the reason I have put it in the marketing section is because it is used by marketing to help compensate the marketing people. Also, information about sales volumes and the sources that produced them is relevant for the previous marketing reports.

When Received—This report is received at the end of each month.

Who's Responsible—The site is responsible for the timing and accuracy of this report. The lead bank must reconcile the report and ensure its accuracy in terms of revenue, the sales person, and marketing channel source.

Monthly Inventory Control—Report #10

Residence Club—Inventory Control

Updated - 8/01/08

	Total Homes	Total Frac.	Ideal Mix	Total Released	% Realst	Ideal Sold	Cur Sold	Cur Var	Total Left	% Sold
Premier Ownership										
Two Bedrooms										
Winter Preferred	9	54	49%	54	100%	37	51	14	3	94%
Summer Preferred	9	45	41%	45	100%	31	24	-7	21	53%
Winter Lifestyle	1	6	6%	6	100%	4	5.5	1	0.5	92%
Summer Lifestyle	1	5	5%	5	100%	3	1.5	-2	3.5	30%
Totals	10	110	100%	110	100%	76	76	0	34	69%
Three Bedrooms										
Winter Preferred	6	36	55%	36	100%	29	31	2	5	86%
Summer Preferred	6	30	46%	30	100%	24	22	-2	8	73%
Winter Lifestyle	0	0	0%	0	0%	0	0	0	0	0%
Summer Lifestyle	0	0	0%	0	0%	0	0	0	0	0%
Totals	6	66	100%	66	100%	53	53	0	13	80%

Figure 10-11

	Total Homes	Total Frac.	Ideal Mix	Total Released	% Realst	Ideal Sold	Cur Sold	Cur Var	Total Left	% Sold
Fixed Ownership										
Two Bedrooms										
Winter Preferred	5	30	55%	30	100%	21	25	4	5	83%
Summer Preferred	5	25	46%	25	100%	17	13	-4	12	52%
Totals	5	55	100%	55	100%	38	38	0	17	69%
Three Bedrooms										
Winter Preferred	4	24	55%	24	100%	16	19	3	5	79%
Summer Preferred	4	20	46%	20	100%	14	11	-3	9	55%
Totals	4	44	100%	44	100%	30	30	0	14	68%
Totals	25	275		275			197		78	72%

Figure 10-11 (continued)

The Report—The monthly inventory control report in figure 10-11 is also more of a sales report, but from a pure marketing prospecting viewpoint sometimes you will have your marketing team drive specific clients who purchase specific inventory. Coordination between marketing and sales in the case of inventory that is out of balance is critical. If you are selling multiple products, customer interest levels may vary widely between or among them. You must sell all of them to have a balanced inventory. An example of inventory out of balance in real estate would be if you had ten two-bedroom units and ten three-bedroom units to sell and you had sold nine three-bedroom units and only one two-bedroom unit. Then your two-bedroom units would be "out of balance," and you would need to correct this problem. This report compares the ideal mix of inventory sales to the actual mix of inventory sold.

When Received—This report is received at the end of each month. You need it no later than seven business days after month's end.

Who's Responsible—The site is responsible for the timing and accuracy of this report. This report is then reconciled by the lead bank.

Quarterly Sales and Marketing Engagement Reports—Report #11

Sales and Marketing Engagement Survey
Q1 2008 vs. Q2 2008 Questions 1–22

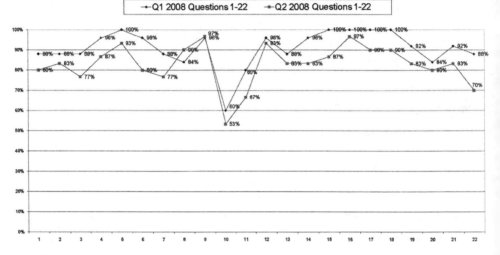

Figure 10-12

Finally, figure 10-12 shows the sales and marketing engagement report produced by the Gallup Organization. Team culture is, I believe, very important and maybe not as much of a priority as it should be in our sales and marketing enterprises. You can see the quarterly results in this report and the numbers on the bottom of the report showing the results of questions we had asked the employees. These responses need to be reviewed, and you should formulate a plan of action for improving low scores and promoting high scores. I will share with you the questions asked in a minute.

This report provides leadership with some very important insight on how the business culture of the team will need to be improved. Most importantly, it tells you what you are doing right and what needs to be improved. Pay attention to this report and respond accordingly to maintain high scores and improve low scores with your team. If you do, I promise you will see better performances from your sales and marketing enterprises.

When Received—The report should be completed at the end of each quarter. As you can see, your scores are compared to those you received in the prior quarterly review.

Who's Responsible—I would engage a third party that is distant from the team. The people who rate you and others need to know that their scoring is strictly confidential and that no one will know who scored whom what. This is the way it must be done to work. Ask employees to be as accurate as possible and remind them each time how important it is that they complete this report and do it as accurately as possible.

Statements in the quarterly sales and marketing engagement report:

1. I know what is expected of me at work.
2. I have the materials and equipment I need to do my job effectively.
3. At work, I have the opportunity to do what I do best every day.
4. In the last seven days I have received recognition or praise for good work.
5. My supervisor seems to care about me as a person.
6. There is someone at work who encourages my development.
7. At work my opinions count.

8. The mission or purpose of my company makes me feel my job is important.

9. My fellow employees are committed to doing quality work.

10. I like going to work.

11. In the last six months someone from work has talked to me about my progress.

12. This last year I have had opportunities at work to learn and grow.

13. I have the training I need to do my job effectively.

14. My immediate supervisor's actions match his/her words.

15. I feel like part of the team.

16. Our team is committed to innovation and continuous improvement.

17. My immediate supervisor is honest and ethical in his/her business practices.

18. My work gives me a feeling of personal accomplishment.

19. My immediate supervisor treats me fairly.

20. I have the opportunity to advance my career.

21. I can ask management any reasonable question and get an honest answer.

22. We regularly celebrate business success in my work group.

Key Notes for Lead Performance Reporting

1. Make sure you have culture performance reports.

2. Consider the lead bank to be the company and all who receive performance reports to be customers. There should also be a check on how satisfied the "customers" are with the reports.

3. Performance reports must be delivered on time so the leader can react appropriately and productively. These reports are critical to performance.

4. Performance reports must be accurate, so each month a review of timing and accuracy should be completed by whoever oversees the lead bank.

5. The performance reports must be correlated with any corporate reports that are being produced.

6. Special request reports need to be completed after the standard reports have been produced and distributed.

Let's hear from our characters about *lead performance reporting.*

Chapter 10: Lead Performance Reporting

Here is an action scene with our characters reviewing their marketing lead performance reports.

Lead domination means understanding the score today and forecasting the score tomorrow. Put your marketing offense and defense in gear to act accordingly. The marketing performance scores must be kept accurately and in a timely fashion and must be reviewed constantly.

Performance and Direction Reports

If you do not know where you are going, any road will take you there

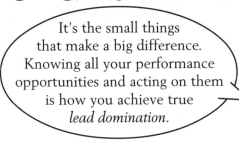

It's the small things that make a big difference. Knowing all your performance opportunities and acting on them is how you achieve true *lead domination.*

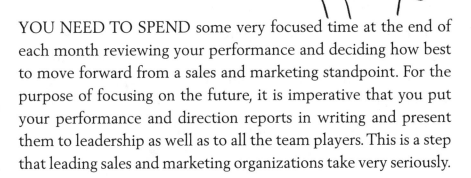

YOU NEED TO SPEND some very focused time at the end of each month reviewing your performance and deciding how best to move forward from a sales and marketing standpoint. For the purpose of focusing on the future, it is imperative that you put your performance and direction reports in writing and present them to leadership as well as to all the team players. This is a step that leading sales and marketing organizations take very seriously.

In the previous chapter we talked about performance reports. Imagine if you produced great performance reports but never really took strong strategic sales and marketing advantage of them. The performance and direction reports ensure that you will take the time not only to review your performance reports but also to plan your strategic sales and marketing future. The importance of this process can hardly be overstated.

I will make comments about the performance and direction report as we go through it section by section. The comments are highlighted at the end of each section and are not part of the regular report. They are there to provide further explanations about each section. The vital statistics we have talked about throughout this book are all featured in this report:

1. Number of leads

2. Cost per lead

3. Volume per lead

4. Cost as a percentage of revenue

All numeric reports in this performance and direction report should be provided by your lead bank team. These reports provide the type of performance orientation that is essential in this business. Select your most qualified leader to produce the performance direction report we are about to cover. It should be completed and reviewed every month.

I find the performance and direction report to be a great communication tool for all parties interested in the current performance and future direction of your enterprise's sales and marketing performance.

We'll start with the revenue section of a performance and direction report:

February 2008 Performance and Direction Report

Revenue Performance

VPL Actual Was $22,735 or 95 Percent of Budget

The total revenue production for the month was 13 net sales, $5,274,409 in net revenue, with an average price of $405,723. The forecast for the month was $5,000,000. The budget for the month was $7,083,492. This performance produced 75 percent of the revenue budgeted for the month. The shortfall in revenue was due to acquiring fewer leads than had been budgeted and a slightly lower VPL than had been budgeted. The VPL for the month was $22,735 against a budget of $23,850—95 percent of what had been budgeted. The sales team did an outstanding job with new leads: 94 percent of the revenue produced was with leads that were ninety days or less old. The closing percentage of 18.3 was 4 points ahead of budget.

Revenue Direction

VPL Is Forecasted to Be $35,000 in March

As we look ahead to the month of March, we are forecasting, based on trends and the lead pipeline reviews, that we will produce 250 leads and a VPL of $35,000. We forecast $8.7 million for the month of March, which is 110 percent of budgeted revenue. We see strength in the hotel integration and broker programs for the month; we also have ten pending sales in the pipeline as additional potential revenues to hit our targets. We believe that half of these will come good in the month of March.

Comments:

Current Revenue Performance

The revenue section of this report focuses on the sales revenue you produced for the month. The key vital statistic in revenue production is volume per lead generated. Although net sales volume takes center stage, we also review the number of sales, the average price, and the volume per lead. The sales volume is always compared to budget and the forecast you had made for the month. If you were over or under in revenue, a short explanation as to why is needed in this section.

Future Revenue Direction

The future revenue section forecasts the revenue for the up-coming month by looking at your pipeline of pending sales and the number of leads you believe you will produce. Multiply the number of leads by the volume per lead forecast to obtain the anticipated sales revenue for the month.

Marketing Performance

Number of Leads: 232 or 78 Percent of Budget

We produced 232 leads in February, which was 78 percent of budget, with a 31 percent conversion to presentations or 77 percent of budget. The lead performance was behind budget by 65 leads due to a shortfall in broker, local marketing, and direct mail lead performance. Conversion to presentation was behind budget by 9 percent because of the lead mix. We had forecast 200 leads for the month. High closing percentages were the big plus for the month, but lower lead flow and conversions to presentations prevented us from hitting our revenue target. Considering that of the 232 leads we produced only 71 took presentations, we will be focusing our efforts on the 161 leads still in progress. We continue to work with our goldmine lead tracking, performance reporting and review lead performance by each sales agent each week.

Marketing Direction

Number of Leads: 250 or 84 Percent of Budget

We are forecasting that we will produce 250 leads in March, which is 84 percent of budget, with a 40 percent conversion to presentations or 100 percent of budget. The lead performance will still be a little behind budget by 50 leads due to an antici- pated shortfall in local marketing and direct mail lead performance.

Comments:

Current Lead Performance

This marketing section is all about the vital statistic of the number of leads you produced compared to budget. We also look at the conversion from lead to presentation, another im- portant performance number for marketing and sales. The lead numbers are always compared to budget as well as forecast, showing whether you were over or under in leads. A short explanation as to why is needed in this section.

Future Lead Direction

In the future marketing section you are forecasting the num- ber of leads for the upcoming month. This is done by looking at your marketing trends on lead flow. You will also need to forecast the percentage of leads that will convert to presenta- tions for the month. That will give you the forecasted leads and presentations compared to budget. I would give a short explanation as to what your team will be doing to meet lead and presentation forecasts.

Marketing Cost per Lead Performance

Cost Per Lead Was $494 on a Budget of $1,090 or 45 Percent of Budget

We produced a cost per lead for the month of only $494 dollars because of outstanding cost savings in hotel integration and an accounting adjustment that was made on the broker program. Without the accounting adjustment the cost per lead would have been around $850. The forecast was $900 for the month.

Marketing Cost per Lead Direction

Cost per Lead in March Forecast to Be $1,000 on a Budget of $1,100 or 84 Percent of Budget

We are forecasting that we will produce a $1,000 cost per lead average based on our pipeline of advertising and current responses we are receiving. We have reviewed cost and lead flow on each of our marketing channels to estimate this future cost per lead for March.

Comments:

Current Cost per Lead Performance

This marketing section is all about the vital statistic of the cost per lead you produced compared to budget and forecast. If you were over or under in cost per lead, a short explanation as to why is needed in this section.

Future Cost per Lead Direction

In the future marketing section you will be forecasting the cost per lead for the upcoming month, which is done by looking at your marketing trends on lead flow and reviewing your spending plan for the upcoming month These indicators will help give you an anticipated cost to compare to budget.

Sales and Marketing Cost Performance

The total cost for February was $360,707 on a budget of $876,701, so costs were under budget by $515,994. The main variances were marketing dollars saved because of commissions not earned by the sales executive and a large broker saving due to some accrual credits.

Sales and Marketing Cost Direction

We are forecasting the total cost for March to be $850,000 on a budget of $880,000—or 96 percent of budgeted dollars spent. The main variances are marketing dollars saved because of the hotel and broker programs. A short explanation as to why you are going to save on the hotel and broker program will be needed here.

Comments:

Current Sales and Marketing Cost Performance

In this section we look at *all* costs, including sales and marketing costs of the entire operation. We compare these overall costs to budget and our forecast. This is the cost number most developers are most interested in. There should be a brief explanation if the amount spent is over or under budgeted dollars.

Future Sales and Marketing Cost Direction

The sales and marketing costs for the upcoming month are reviewed by checking all cost line items and then forecasting the total cost for the month.

Key Metrics: February

	ACTUAL	BUDGET	VARIANCE	YTD
Leads	232	297	(65)	399
Leads % to Pres.	31%	40%	-9%	38%
Presentations	71	119	(48)	153
Gross Sales	14	18	(4)	30
Sales Canceled	1	1	0.0	1
Percentage Canceled	7%	6%	1.6%	7%
Net Sales	13	17	(4)	28.5
Net Closing Percentage	18.3%	14.3%	4.0%	18.6%
Average Price	$405,724	$416,676	($10,952)	$453,458
Net Volume	$5,274,409	$7,083,492	($1,809,083)	$12,923,559
Volume per Lead	$22,735	$23,850	($1,116)	$32,390
Total Marketing Dollars	$114,572	$323,772	$209,200	$361,109
Cost per Lead	$494	$1,090	-$596	$905
Cost As % of Volume	7.0%	13.4%	-6.4%	10.0%

Comments:

Key Metrics for February

In this section you show your key performance metrics compared to budget for the current month as well as the year-to-date performance. This is an easy and outstanding way to review performance. It is great to look at all the vital statistics for the month and year on this simple report. Be prepared to deliver a short presentation on this performance based on what the report is showing you.

Key Issues:

– Our owner experience has not met expectations. Apply the four-legged stool concept: If one leg is broken, the stool will fall. We do not have a stool that is standing today. You need to have a meeting with the following operations to review how each, both separately and together, will improve owner experience:

- Sales
- On-site Operations
- Service Operations
- Hotel Operations

– Our broker program lead flow has dropped because the resale market is starting to compete.

– It is critical that we identify a second fractional development in order to maintain the positive pace and keep the current sales talent focused on performance.

Comments:

Key Issues

In this section you can review key issues that could affect performance as you move ahead. This is a great way to get your team all moving in the right direction to deal positively with these issues for the future. Be prepared to deliver a short presentation on this subject.

Closing Forecast for Next Month:

We are also forecasting fifty closed sales with a net volume of $20 million by quarter end. The target was thirty-five sales at $14 million.

Comments:

Closing Forecast for Next Month

These are the sales you are closing for the quarter compared to target. From a company standpoint it is not the sales you make that count; it's the sales that close. Be prepared to deliver a short presentation on this subject.

Marketing Program Trend—February

	Hotel	Broker	Owner	Local	Web-Site	D. Mail	Self-Gen	Advertising	Other	Totals
Leads	87	108	12	5	10	0	0	9	1	232
Leads % Pres.	63%	5%	42%	60%	0%	0%	0%	22%	100%	31%
Presentations	55	5	5	3	0	0	0	2	1	71
Gross Sales	4	3	5	0	0	0	0	2	0	14
Canceled	0	0	1	0	0	0	0	0	0	1
% Canceled	0%	0%	0%	0%	0%	0%	0%	0%	0%	7%
Net Sales	4	3	4	0	0	0	0	2	0	13
Net Closing	7%	60%	80%	0%	0%	0%	0%	100%	0%	18%
Average Price	$358,867	$397,437	$404,509	$0	$0	$0	$0	$514,297	$0	$405,724
Net Volume	$1,435,468	$1,192,311	$1,618,036	$0	$0	$0	$0	$1,028,594	$0	$5,274,409
VPL	$16,500	$11,040	$134,836	$0	$0	$0	$0	$114,288	$0	$22,735
Total Marketing	$29,740	-$3,725	$30,102	$41,006	$0	$0	$0	$0	$17,449	$114,572
Cost per Lead	$342	-$34	$2,509	$8,201	$0	0%	$0	$0	$0	$494
Cost As %	2.1%	-0.3%	1.9%	0%	0%	0%	0%	0%	0%	2.2%

This report gives you all your performance broken down by marketing channel. This is very important to review as you soon will be writing down the individual direction of each of your funded marketing channels.

Comments:

Marketing Program Trend

This is the best simple report that enables the marketing team to understand how its performance by marketing channel has played out for the month. It is a helpful report for forecasting as well as for redirecting marketing dollars based on individual marketing channel performance. Be prepared to deliver a short presentation on this report.

Comments:

Each Marketing Channel Gets Reviewed

The marketing leader now gets to comment on each marketing channel and how it has and will be performing. Be prepared to deliver a short presentation on each marketing channel.

➤ **Hotel Integration**

In February we had 1,048 arrivals, 504 of which were group guests and 544 of which were FIT. We generated 87 total leads; our budget was for 85. Leads were produced in these areas: 3 from groups, 42 from FIT, and 42 from people not staying in the hotel. Our hotel penetration for FIT guest was 7.7 percent for the month, which is .7 percent above our target of 7 percent FIT penetration. We need to work on improving group guest penetration where we had .6 percent penetration against a goal of 2 percent. We converted 63 percent of these leads to presentations, which is low for the month as our target was 69 percent. The 55 presentations we produced created 4 net sales and a net volume of $1,435,468. This is a closing percentage of

7.3 percent versus a budget of 4.0 percent. The hotel program produced 27 percent of our net revenues for the month.

➤ Broker Program

We have currently have 13 premier VIP brokers, 2 VIP brokers, and 10 standard brokers' offices under contract and receive 108 leads for the month. This is just below our budget of 117. The broker program is challenged this year because of the re-sale market, which is being operated by our best past brokers. Our broker team leader is driving *all* the lead flow from the broker premier, VIP, and standard programs. The broker program converted 5 percent of its leads to presentation whereas the budget called for 20 percent. The 5 presentations converted to 3 net sales and a volume of $1,192,311. This is a closing percentage of 60 percent versus a budget of 12 percent. The broker program produced 23 percent of our net volume for the month.

➤ Owner Referral Program

We are accelerating our focus on this program in hopes of generating strong leads, presentations, and sales from owner marketing. Here is the approach we are taking: *First*, we have one person dedicated to this program, the owner team leader. *Second*, we have created a "Just One Survey" that will be used to compare experience levels to leads, presentations, and revenue production. We will create an individual marketing program for each owner that focuses first on high experience level ratings, then on leads, presentations, and sales from re-loads and/or referral business. *Third*, we have a "Just One Incentive" program for all net closed sales on this program. The incentive gives owners who makes the referral a 50 percent credit on their maintenance fees.

We produced 12 leads versus a budget of 21. We converted 42 percent to a presentation versus a budget of 50 percent and produced 5 presentations versus a budget of 11. These 5 presentations converted to 4 sales for a closing percentage of 80 percent versus a budget of 11.4 percent. This program produced $1,618,036 in net revenue versus a budget of $953,547. It was the number one program for the month on net revenue at 30 percent of the net volume for the month.

➤ Local Programs

We produced 5 leads versus a budget of 28. We converted 60 percent to a presentation versus a budget of 55 percent and produced 3 presentations versus a budget of 15. These 3 presentations converted to 0 sales. We are looking to cut back in cost on this program as our new local advertising campaign is not working as well as we had hoped. Year-to-date this program is 3 percent over in percentage of revenues versus cost.

➤ Website Leads

We produced 10 leads versus a budget of 11. The website was down for updates for most of the month. We converted 0 percent to a presentation versus a budget of 30 percent and produced 0 presentations versus a budget of 3. This is not a big revenue program, but the little volume that is produced is very cost effective.

➤ Direct Mail Programs—Registered and Non-Registered

We need to review our direct mail strategies with the best minds in the company. This marketing source has not been successful at all. We need to review all that was done and see whether there is a better game plan for using this marketing channel in the future. A meeting has been set for March 22 to see whether we are going to try a new approach.

Below is the performance report for our direct mail program so far. As you can see, this program has a 67% marketing cost which is completely unacceptable.

Direct Mail Programs

Updated 1/28/05

	REGISTERED	UNREGISTERED	TOTALS
Direct Mail Pieces Sent	30,600	9,200	39,800
Total Leads Generated	84	20	104
Percentage of Presentations	0.27%	0.22%	0.26%
Total Presentations Generated	3	2	5
Total Leads Still Working	8	5	13
Total Leads Not Interested	73	13	86
Number of Sales	1	0	1
Net Sales Volume	$317,312	$0	$317,312
Total Direct Mail Sent	39,800		
Total Leads Received	104		
Total Direct Mail Costs	$212,932		
Cost per Piece	$5.35		
Cost per Lead	$2,047		
Cost per Presentation	$42,586		
Cost per Sale	$212,932		
Marketing Cost for DM	67.10%		

➤ Self Generation

No leads were produced, and there was nothing budgeted for this source in the month.

> ➤ National Advertising outside of Colorado

We produced 9 leads versus a budget of 4. We converted 22 percent to a presentation versus a budget of 25 percent and produced 2 presentations versus a budget of 1. These 2 presentations converted to 2 sales for a closing percentage of 100 percent versus a budget of 12 percent. This program produced $1,028,594 in net revenue versus a budget of $0 or 19 percent of the net volume for the month. This program has been cut back because of a strong trend of increasing costs per lead.

Cancellation Review

Project to date we have 2 cancellations out of 167 (.12 percent) sales we have made project to date. We have 199 reservations and 59 cancellations (29.6 percent) as of the end of this month.

Comments:

Cancellations

A quick review of any of the cancellations and a quick explanation if needed.

Inventory Control

Premier—Premier has 176 fractionals to sell, including the lifestyles in this category. So far we have sold 116 or 65.9 percent. The ideal mix is 64 percent. We have 60 premier fractionals to sell.

Fixed—Fixed has 99 fractionals to sell. So far we have sold 51 or 30.5 percent. The ideal mix is 36 percent. We have 48 fixed fractionals to sell.

Below is an inventory mix report. Lots of good information, but if you compare the ideal sold and the current sold, you can see which categories in the inventory mix are in or out of balance.

Residence Club—Inventory Control

Updated 3/01/05

	Total Residences	Total Fractionals	Ideal Mix	Total Released	Percentage Released	Ideal Sold	Current Sold	Inventory Variance	Inventory Left	Percentage Sold
Premier Ownership										
Two Bedrooms										
Winter Preferred	9	54	49.1%	54	100%	37	49	12	5	91%
Summer Preferred	9	45	40.9%	45	100%	31	21	(10)	24	47%
Winter Lifestyle	1	6	5.5%	6	100%	4	5	1	1	83%
Summer Lifestyle	1	5	4.5%	5	100%	3	0	(3)	5	0%
Totals	10	110	100.0%	110	100%	75	75	(0)	35	68%
Three Bedrooms										
Winter Preferred	6	36	54.5%	36	100%	22	25	3	11	69%
Summer Preferred	6	30	45.5%	30	100%	19	16	(3)	14	53%
Winter Lifestyle	0	0	0.0%	0	0%	0	0	0	0	0%
Summer Lifestyle	0	0	0.0%	0	0%	0	0	0	0	0%
Totals	6	66	100.0%	66	100%	41	41	0	25	62%
Fixed Ownership										
Two Bedrooms										
Winter Preferred	5	30	54.5%	30	100%	16	24	8	6	80%
Summer Preferred	5	25	45.5%	25	100%	14	6	(8)	19	24%
Totals	5	55	100.0%	55	100%	30	30	0	25	55%
Three Bedrooms										
Winter Preferred	4	24	54.5%	24	100%	11	13	2	11	54%
Summer Preferred	4	20	45.5%	20	100%	10	8	(2)	12	40%
Totals	4	44	100.0%	44	100%	21	21	0	23	48%
TOTALS	25	275		275			167		108	61%

Comments:

Inventory Control

Inventory control and reporting on the current status of inventory are very important. In this section we will review where we are and our strategy for moving ahead to ensure that the selling mix stays healthy.

Lead Database Report

Because database management is one of our sales and marketing strategies, I will include it in our monthly reviews. Our database is managed by marketing channel as well as in three specific categories: *unregistered leads* in unregistered states we do not work at this time, *unassigned leads*, which are leads in registered states that are on the DNC list, and *assigned leads*, which are in registered states and not on the DNC list. Note that unassigned leads are not given to sales executives but are sent a mailing. Assigned leads are given to sales executives to follow up on.

Updated 3/2/05

UNREGISTERED	MTD	%	YTD	%	PTD	%
Hotel Int.	2	3.0%	3	2.3%	7	2.0%
Broker Program	62	92.5%	119	92.2%	311	90.7%
Direct Mail	0	0.0%	0	0.0%	0	0.0%
Local Marketing	0	0.0%	0	0.0%	6	1.7%
Other	0	0.0%	0	0.0%	0	0.0%
Owner Referral	0	0.0%	1	0.8%	1	0.3%
R&D Advertising	0	0.0%	0	0.0%	0	0.0%
Web Marketing	3	4.5%	6	4.7%	18	5.2%
Self-Generation	0	0.0%	0	0.0%	0	0
TOTAL	67	100.0%	129	100.0%	343	100.0%

UNASSIGNED	MTD		YTD		PTD	
Hotel Int.	0	0.0%	0	0.0%	2	0.6%
Broker Program	76	100.0%	120	100.0%	306	97.1%
Direct Mail	0	0.0%	0	0.0%	0	0.0%
Local Marketing	0	0.0%	0	0.0%	2	0.6%
Other	0	0.0%	0	0.0%	0	0.0%
Owner Referral	0	0.0%	0	0.0%	0	0.0%
R&D Advertising	0	0.0%	0	0.0%	0	0.0%
Web Marketing	0	0.0%	0	0.0%	4	1.3%
Self-Generation	0	0.0%	0	0.0%	1	0.3%
TOTAL	76	100.0%	120	100.0%	315	100.0%

ASSIGNED	MTD		YTD		PTD	
Hotel Int.	88	56.1%	173	51.2%	646	34%
Broker Program	32	20.4%	67	19.8%	638	34%
Direct Mail	0	0.0%	8	2.4%	82	4%
Local Marketing	5	3.2%	17	5.0%	147	8%
Other	1	0.6%	1	0.3%	36	2%
Owner Referral	12	7.6%	26	7.7%	99	5%
R&D Advertising	9	5.7%	17	5.0%	35	2%
Web Marketing	10	6.4%	28	8.3%	172	9%
Self-Generation	0	0.0%	1	0.3%	19	1%
TOTAL	157	100.0%	338	100.0%	1874	100%

Customer Focus:

The market is so thin in this price range that this is a key area from a sales and marketing standpoint. How we deal with these customers and the ongoing experiences they have at every touch point is very important for our current and future success. So far there have been some real challenges in this area.

You want to review the challenges and take steps to meet them.

Culture:

So far we have a very positive performance-oriented culture. Now that we are in the true selling cycle, we are working with the team to develop a new operational plan for sales and marketing.

Key Notes for Performance and Direction Reports

1. These reports are part of the written performance reporting that is essential for top performing companies.

2. Be prepared to deliver short but knowledgeable strategic advice in each of the categories of the report.

3. Feel free to work with multiple team members in preparing this report.

4. After this report is presented to the team, please update it if opposing views are shared and agreed upon.

5. The leader who prepared this report should also be preparing the team, based on the recommendations of this report, for the months ahead.

6. This report is detailed, very important, and takes time to produce. I recommend you put it together over several days and make sure you do it in an environment that is conducive to creating a great finished product.

7. The teams that take the time to do this report and follow-up will be the ones that are well on their way to achieving lead domination.

Let's hear from our characters about *performance and direction reports.*

Chapter 11: Performance and Direction Reports

Here is an action scene with our characters setting their future direction based on past performance.

A written direction report on where you are going next based on past performance is a must for teams that truly want to achieve lead domination.

Marketing Addenda

PROSPECTING IS HOW YOU generate qualified leads, so I want to expand on this subject with these additional detailed strategy plans, which can be adapted in a variety of ways and should prove productive in terms of helping you generate quality leads. I highly recommend you read through each of these examples and apply the general plans to your lead business. Each of these is a key for successful lead prospecting.

If you would like to continue with the continuity of the 21 proven strategies, I recommend you put a marker on this page and come back to these important prospecting strategies once you have completed the book. Just jump to page 285 and come back to these addenda after you finish the book.

Hotel Marketing Prospecting

This marketing source is used for shared ownership or real estate sales that have hotel guests who stay on-site. If these conditions do not apply to your product program, you may want to consider a variant of this marketing plan or just review the details as a learning opportunity about marketing prospecting.

Hotel integration is a marketing program and process that allows you to introduce your product to hotel guests. It is a cost-effective way to prospect for leads. Let's start with the assumption that the hotel you're targeting attracts the type of client you are looking for: quality customers who have come to this location because they enjoy the hotel's amenities and location.

Hotel integration marketing programs can provide levels of penetration from between two and twenty percent of arriving guests, depending on the program, the dedication and skill of your employees, the degree of cooperation with hotel staff, and the precise process employed. "Penetration" is a marketing term used to describe the level of interest your prospecting program produces with guests staying in the hotel. The higher your penetration—or percentage of interest generated among guests—the better.

Below, in figure A-1, you see an example of marketing assumptions for a hotel that has 250 rooms and 70 percent occupancy for a period of one year—or a total of 25,550 arrivals in one year. If your program produces a 3 percent penetration of all the arrivals to preview your offering, it would yield 767 leads per year. A more effective plan that penetrates the hotel at a 6 percent rate doubles your lead flow. This lead flow is only calculated on FITs (frequent independent travelers) and group guests. There will also be walk-bys who are not staying in your hotel.

Rooms	250
Occupancy	70%
Days per year	91,250
Room nights	63,875
Average stay	2.5
Arrivals	25,550
Penetration	3%
Leads per year	767
Leads per month	**64**

Figure A-1

Let's review the three different prospecting guest types and then the three different prospecting opportunities available through hotel integration programs. Each of these prospecting types and approaches requires a slightly different strategy for generating lead production, and you should have your teams set up to capitalize on each opportunity.

FIT Guests: These "frequent independent travelers" stay at the hotel by choice, pay on their own the rack rate, and are attracted by the hotel's location and amenities. They are your best bets for conversion from prospects to leads and then from leads to presentations and sales. These prospects should be the primary focus of your marketing efforts.

Group Guests: These guests usually stay at the hotel because they are on a company business trip. Their time is very limited, and for the most part they are not as qualified as the FIT guests because they are not guests by their own personal choice. Still, you will want to contact many of these potential clients because they can be very cost-effective prospects who turn into leads.

Walk-Bys: If you establish a marketing presence in the lobby area of the hotel or other high-traffic area, you will be able to take advantage of this prospecting opportunity. "Walk-bys" are people who just stroll past your marketing area and become interested in learning more about your offering. They aren't even staying in your hotel. Targeting walk-bys is a great way to prospect outstanding additional leads for your hotel integration program.

All three of these prospect types have come to be in this particular location, and most of them will be paying a good rack rate to be there. There are three different prospecting strategies with which you can reach them. Just remember, though, that most of these clients are guests of the hotel. You don't want to do anything to disrupt their stay. Their hotel room is their sanctuary, so you just need to have the information available and let them inquire if they choose to do so. All strategies need to be worked out carefully with the hotel executive team to make sure you are doing the best thing for the customers, the hotel, and your own prospecting program. All three of these considerations need to be kept in mind while you design your hotel integration program.

The three primary hotel integration strategies can be classified as pre-arrival, on-site, and post-arrival. Also, innovation is the name of the game with hotel integration programs. Your innovations should always take into account the guests' hotel experience, the hotel executive team's approval, and your leadership team's approval. Here is an overview of the three types of strategies:

Pre-Arrival: Making something available about your offering for the hotel guests to review during the pre-arrival process is important. This can be done right after they make reservations for their stay. Your product and a short compelling prospecting message should be part of their confirmation materials.

Then you should consider sending an additional prospecting piece to guests a week or two before they arrive with a more compelling message and an exclusive focus on your product opportunity. It could be as simple as a postcard offering a view of your newly decorated models. It could also be a full brochure about the offering, providing significantly more detail. Either way, this piece will be a very important part of your hotel integration program. You want to make contact with guests before they arrive and at least introduce your offering as an option to consider when they are on-site. By doing this, people who are interested can set aside the time to view your offering while they are on-site. Pre-arrival marketing will create a first impression about your product offering. Additional messages, after guests have arrived on-site, will reinforce your message, but you only get one chance to create a first impression. A good pre-arrivals program can generate an additional one to three percent in hotel marketing penetration. At 1 percent, using our hotel example in figure A-1, that means an additional 250 very qualified leads.

On-Site: The most important part of the hotel integration program is to have the marketing leader in charge of the program work closely and build a rapport with the executive hotel team. Your marketing leader needs to be very supportive of the hotel executive team. He or she can volunteer some lobby duty time, help in special projects that benefit the hotel, be concerned and aware of hotel issues, and generally provide support. If you win the support of the hotel team because they see you are willing to support some of their activities and you can communicate well with the executive team, then this program has great potential for success. If not, then this program will be extremely handicapped.

You must work with the hotel executive staff on your important on-site strategies. Here are a few great prospecting ideas for on-site hotel lead generation:

1. **Marketing coordinators in the lobby:** Have some attractive, well-dressed marketing coordinators work the high-traffic areas of the hotel lobby. Provide them with concierge desks and phones. When prospects walk by these desks, they should clearly be able to see your product offering. You should make

plenty of information about your offering available; be sure, however, that your marketing people remain engaged in marketing-driven activities, not sales. Your marketing coordinators should understand and be able to perform all the duties of a concierge in the hotel when needed.

Part of the marketing coordinators' compensation should be determined by their ability to deliver qualified leads to the sales team. Each hotel integration employee should be managed on the basis of performance on a monthly basis. This is best done by reviewing how each marketing coordinator mixes with the hotel team, handles the guests they service, and produces both leads and presentation opportunities. In figure A-2 on the next page you can see that a coordinator's base salary is about 55 percent of his or her total compensation; the rest of his or her compensation consists of bonuses based on his or her lead and presentation production. A coordinator who can produce a 5 percent rather than a 3 1/2 percent penetration number will see a 20 percent increase in compensation.

2. **Brochures in the room:** In a well-run hotel integration program you will have product brochures in hotel rooms. Customize the piece just for the arriving guests staying at the hotel. Be sure you have the hotel team involved in the creation and production of this brochure. What is perhaps most important—and often overlooked—is where you place the brochure in the room. You also need a process to guarantee that brochures get into the rooms.

Making sure brochures get into rooms and are replaced if guests take them is very important to the program. I recommend that you train the hotel housekeeping team to do this as part of their room cleanup. They will need to make sure not only that brochures are in rooms but also that brochures are in

Marketing Coordinators Compensation

Rooms	170		
Days per year	365		
Occupancy	63%		
Average stay	2.5		
% Qualified	90%		
Arrivals	14073		
Penetration	**3.50%**	**5.00%**	
Total leads	493	704	
Leads to presentations	60%	60%	
Total presentations	296	422	
Closing percentage	7%	7%	
Total sales	21	30	

Compensation for Two Marketing Coordinators @ 3.5% Penetration

PERFORMANCE		PLAN	DOLLARS
2080	Base	$16	$33,280
493	Leads	$10	$2,463
296	Presentations	$110	$16,254
21	Sales	$0	$0
			$51,997

Compensation for Two Marketing Coordinators @ 5.0% Penetration

PERFORMANCE		PLAN	DOLLARS
2080	Base	$16	$33,280
704	Leads	$10	$3,518
422	Presentations	$110	$23,220
30	Sales	$0	$0
			$60,019

Figure A-2

good shape and placed strategically. You should spot check a few rooms each week to make sure everything is in order.

3. **Turn-down pieces:** These can be very creative pieces that go on the pillows of each of the guests during the turn-down process. They usually provide the next day's weather report.

The hotel team usually likes this concept because it is an upgrade to what is currently being provided and is fully funded by your sales and marketing hotel integration channel. They can be beautiful watercolor cards of the area with the next day's weather and a small note about your product. These pieces can be a great additional way of improving your hotel integration lead production.

4. **Invitations to wine parties:** These invitations to wine parties held in the sales gallery of your offering are usually given out at check in, if the hotel is willing to work with you on this strategy. These parties need to be well coordinated. Marketing specialists and sales agents must make sure the invitations go out and that the wine parties are staged correctly. My experience has been that although relatively few people show up, the quality of the leads tends to be outstanding.

   These wine parties are also great opportunities if you are operating a broker network in your area. They will give brokers the chance to view models of your product offering. I have found these opportunities work well to stimulate broker lead generation opportunities.

5. **Key cards:** If the hotel will allow it, another opportunity is to pay for all the hotel key cards for rooms and have a message on them about your offering.

6. **Concierge support:** If you have hotel concierge support, this strategy can be outstanding. A great way to motivate the concierge is to offer some kind of a referral fee for generating leads. The concierge is used to receiving fees for booking activities for hotel guests. A tour of the residence models should be viewed as an additional activity. So make your referral incentive available and support this strategy with a highly visible sign encouraging guests to come see the models. In some cases the hotel team may allow you to take over the concierge pro-

gram and pay for it on behalf of the hotel. If you ever get this chance, it is a win/win for the hotel and your sales and marketing teams.

7. **Employee Awareness Program:** This is an important strategy that is sometimes overlooked. Make sure hotel employees know about your offering and know where to send an interested hotel guest for more information. Make sure you develop a presentation that is delivered on a regular basis to all hotel employees at their meetings, especially hotel employees who talk regularly with hotel guests. This can be done at the hotel team's regularly scheduled meetings. You can provide give aways, which will make you a welcome part of these meetings. You should also be involved in new employee hotel orientation so all new employees know you are part of the hotel operation and can direct hotel guests accordingly. The main goal is to reinforce the importance of the hotel team's participation in the hotel integration program.

8. **Employee Referral Program:** If you establish effective communication between hotel staff and the sales and marketing teams, you may have an opportunity to offer a referral incentive to hotel employees. Employees can give referral cards to clients that can be turned in when clients show up at the sales office. You can offer something as simple as an American Express gift card to the referring hotel employee. If you do this, you will see some very productive results.

9. **FIT amenities:** A great way to stimulate business is to provide an in-room amenity only to the very best of the FIT guests. This amenity would have a special welcome card attached offering guests a private viewing at their convenience to see your decorated models.

10. **Owner breakfasts:** Another great idea is to do a continental breakfast once a week for the owners who are on-site to re-

view new and exciting opportunities that come with their ownership. These can be great opportunities for owners to meet other owners. Most importantly, you can discover whether your owners are happy with what they have purchased and whether you are exceeding their experience expectations. If so, you will find that owners will purchase additional interests and refer to you friends who may be interested in your offering.

11. **Displays:** Sometimes a well-placed display in or around the hotel works very well to support your marketing efforts.

You do not need to implement all these strategies, but the more you have in place, the more leads you will generate. Think about the hotel as your partner and work together with its staff. See whether you can print all the key card folders for the hotel for a year or the turn-down cards, or help sponsor the employee rallies and/or team meetings. The hotel will be your partner in this program if you work well with the staff, and both of you will benefit. Most of all, the hotel guests will have a first-rate experience.

Most of the prospecting ideas mentioned above are self-explanatory; however, the hotel marketing coordinators require some further explanation. All in-room collateral mentioned above, wines parties, and meetings with hotel employees to generate interest in the property should be under the direction of your marketing coordinators. They need to blend in with the hotel staff, be professionally dressed, and have very pleasant, engaging personalities. They are responsible for giving information to guests who just walk by their desks, taking all inquiries, and making a smooth handoff of interested clients to your sales team.

Post-Arrival: After guests have left the site and if they have not visited your offering, it is nice to send them a thank-you card for visiting the hotel and a brochure about your offering with an opportunity to return to the hotel to see the models and learn more about your product. This post-arrival should only be sent to a select few of the best FIT guests.

Below, in figure A-3, you can view a hotel integration lead performance report. This report will give you vital information about the percentage of people who have viewed your offering from the total number of guests who stayed in the hotel. Remember that hotel arrival penetration is the key to success. This report allows you to review the penetration levels for FIT, group, and any additional leads you have harvested from walk-by traffic.

otel Integration Penetration Performance Report

2008	FIT Arrivals	Group Arrivals	Total Arrivals	FIT Leads	Group Leads	Non-Hotel Leads	Total Leads	FIT Pen	Group Pen	Total Pen	VPL	Revenue
January	723	699	1,422	65	5	24	94	9.0%	0.7%	6.6%	$32,000	$3,008,000
February	716	577	1,293	55	5	18	78	7.7%	0.9%	6.0%	$25,000	$1,950,000
March	897	577	1,474	50	4	29	83	5.6%	0.7%	5.6%	$33,000	$2,739,000
April	543	300	843	35	3	12	50	6.4%	1.0%	5.9%	$24,000	$1,200,000
May	970	550	1,520	75	5	15	95	7.7%	0.9%	6.3%	$18,000	$1,710,000
June	316	250	566	30	6	18	54	9.5%	2.4%	9.5%	$21,000	$1,134,000
July	652	642	1,294	45	7	16	68	6.9%	1.1%	5.3%	$18,000	$1,224,000
August	1,032	823	1,855	65	8	35	108	6.3%	1.0%	5.8%	$19,000	$2,052,000
September	720	759	1,479	55	9	10	74	7.6%	1.2%	5.0%	$24,000	$1,776,000
October	420	377	797	35	10	11	56	8.3%	2.7%	7.0%	$25,000	$1,400,000
November	559	405	964	45	11	11	67	8.1%	2.7%	7.0%	$32,000	$2,144,000
December	833	350	1,183	55	4	10	69	6.6%	1.1%	5.8%	$33,000	$2,277,000
TOTAL	8,381	6,309	14,690	610	77	209	896	7.3%	1.2%	6.1%	25,239	$22,614,000

Q1	2,336	1,853	4,189	170	14	71	255	7.3%	0.76%	6.1%	30,184	$7,697,000
Q2	1,829	1,100	2,929	140	14	45	199	7.7%	1.27%	6.8%	20,322	$4,044,000
Q3	2,404	2,224	4,628	165	24	61	250	6.9%	1.08%	5.4%	$20,208	$5,052,000
Q4	1,812	1,132	2,944	135	25	32	192	7.5%	2.21%	6.5%	30,318	$5,821,000

igure A-3

One of the most important statistics on this report to review is the number of FIT guests who arrived and what percentage of penetration you achieved. These FIT guests have the highest yield from lead to sale. Figure A-3 shows a year-to-date conversion rate of 7.3 percent. You always need to ask how you can increase this number.

A necessary step toward that goal will be to review your pre-arrival, on-site, and post-arrival prospecting strategies. The better you are in all three of these areas, the higher your penetration numbers will be.

Key Notes to Hotel Marketing Prospecting

1. You must have a plan for developing a relationship with the hotel team.

2. Communicate with the hotel team about your entire program, strategies, and the collateral you are going to use.

3. Focus your strategies on the three clients: FIT, group, and walk-bys.

4. Have your full pre-arrival strategy in place.

5. Have your full on-site strategy in place.

6. Have you full post-arrival strategy in place.

7. Make sure your hotel integration employees are fully trained and that you work with them on their marketing skills daily.

8. Have all of your hotel integration performance reporting ready to go before you start this program.

9. Use as many of the marketing strategies as makes sense and as you can get approved. The more you use, the more leads you will generate.

10. The main focus of this prospecting program is to deliver presentations to sales from people staying in the hotel or visiting the hotel.

Broker Networking Prospecting

If you cannot use a real estate broker to help generate qualified leads for your product, you should consider some kind of a networking and/or partnering program, which can be an outstanding prospecting opportunity.

I would have loved to put in this book my entire broker referral prospecting training manual, but it is a bit long and needs some explanation before its exercises make sense. I have made this section complete, but if you want more information or clarification, please contact me at leaddomination@loreinstitute.com.

Here are some important things to put on the top of your checklist as you start a broker referral program. Make sure all of these have been taken into account before you launch your broker program.

1. You need to understand and follow the four sequences I outline for you in this section.

2. You need two people to work full-time running a specific broker area, a broker manager and a broker administrative assistant. Each morning they should wake up thinking about their broker strategies and responsibilities. The bottom line for these two people is to produce what we will call HOT leads. Their HOT leads will be given to sales to convert to sales revenue.

3. You need to register and protect the broker agents on the HOT leads your broker agents give you.

4. You need a broker referral legal agreement that outlines the rules of the offering, the registration process, the agent lead protection process, and the commission you are offering for referring clients.

5. Make sure you understand the difference between a prospecting lead and a HOT lead.

6. Understand that this is a broker referral program, not a broker sales program.

7. Review the important lead follow-up process.

In addition, there are four broker referral sequences:

1. Broker office selection

2. The icebreaker

3. The presentation

4. The lead follow-up

Broker network prospecting, like most marketing programs, begins with a specific targeted marketing plan. In what offices are you going to invest your money, time, and resources? Also, which offices and agents are most likely to give you the best return on your investments in time, money, and resources?

The broker networking program is one of my favorite marketing prospecting programs because with the correct prospecting strategy in play you can control the number of leads you harvest better than with almost any other prospecting marketing program. I have run brokers programs and written training manuals on the best way to execute these programs, so I am talking from experience, not theory. The training can be modified to meet different situations, but here are the four important sequences you should know:

Sequence One—Broker Office Selection

We begin with the important question of how to select a broker office. Why choose one rather than another? What makes you think a particular office is talking to the same buyers you are looking for?

After reviewing the marketplace in your area for the broker offices that have the highest potential, you should identify offices to target, leaders to contract, and the number of agents who work in the offices. Your broker manager should pick enough offices to be able to get you through twelve months of sales.

I would recommend using a very simple form for identifying the broker offices you are going to invest in. You need this kind of a list to review individual office performance.

List of Broker Offices

1. Office Name _____

Number of Agents _____ Office Leader _____

Notes on the leader _____

Figure A-1

You also need to keep track of the number of offices selected and number of agents that these offices represent. These statistics are among the metrics that will guide you in your broker network prospecting performance. Figure A-2 is a sample performance report completed by the broker manager, designed to ensure that a company meets or exceeds its broker target.

Broker Program Vital Statistics

Sequence One—The Market Target	NUMBERS	PERCENTAGE	
Number of Broker Offices Targeted	75	100%	of targeted
Number of Agents Offices Represent	3,750	100%	of targeted

Figure A-2

After you have established and recorded the targeted number of broker offices you will need for twelve months, it is time to set up appointments with the broker leaders of these offices. The broker leaders must understand and endorse your broker referral program to reach your next target. This is done through the ice-breaker.

Sequence Two—The Icebreaker

There are three important pieces to this sequence. First is the icebreaker phone presentation you will make to the broker office leader to set up the appointment to meet face to face. If this discussion goes well, you will be set for a second presentation, this time face to face with the broker office leader to present your program. Third, if the face-to-face meeting goes well, you will have established a date, time, and place to deliver your broker referral presentation to all the agents in the broker leader's office. This icebreaker process should be the responsibility of your broker manager.

Below in figure A-3 is a visual of what I just described.

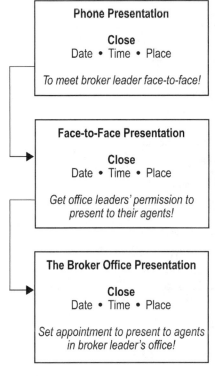

Figure A-3

As part of your broker referral prospecting vital statistics, you need to keep track of the number of icebreakers performed, brokers not interested, brokers you are still working with, scheduled icebreaker presentations, and icebreakers that convert into office presentations.

Figure A-4 shows reports for tracking these statistics.

Broker Program Vital Statistics

Sequence One—The Market Target	Numbers	Percentage	
Number of Broker Offices Targeted	75	100%	of targeted
Number of Agents Offices Represented	3,750	100%	of targeted

Sequence Two—The Icebreakers			
Number of Phone Icebreakers Performed	70	93%	of targeted
Number of Brokers Not Interested	3	4%	of phoned
Number of Brokers Still Working on Scheduling	5	7%	of phoned
Number of Brokers Scheduled Face-to-Face Presentations	62	89%	of phoned
Face-to-Face Icebreakers Performed to Brokers	58	94%	of phoned
Icebreakers Converted to Office Presentations	50	86%	of performed

Figure A-4

Sequence Three—The Presentation

After a successful face-to-face icebreaker presentation, the broker office leader will have agreed to set up a date, time, and place for you to make a presentation of your broker referral program to the office's agents.

There are seven important parts of this presentation sequence. First is the *place* of the presentation, second is the *preparation* of the place for the presentation, third is the *invitation* and the way it is distributed, fourth is the *RSVP* process to the presentation, fifth is the *audio visuals* of the presentation, sixth is the *lead harvest tool* used at the presentation, and seventh is the *room coverage* of the presentation.

Let's review the key highlights of the broker referral presentation that you deliver to these broker offices and specifically their agents in the offices:

1. The Place—I would highly recommend that the presentation not be made in the broker office as part of an office meeting. You want the undivided focus and attention of the agents. I recommend you take them off-site to a convenient location, with a nice spread of cheeses and wines. Your broker referral presentation should be the only reason they are there and the only piece of business they have to consider. It should be the responsibility of the administrative assistant to secure the off-site location in coordination with the broker manager.

2. Preparation—Make sure the place you pick will accommodate the agents, along with the food and drinks, and will offer a comfortable environment for your approximately twenty-minute presentation on your broker referral program. Preparation should be a responsibility of the broker administrative assistant. Preparation includes all materials for the event, collateral, and audio-visual necessary for the presentation.

3. Invitation—The invitation to this event should be in color and be attractive enough to entice broker agents to attend the presentation. I recommend having the office manager send each agent an email inviting and encouraging them to attend this informative presentation. Include an RSVP. Only agents on the list who RSVP will have a reserved seat for the event. The invitation should be the responsibility of the administrative assistant.

4. RSVP—Make sure your broker administrator keeps track of the RSVPs so you can guarantee the space for the presentation will accommodate all attendees.

5. Audio visuals—The presentation is the responsibility of the broker manager, but it is always a good idea to have the administrative assistant be present as well. The presentation needs to have effective visuals, and the audio must be well rehearsed and presented to motivate brokers to produce leads.

6. Lead harvest tool—Make sure you are well prepared with the most creative and simple lead harvest tool for the agents. An example of a lead harvest tool is a very simple form that the broker agents can use to start filling in information about their referrals. I have even seen agents put referral names on the back of their business cards and turn them in. These are two examples of simple harvest tools. You want it to be extremely simple for the agents to deliver names of clients you are interested in.

7. Follow-up—At the presentation you will receive leads, and the way you follow up with these leads will be critical to the success of your program.

As part of your vital statistics, you need to keep track of the number of broker presentations performed, the number of agents invited to your presentations, the number of agents who RSVP, the number of agents who attend the presentation, the total leads you harvest from the presentation, and total number of leads harvested per presentation. See figure A-5.

Broker Program Vital Statistics

Sequence One—The Market Target	Numbers	Percentage	
Number of Broker Offices Targeted	75	100%	of targeted
Number of Agents Offices Represent	3,750	100%	of targeted

Sequence Two—The Icebreakers			
Number of Phone Icebreakers Performed	70	93%	of targeted
Number of Brokers Not Interested	3	4%	of phoned
Number of Brokers Still Working on Scheduling	5	7%	of phoned
Number of Brokers Scheduled Face-to-Face Presentations	62	89%	of phoned
Face-to-Face Icebreakers Performed to Brokers	58	94%	of booked
Icebreakers Converted to Office Presentations	50	86%	of performed

Sequence Three—The Office Referral Presentation			
Office Broker Referral Presentations Performed	45	64%	of ice breakers
Office Broker Referral Presentations Performed	45	90%	of scheduled
Number of Agents Invited to Broker Presentation	4,500	100	per office
Number of Agents who RSVP to the Presentation	1,800	40%	rsvp of agents
Number of Agents who Attended the Presentation	1,125	63%	rsvp showed
Number of Leads Harvested in *Total*	1,012	0.9	per agent show
Number of Leads Harvested per *Presentation*	22		

Figure A-5

Keep in mind that the goal of your presentation is to harvest leads from the broker agents. These leads are customers the broker agents have developed relationships with and feel might be interested in your offering.

There are very specific strategies for delivering a broker presentation that will create a strong lead flow. You get leads from the broker agents, and they get commissions if the leads purchase at the close of escrow. This is a win/win program.

Sequence Four—The Lead Follow-up

A successful presentation will produce quality leads. The number of leads you have produced is important, but more important is your ability to convert these harvested leads into HOT leads. A HOT lead is a lead who has been given a warm introduction to the product and wants more information from one of your sales agents. Sales will also need to have harvested the name, address, and phone number of these leads for them to qualify as HOT. This is done through the sequence we call the lead follow-up process.

What you harvest from a broker prospecting program are not really leads but prospects. Do not give these prospects yet to sales; they need to be more qualified first. The way you qualify them is by having either the agent who gave you the leads or your broker assistant call them and provide a warm introduction.

Figure A-6 shows an example of a warm introduction presentation by a real estate office agent.

Hello X,

How are you?

Do you have just a minute for me? I have something I want to share with you.

Our office has received an exciting partnership with (*name of property*) offering (*location of property*). When I received and reviewed the details of this second home offering at the (*name of property*), I immediately thought of you.

X, this is the opportunity to own a shared interest at the (*name of offering*). I know you spend time in (*location*), and this offering is nothing short of a perfect second home alternative. I would love to set up a call and get you all the information on this offering so you and your family can take a look at this. It is very exciting and very different than most second home offerings. Again, I think it is the perfect second home. Can I set up a time to have my partner at the (*name of property*) call you and give you an update?

Figure A-6

If the answer to this script is yes, you have now turned a broker prospect lead into a broker HOT lead. Once the lead has been turned HOT it goes to sales for follow-up.

There are seven important parts to this sequence:

1. Count and review all leads you have harvested. This is a vital statistic that needs to be recorded.

2. Call agents who attended your presentation to gather additional information about the leads you harvested, to obtain new leads, or to get back to agents who have asked you to call them for leads. The sooner you do this after the presentation, the more additional leads you will harvest.

3. Put all leads harvested into your lead follow-up software so you can check whether they are currently in your database or on a "do not call" list.

4. Get back to the agents and let them know if the leads they gave you can be protected. This protection should be provided as soon as the clients have been contacted, given a warm introduction to the product, and indicated they would like to talk to a sales agent. You will also need a name, address, and phone numbers for each client.

5. Follow up on the warm introductions and record all HOT leads. HOT leads need to be put in the system by the administrative team and given to sales.

6. Stay close to your sales team and the real estate agents on the follow-up with your HOT leads.

7. Convert HOT leads to sales.

You need to keep track of such vital statistics as the number of leads harvested, leads not interested, leads still working, HOT leads in the system, HOT to presentation percentages, number of presentations, HOT leads closing percentages, net sales, HOT lead VPL, and HOT lead net volume.

See figure A-7 on the following page.

People You Will Need to Hire

The two people who run the broker program are the broker manager and the broker administrative assistant. They will always report to a director of marketing or a project director. Their compensation will have a lot to do with the HOT leads and revenues that their broker network produces. Obviously, the higher the sales revenue, the higher their compensation. I would recommend 50 percent of their compensation be base salary, 25 percent be based on HOT leads, and the remaining 25 percent be based on net sales revenue produced by their broker network.

The broker manager is the leader of the program, so this person needs to be someone who is highly social, a great presenter, well organized, responsible, and has a desire to meet or exceed all bud-

Broker Program Vital Statistics

Sequence One—The Market Target	Numbers	Percentage	
Number of Broker Offices Targeted	75	100%	of targeted
Number of Agents Offices Represent	3,750	100%	of targeted

Sequence Two—The Icebreakers			
Number of Phone Icebreakers Performed	70	93%	of targeted
Number of Brokers Not Interested	3	4%	of phoned
Number of Brokers Still Working on Scheduling	5	7%	of phoned
Number of Brokers Scheduled Face-to-Face Presentations	62	89%	of phoned
Face-to-Face Icebreaker Performed to Brokers	58	94%	of booked
Icebreakers Converted to Office Presentations	50	86%	of performed

Sequence Three—The Office Referral Presentation			
Office Broker Referral Presentations Performed	45	64%	of icebreakers
Office Broker Referral Presentations Performed	45	90%	of scheduled
Number of Agents Invited to Broker Presentations	4,500	100	per office
Number of Agents who RSVP to the Presentations	1,800	40%	Rsvp of agents
Number of Agents who Attended the Presentations	1,125	63%	Rsvp showed
Number of Leads Harvested in *Total*	1,012	0.9	per agent show
Number of Leads Harvested per *Presentation*	22		

Sequence Four—The Lead Follow-up Process			
Leads Harvested	1,012		
Leads Not Interested	582	58%	of Leads
Leads Still Working	250	25%	of Leads
HOT Leads in the System	180	18%	of Leads
Performance from Lead to HOT	18%		
Performance from HOT to Presentation	40%		
Presentations	72		
HOT Leads Closing Percentages	22%		
Net Sales	16		
HOT Lead to VPL	$35,556		
HOT Leads to Net Volume	$6,400,000		

Figure A-7

geted targeted numbers. This is a very important hire. I have listed throughout this chapter the different areas of the program the broker managers are in charge of. He or she must be trained before they start. The success of the whole broker prospecting network has everything to do with this leader. He or she must be able to lead, delegate, and execute all four sequences outlined earlier in this section.

The broker administrative assistant is also very important and needs to be a well-compensated position. This person must love organizing and juggling multiple tasks with great skills and organizational ability. You have already seen all the different duties this assistant will have with respect to the sequences. The biggest role he or she plays, though, will be on the follow-up of the lead production. Even though there are many tasks to perform, the broker manager must be able to produce the leads, and the administrative assistant must be able to help turn these leads HOT for the program. I would suggest compensating this person 60 percent in terms of base salary, 20 percent on HOT leads, and the remaining 20 percent on net sales volume.

Registration of Your Broker Leads

In my view you cannot have a successful broker prospecting program without being able to register and protect your broker agents on the leads they harvest that are HOT. You need a database that includes *all* the leads you harvest from *all* channels. It will allow you to check on the leads that broker agents give you. If the leads they give you are not in the database, they can register them. If the leads are already in the database, they cannot. To ensure the success of your broker program, you must be able to check on leads accurately and quickly. If leads are not in your database, the broker agents can register them only if they are turned HOT. When you register a lead in the broker agent's name, the lead is protected in that agent's name in your database for a period of time. I recommend two years. Once the lead is registered, no other broker or marketing program can claim that lead. If the lead purchases from you, that broker office and agent will be paid their commission.

Figure A-8 shows an example of the broker registration form.

Broker Referral Registration Form

Fax to (212) 835-xxxx

CLIENT INFORMATION

Name: _____

Address: _____

City:_____ State:_____Zip: _____

Telephone:_____Fax: _____

Email: _____

      ASPEN: ❑   NEW YORK: ❑ Fractional   ❑ Whole Ownership

BROKER INFORMATION

Initial Client Contact Preference: Whole Ownership ❑   Residence Club ❑

Referring Real Estate Office: _____

Referring Broker: _____

Address: _____

City:_____ State:_____Zip: _____

Telephone:_____Fax: _____

Email: _____

       THIS CLIENT HAS BEEN APPROVED AS A REGISTERED CLIENT
              FOR THE ABOVE BROKER OFFICE.

_____   _____

Name of Broker Manager—Name of Offering   Date

By signing below, I give [offering name®] and its affiliates ("Name") permission to contact me about the [name of offering] using the information I have provided above. I understand that this permission overrides my listing on any state and federal do-not-call list. I can opt out of future calls at any time by requesting to be placed on the company do-not-call list by calling 1-800-xxx- xxxx.

_____   _____

Client's Approval   Date

Figure A-8

Legal Broker Agreement

You need to meet with your legal department and draft an agreement that spells out the rules of your broker program, such as how to register and protect your leads, commissions amounts, when they are earned, how they are paid, start and stop date of the agreements, how you resolve disputes, and some performance criteria. Consult with your legal team, as there will be plenty of other categories to cover. Make sure you have your legal broker agreement signed by the office before you start harvesting leads.

Brokers Referrals and Do Not Sell

An effective broker program must be simple for the broker. The program cannot in any way interfere with the broker's real responsibilities, which usually include selling homes. Offer brokers a good commission, and limit their responsibilities to providing you with a name, registering that name, and helping you turn the prospect into a HOT lead. You and your team must do all the rest. You and your team must communicate what you are doing in the follow-up so the broker agent remains informed. He or she will receive a commission at the close of escrow. If it's not simple for the broker to earn commissions by referring leads, then the program will not work.

The Follow-up Process

The follow-up process is so very important for a successful broker networking program that I want to provide a little more detail about this subject. First, it requires a person who is very well organized as well as who loves to follow up on the phone. Follow-ups are the responsibility of the broker assistant, who is a very important part of the success of this program. Broker managers need to focus on lead production, and broker assistants need to focus on converting the prospects into HOT leads.

The International Opportunity

There are some very good broker lead opportunities in the international market. I have done some work in Europe and found it to be very productive. Just be sure to cover all registration and legal issues before you begin investing in overseas opportunities.

The great thing about dealing with international brokers is their interest level. These brokers will make the commitment to come out and review your resort, and you will find that the quality of lead production they provide will be very high. Keep in mind that some of the countries that you will be dealing with will have great dollar exchange opportunities, which can make owning in the United States a very welcome proposition.

Figure A-9 shows a flowchart of a lead going through the broker process. Maybe it will help you conceptualize more clearly how to process leads though this important system.

Broker Network

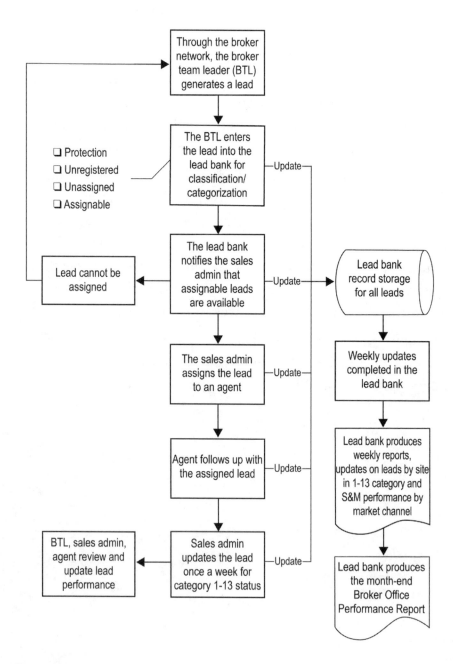

Figure A-9

Key Notes to Broker Networking Prospecting

1. You must have an expert on the four broker referral sequences.

2. Your broker manager and assistant must be thoroughly trained on sequences and all broker networking processes.

3. Define and write out your standard operating policies.

4. Complete your broker referral agreement.

5. Create your database and software strategy.

6. Make sure you have clear rules for your database, how you are going to protect broker leads, and when you are not going to protect broker leads. Also, make sure you do not call on unregistered states.

7. Protecting the agents' leads is an important part of this program.

8. Turning broker leads into broker HOT leads is vital; make sure you have the best process to achieve this goal in place.

9. Put together your yearly forecast by month using the vital statistics reports.

10. Be ready to start to execute this forecast on a monthly basis.

11. Have your written broker referral program description and purpose paper completed.

12. Focus on generating HOT leads though the system.

13. Update brokers on the status of their HOT leads.

14. Review with the sales team the status of the HOT leads they have received.

Web Marketing Prospecting

Web marketing is a very valuable method of cost-effective prospecting. You should be sure to develop at least a reasonably good website promoting your products. Make sure your site is easy to navigate, has a compelling visual style and written narrative about your product, and makes it easy for your prospect to request additional information.

A standard web hit to lead conversion percentage is about fifteen to thirty percent. Obviously, there is a significant difference between a fifteen and a thirty percent conversion rate. The variation will depend on how interesting and enticing your website is and the diligence of your sales team in working web leads and making follow-ups.

A web lead will probably be your lowest in terms of cost from all your marketing channels. Before you go crazy trying to generate a bunch of these leads to reduce your overall CPL, though, you should be aware of the following: A web lead generally takes more follow-up to convert to a presentation and then to a sale than almost any other lead that marketing can generate. The reason these leads require more follow-up than most is they tend to communicate through email until they have enough information to feel comfortable talking with a live person. This process takes way more time than if someone simply calls in the first place. This channel will also have one of your lower VPL ratings. So although very cost effective, web leads can cause wear and tear to your sales teams. You should therefore use this method but be careful about the percentage of leads you send up to sales from the web channel. Determine the right percentage so sales can do the required follow-up without becoming overloaded.

Keep in mind that most advertising in your other marketing channels can receive your website URL (uniform resource locator). Pure web leads are generated by Internet advertising. For example, you can place web banners in online newspapers. Customers who come to you by clicking on these banners definitely count as web leads. By contrast, leads supported by the website but driven to it by another channel should be credited to that other channel. To refine your marketing strategies, it is very important to keep accurate records about what channels are actually driving leads. For instance, when you advertise for leads in different marketing channels, such as newspapers and magazines, and provide your URL, you will see an increase in activity on your website. But how can you know which channel is directing leads to your website?

The answer is that URLs can allow you to track where your leads are coming from. So a newspaper ad should provide a different URL than a magazine or a pure web advertising program. These URLs function like sub-marketing source codes for you. So you could generate three hundred leads to your website from an ad in *The New York Times,* and the hits on the page from the website with the specific URL you ran in your ad would allow you to determine the channel that directed these customers to your site. This URL tracking will help you understand which source has created the best leads for your marketing dollars invested. Notice, however, I did not say the *most leads;* I said the *best leads.*

Always remember when you are prospecting for leads to calculate how many leads you are getting for the dollars you've invested—this is your quantity metric. But don't stop there. Next you need to know the quality of the leads you've generated, which is determined by looking at your VPL (volume per lead). Divide the CPL by the VPL to determine what you are paying for marketing compared to the revenue you produced. Compare these figures to your budget or targets, and you will know how good your leads are. Higher percentages than targeted indicate lower quality leads whereas lower percentages indicate higher quality leads.

Below in figure A-1 are three examples: the first is on budget, the second represents high-quality leads, and the third low-quality leads. In each of these examples the lead amounts are the same and the cost per lead is the same. From a pure marketing standpoint there is no difference among them. Where the difference becomes apparent is in the sales conversion from lead to sale. You will see a budgeted VPL of $4,500. The high-quality leads produced a $5,000 VPL whereas the low-quality leads produced a VPL of $3,000. From a sales standpoint the quality of these leads is different. Look at the percentage of expense compared to revenue produced: 8.2 percent is on budget, but the high-quality leads produced 7.4 percent, and the low-quality leads produced 12.3 percent.

	LEADS	VPL	CPL	VOLUME	EXPENSE	%
Budget	1,200	$4,500	$370	$5,400,000	$444,000	8.2%
High Quality Leads	1,200	$5,000	$370	$6,000,000	$444,000	7.4%
Low Quality Leads	1,200	$3,000	$370	$3,600,000	$444,000	12.3%

Figure A-1

When you develop your website, take your time and remember that you are building it for the customer. You want to create something that is compelling to look at, presents your product in the best light, and is easy to navigate. Take a look at your competitors' websites to get ideas about what works and what doesn't work.

Also, make sure you have someone looking into key words, so that when people search the web, your product shows up. If you can, you should appear in the top five results when the key word is typed into a search engine. If you have a direct competitor with more exposure than you do, then consider purchasing an advertisement on your competitor's pages. Key word buys and strategic placement of ads are important for increasing your lead production.

The number of web leads can be quite substantial, but if you just turn these leads over to your sales team without any qualifications, sales will soon discover they are a lot more work than most other kinds of leads. If you are getting a lot of web leads and you do not filter any of them, your sales team will only be able to convert a small percentage into sales. Web leads then usually end up in the bottom of the sales team's follow-up pile or, in some cases, in the trash can. That is why I recommend appointing a web concierge.

A web concierge responds to a web inquiry as soon as it is received with a personal message. An example would be:

Hello, my name is Doug. I see you inquired about our Santa Barbara Residence Club. So I can help meet your needs, please respond to the following:

1. Which of these options best describes how we can help you, A, B, or C?

A. Just curious about your offering. Please send me information.

B. I would like to speak with someone in sales to get pricing and other specific information.

C. I would like to get information on visiting the property.

> 2. I live in the state of _____.
>
> 3. My phone number is _____.
>
> 4. The best time to contact me is _____.
>
> Thank you for your time and interest.

With this type of concierge follow-up before you send the lead to a sales person, you will obtain better results from your website.

The keys to web marketing are a well-developed website, diversification of your web marketing investment, use of different URLs to pinpoint where your leads are coming from, strategic investment in key words, web concierges, and training your sales team about how to convert these leads to presentations and sales. You need to prepare your team thoroughly, or you may find this source to be the least desirable of your marketing channels.

In summary, your website is very important. Not only does it generate pure web leads, but it also provides strong support for most of your other marketing programs. Make sure someone is overseeing the marketing side of your website and that you are leveraging this important technology.

Key Notes to
Web Marketing Prospecting

1. You need to develop and continually update your website so it is compelling to a potential purchaser and easy to navigate.

2. Have a well-thought-out plan for using URLs to track the different channels that are directing clients to your website.

3. Purchase key words to improve your ranking on search engines, and place ads in strategic spots on the Internet.

4. Have web concierges gather more information on leads before they are sent to sales.

5. You must train your sales team on follow-up processes as these leads are more difficult to convert than most.

6. Have web performance reports to update your progress on a monthly basis.

7. Your website not only will produce its own leads but will also support other marketing channels and increase their lead production.

Local Marketing Prospecting

Advertising campaigns can be divided into three areas. The first is local, which means the state where your product is being offered. The second is national, and the third is international. In this section we will focus on local advertising opportunities.

First, your marketing team should put together a report covering all the advertising that is appropriate and meets your qualified lead parameters locally. An analysis of what all competitors in your state have done with their local marketing dollars should be part of this report. Then, your marketing team should work on determining the marketing dollars you will need to invest in your local campaign.

Local advertising means first and foremost advertising in newspapers and magazines. Since a huge number of newspapers and magazines are published in virtually every state, you will obviously need to evaluate which ones will be most likely to end up in the hands of your targeted leads. When you choose to advertise locally in either newspapers or magazines, be sure your advertising is being targeted to the end user. It is expensive to advertise in publications just to inform the local market, so be sure to craft an effective message with a local appeal. It will likely be quite different from your national or international messages.

Some of the most productive local advertising can come from niche marketing and creative local activities. When you have people on your marketing team who can deploy these kinds of marketing approaches, additional leads can be produced. For instance, I was involved with a project that had quite a bit of local notoriety and press when it was going through the planning and approval process. It was a very nice resort, and I think for the most part the local people were proud it was part of their community. Our marketing team generated some very cost-effective and productive leads through a number of strategies. Evening wine and cheese parties, along with continental breakfasts, were planned and held, giving local people the opportunity to learn more about the new resort. At these events complimentary stays at the resort were given away in drawings so some of the local people could experience what the place would be like for guests.

We also delivered an informative, well-executed presentation about the resort and what it meant to the community, as well as about what it would be like to stay there. At the end of the presentation we offered attendees three special things, including preferred pricing for sixty days for them and their friends and family and a special promotional deal for guests of the local people who might want to experience the property. Lastly, if any of the guests referred to us by locals purchased the offering, we would give the people who had made the referral random credits that could be used at the resort. Note that if you plan to make these kinds of offers, you should check with your legal department first since different states have different laws governing such matters.

Our marketing strategies enabled us to teach local people about the resort and made them local ambassadors of the property. Overall, our programs were highly successful and cost-effective. It took some work by marketing, but the programs produced a much better result than just running ads in local newspapers and magazines would have.

You need to be extremely careful in this marketing channel because it is a fully reactive marketing program. You advertise and wait for a response. This type of lead generation has great vulnerabilities. Unlike hotel, broker, and owner programs, in which you can be much more proactive in your lead production, or web programs, which have much less spending risk, local advertising requires marketing dollars up front. You are counting on your investment in ads or events to produce leads.

The first rule of thumb is if you cannot measure it, do not spend money on it. I have heard marketing people say local advertising is all about making the local community aware of your presence, not getting leads. If it is really only about awareness of your product, though, it is a matter for public relations, which should not be part of your marketing channel and lead production budget. For your marketing channel budget you must be able to get leads and report on their quantity and quality. That means you need an accurate accounting of the number of leads each ad or event produces. You also need to be able to calculate the cost per lead and the volume per lead.

Pick your opportunities carefully, track the results, and keep the local marketing channel on a constant red alert. I have worked many sites where after investing in the local market we decided to allot funds to another marketing source that was much more productive in terms of cost-effective lead generation.

Key Notes to Local Marketing Prospecting

1. Local marketing consists of prospecting in the state where your product is.

2. Try to think out of the box when it comes to generating local interest in your product. There are great opportunities all around you in the local market. You and your team just need to be clever enough to tap into them.

3. If you cannot track it, do not invest in it.

4. Review lead qualities against budget on daily, weekly, and monthly bases.

5. Review lead quality by dividing your cost per lead by your volume per lead. Compare the resulting percentage to what you budgeted.

6. Higher percentages mean there is a problem in the quality of the leads. Lower percentages mean you are producing quality leads.

7. Put this reactive marketing channel on a red alert status and make sure you are getting a return for the dollars you have invested.

National Marketing Prospecting

If you need additional leads for hitting your targets and your state advertising isn't doing the job, then consider national advertising. A national advertising campaign will require a fair bit of preparation. You need to make sure you do extensive market research to ensure your best leads, or the additional leads you are going to need, truly are in other states. Verify with hard data that your buyers are located outside your home state. This should be fairly easy to do. Just confirm that there is a healthy prospecting market before you invest in expensive marketing programs.

After you have done your due diligence, you need to pinpoint the states these leads are in, the area in the states where most of these leads reside, and the best marketing tool to reach out to these leads. Believe me, this is no place for guessing or experimentation. Ads in major national publications can cost $25,000 to $50,000 apiece. You are now entering the big league of costs, and a month or two of bad marketing strategies can put you so far in the hole that it could be hard to recover.

National advertising, like local advertising, is usually done in media print sources such as newspapers and magazines. There are other ways to market, but this channel provides wide distribution. National advertising can produce a large lead flow for your sales team, but it will be one of your more expensive leads. When leads resulting from national ads slow down, you need to be ready to make adjustments, or your lead cost can get way out of the targeted range. I have seen lead costs when not monitored carefully rise to more than $4,000 per lead.

The only way lead costs like this should be acceptable to you is if cost per lead and volume per lead are both high. Take a look at your report card, which is the percentage of expense compared to revenue or the percentage of your marketing cost. If it is at or under budget, you can live with high marketing costs. Just keep a close eye on the situation.

This is clearly a channel that requires a great amount of marketing experience or at least homework to ensure the best selection and placement of advertising. Networking is one important key to success. I have seen $50,000 ads be purchased for $10,000 because a marketing expert was able to network with the right people. A last-minute insertion can be an outstanding discount opportunity. Good opportunities are available all the time—you just need to have the right connections. Just imagine what a $50,000 ad purchased for $10,000 in the right paper, with the right message and the right placement, will produce. This is pretty exciting stuff, but it takes a smart marketer to ensure you capitalize on such opportunities.

Most states have laws about marketing and selling property, so you need to take time to familiarize yourself with those and to complete any registration process that may be required. Once a state has signed off on your registration, you can begin to market and sell your product in that state. The registration process, though, may take from ninety days to a year, depending on the state and the product you are trying to register. Be sure your legal team works closely with your sales and marketing teams as you go through the registration process.

When reviewing the performance of a national advertising campaign, keep one eye on when ads run and what happens to your web count. I have seen web counts really increase when these ads hit, so you need to make sure you are crediting the national ads with these inquiries. If you are not set up to count web leads generated by national advertising as such, you can never really measure the true effectiveness of your campaign. So be sure to use a special URL for your ads to capture hits directed to your website by this channel.

If you have a product with broad appeal and your budget calls for significant lead production, national advertising probably needs to be part of your diversified marketing strategy.

Key Notes to National Marketing Prospecting

1. Prepare well in advance if some of your best leads are in other states. The registration process, if required, can take months.

2. Review cost versus production carefully before embarking on a national advertising campaign.

3. If you cannot track it, do not invest in it.

4. Review lead qualities against budget on daily, weekly, and monthly bases.

5. Review lead quality by dividing cost per lead by volume per lead. Compare the resulting percentage to you budget.

6. Higher percentages mean there is a problem in the quality of the leads. Lower percentages mean you are producing quality leads.

7. Put this reactive marketing channel on a red alert status and make sure you are getting a return on the dollars you have invested.

8. Generate national advertising performance reports to update progress on daily, weekly, and monthly bases.

International Marketing Prospecting

Today's global economy means international advertising can play a major role in your lead production. There are many new and different processes to deal with if you decide to take your marketing into a foreign country. Just remember that if you do that, you must also be prepared to take your sales team into this environment.

Obviously, you need to start by selecting countries where you think there will be a demand for your product. When you begin your due diligence in the market, get your legal, tax, and financial teams involved. You will need legal advice about the registration laws, if any, for the countries you're targeting. Understanding what the cost and timeframes are going to be to get permission to market in a country is important before you start. Some countries are almost impossible to sell in whereas others are easy. For some countries you are going to find it is so difficult and expensive to sell there that there is no reason to start reviewing their marketing potential.

Next, look carefully at the tax laws for selling products to international citizens. You may find no problems here, but you may discover that a country's tax laws make it impossible for you to meet your margins. You obviously do not want to play in that market. Also make sure that from a financial standpoint there are no complications in reporting revenue. If international markets pass these tests, then you can start prospecting for potential leads.

I want to be positive about international marketing because I have seen some outstanding results when the right product has been introduced into the right market. You just need to understand that it is a different situation than when you are selling in the United States. The discovery planning is definitely more complicated.

While you are reviewing regulations, taxes, and reporting revenue, you should also determine whether you are going to need to translate your marketing materials into another language and what the cost of that will be. Will your sales staff be able to communicate with the potential buyer? That's an important question, obviously.

Additional research is necessary before you start allocating and spending dollars in an international market. Each product you would like to offer internationally will require a different approach, but let's take an example of a real estate product. I would recommend that you first spend time with high-end real estate broker offices to determine just how much potential international markets may have. If you launch first in the international market with a broker program offering mostly commissions to the brokers, the risk will be very small from a financial standpoint. Find the right international broker offices in the right countries for your product and see what kind of lead generation they produce.

International marketing can have a great beneficial impact on sales, especially real estate whole ownership and high-end shared ownership sales. The enormous opportunities for attracting potential clients from foreign countries can make it worth the investment if regulation, taxes, and so forth won't undercut your profits. If you do your up-front work on international markets, they could be an outstanding source of business.

Key Notes to International Marketing Prospecting

1. Do your homework far in advance to ensure you can sell profitably in your chosen international markets.

2. Consult your legal, tax, and finance teams early in the discovery process.

3. Make sure there are no language barriers preventing you from marketing your products successfully.

4. The above considerations can impose extra costs. Make sure these dollars are well spent and that the lead generation is worth the added expense.

5. Plan well in advance of marketing for the registration process, which can take several months.

6. If you cannot track it, do not invest in it.

7. Review lead qualities against budget on daily, weekly, and monthly bases.

8. Review lead quality by dividing cost per lead by volume per lead. Compare the resulting percentage to you budget.

9. Higher percentages mean there is a problem in the quality of the leads. Lower percentages mean you are producing quality leads.

10. Put this reactive marketing channel on red alert status and make sure you are getting a return for the dollars you have invested.

11. Have international performance reports to update progress on a monthly basis.

Direct Mail Marketing Prospecting

Direct mail used to be a favorite marketing channel in most lead campaigns. But a lot has changed in the direct mail world. Today, with e-marketing, web marketing, and other available marketing programs, the popularity of direct mail is not what it was. In addition, do-not-call regulations have created an additional setback for this approach. In the old days you could chase your mailing with a phone call. You can still adopt this approach, but the number of people you can reach now has been substantially reduced.

Today, you can use many different marketing channels to generate leads more quickly and with less risk. You can also start and stop other marketing programs if they are not performing well—but direct mail is not a flexible channel. At one point direct mail was also just so overused in the marketplace that response percentages declined sharply. Couple that with the time it takes to do a direct mail campaign, and it appears not to be one of your better marketing options.

Direct mail entails some real risks. You do most all your spending up front, before you start generating any leads. So before you send the mailing out, you need to develop your target lists in a very strategic manner. The investment of time and resources can be considerable, as you have to design the piece, print it, and pay for postage. If a campaign has gone through a branding and/or image review—which it should—the timing from the start of the campaign to the actual mailing can be months.

So you really want to make sure you are targeting the very best prospects when this mail is dropped. If the program gets a poor response after you mail your piece, and the percentage of responses comes in below targets or the conversions from lead to presentation to sales do, there is not much you can do to recoup your investment. This is a very reactive program. You have to wait and hope that all your due diligences pay off.

Before you move ahead with a direct mail campaign, make sure you have asked and answered the following question: Is this the best way to reach prospects? Make sure you have explored all other options and that direct mail has the potential to deliver what you want.

All that being said, however, direct mail is still being used with success, and I have seen well-planned direct mail programs produce great results. In the right numbers, to the correct targeted prospects, and with the right message, direct mail can still generate sales successes.

Direct mail has the advantage of targeting your leads. You send your information straight to your prospects' homes and hope for a response to your offering. Responses can be made through the mail with a business reply card, on the phone, or on your website. Sometimes you can increase your response rate by following these direct mail pieces up with an email.

The idea behind the direct mail approach is to elicit a response from your targeted prospects that will lead to presentations and sales of your product. The responses to direct mail can be between .15 and 10 percent. Your response rate will depend on to whom you are sending the mail, what you expect the prospect to do, and how compelling your offer is.

When a direct mail program is reviewed for approval, you will need to be able to forecast as accurately as possible the following financial numbers:

1. **Number of pieces you plan to send**—This number should depend on the best target market of buyers and the number of leads you think you can generate from these buyers.

2. **Percentage of responses**—You need to forecast the number of responses you expect your direct mail piece to elicit.

3. **Percentage of inquiries that become leads**—Most inquires will become leads because most people are looking for information if they respond to a direct mail offering.

4. **Number of leads generated**—You should also forecast the number of leads you are hoping to turn into presentations of your product by your sales team. This includes leads turned over to sales on the phone and complete presentations in the form of an on-site preview package.

5. **Number of leads that convert to presentations**—When you generate a lead, it will either be converted into a product presentation or it will not. Leads that convert into presentations are interested enough that they want sufficient information to make an informed purchase decision. These are usually your best leads, and you really would like the number of leads that elect to receive a presentation to be high.

The reason these numbers are so important is there is a lot of work that goes into getting a direct mail program launched. You really want to make sure you have a viable program before you move forward. Also, because this approach requires a large commitment from your team, if the financial numbers work, I would recommend you put together a description and responsibilities paper before moving ahead (see chapter 7). That way you can better prepare yourself and outline the program to the different team members.

The description and responsibilities paper will cover the following:

1. Program description
2. Who and where the buyer is
3. Objectives
4. Benefits
5. Processes
6. Offer
7. Assumptions
8. Lessons learned
9. Action steps

Once your marketing team has completed the financial review and the description and responsibilities paper, you are ready to launch your direct mail program. Here is a quick summary of the remaining steps leading to your launch, with the team or teams responsible for each step in parentheses:

1. Compliance (legal)
2. Lists (marketing)
3. Look and messaging (legal, marketing)
4. Production (marketing)
5. Response center (marketing)
6. Fulfillment (marketing)
7. Inquiries, leads, presentations, sales (sales, marketing)

Have all specialty teams ready to go the day you mail your piece to drive responses, conversions, and revenues.

Key Notes to Direct Mail Marketing Prospecting

1. You need to do your homework to ensure the list you are using is definitely your buyer profile.

2. You also need to review the buyer list carefully, as it is essential to target the right potential customers.

3. Look and message are also very important.

4. Make sure to establish your financial expectations.

5. Complete your description and responsibilities paper.

6. Mobilize your teams to ensure all essential details have been addressed before your launch.

7. Make sure marketing and sales are ready when you launch your campaign.

Event Marketing Prospecting

Event marketing is a very specialized prospecting program that will enhance your marketing diversification. The first step is to identify local and national events that your potential buyers attend. Then, send your marketing team to these events and make your products available for potential clients to review. Here are some examples of the kinds of events where you might find it advantageous to market your products:

Individual event marketing—Let's say you are selling a high-end real estate product in New York City. Through your marketing research you discover a list of people in Connecticut who vacation regularly in New York City at high-end hotels. You decide you would like to have an event in Connecticut for these qualified clients right in their backyard, introducing a subject they already enjoy: visiting New York City.

You plan this event at a popular museum in Connecticut close to these potential clients. You invite your leads to a special tasting of fine wines and cheeses and at this event introduce your product as an alternative way to visit New York. Marketing specialists should be on hand to answer questions and to invite potential clients to visit the properties in New York. Face-to-face interactions during such events can create very qualified leads.

Group event—This kind of event has already been planned by another organization. It may be an annual event that is well attended. Your marketing team would be dispatched to it because you believe potential clients will be in attendance. The usual strategy would be to set up a booth showcasing your products. Potential clients would have the chance to interact one-on-one with your representatives. The goal, again, is to produce highly qualified leads for your sales team that you probably could not obtain through any other marketing channel.

These events are complicated and require the right presentation strategy. Understand where the potential clients are going to be during the event, what will distract from their attention, and when will they have time to focus on your offering. Marketing companies sometimes spend thousands of dollars to be part of these group events only to discover that their location and their potential clients' activities were not at all conducive to lead generation opportunities. If you can make effective contact with potential customers, you can attend these events frequently, perhaps every other month of the year.

Events, unlike other marketing programs, occur in a short period of time. You must be fully prepared for your marketing event. If you're not ready, there is usually no way to adjust your strategy—you just lose the time and money you have invested and the opportunity. But if your event has been well chosen and your presentation strategy has been well thought out, you can produce some very good cost-effective leads.

This type of activity may be new to your marketing personnel, so you need to make sure they have adequate preparation and the interpersonal skills to be effective. You also obviously need to make sure the event you select lends itself to your product and your approach. Make sure the event does not have too many distractions or your team will not be able to have effective lead-generating conversations with potential prospects. Face-to-face interactions are the key to these events, and your ability to deliver a complete marketing presentation is important. You also need to understand when a marketing presentation stops and a sales presentation begins. Your marketing team must stay on the marketing side of the presentation.

Good planning is essential for success at these events. Be sure you allow plenty of time for organizing all your events. These are not last-minute opportunities. Consider that your image, brand, and product will be on display. Time and dollars must be invested so that prospects have a good first impression.

Start by identifying events your potential customers will actually attend. The biggest mistake I have seen in booking events is that they are chosen because the clients who attend are financially qualified. This single filter will not necessarily produce a favorable result. Potential clients need, of course, to be financially qualified to purchase, but what makes event prospecting work is targeting people who use or need the products you are offering. Some events are expensive, so make sure there is a compelling reason to be there.

Events I have experienced have been either very successful or complete failures—there is little in between. To ensure success, before you choose to do an event you should do two things. First, take time to develop a description and responsibilities paper. Second, spend a little extra time when you create your financial expectations. These exercises will force you to address all the important components of your presentation before you start an event.

Let's take a look at what a description and responsibilities paper for an event should include:

Program description—Review how the prospecting will take place at an event. I have seen events where the booth marketing set up was not located where the potential clients were. I have also seen events where you could not talk to people because of the distractions. Make sure there is time between event activities so your marketing presentation can be given.

Objective—The clear objective is to create leads from an event. Make sure the teams you have to run the event understand how many leads each is responsible for. You do not want your team members to show up and just hope for the best; you want them to show up knowing what lead success is for each of them in terms of actual numbers produced.

Benefits—Try to identify how your product will benefit potential customers. Answer this question: Why should clients attending this event buy your product?

Processes—You will need to go through the processes whereby you will meet, greet, and make presentations to clients and also collect leads from the event. Training and scripting are essential. Have your team ready and eager to start. Be sure to rehearse all processes before the event starts.

Expectations—Make sure all your team members attending the event understand the lead goal and are willing to make intelligent adjustments if necessary while the event is in progress to meet this goal. Spell out your expectations before you start.

Lessons learned—List all the opportunities and challenges of the event before you start and have a plan in everyone's mind of what you are going to do to meet the challenges and make the most of the opportunities.

Action items—This is a detailed list of what needs to be done before, during, and after the event. It specifies who is responsible for each item and under what timeframe each should be completed. This step is very important for assessing the potential of events.

After you have completed your description and responsibilities paper, you should determine your financial expectations.

Attending events can be very helpful for reaching prospects you would not reach otherwise. Just be ready for the work that needs to be completed by marketing to produce leads successfully. Events tend to be time consuming and work intensive, but they are lots of fun for your team, and if done correctly can produce some very qualified leads.

Key Notes to Event Marketing Prospecting

1. Take extra time to make sure potential buyers will be attending the event you are considering.

2. Make sure you have ample time to prepare for the event.

3. Complete all your planning by preparing a description and responsibilities paper and your financial expectations.

4. If you are moving ahead, make sure you communicate the event description and responsibilities to all who will participate.

5. Make sure you have the correct number of marketers and that they are trained about how to make their presentations effectively.

6. Each marketing person who attends an event must not only be prepared but must also know what his or her individual contribution to lead flow will be.

7. Have fun, meet people, tell your story, and produce leads. You will definitely meet some great people at these events.

Exit Marketing Prospecting

After a sales presentation, when a client has decided not to purchase your product right away, is a great time to implement an exit marketing program. The reason it's called "exit marketing" is the client has not yet decided to purchase but has expressed a very high level of interest in your product. The exit program is geared toward the client who really likes your offering but needs to have more information and/or time before he or she moves ahead.

What a great concept for marketing—to offer sales a program that takes the very best leads marketing has generated and gives them the time they need to make a comfortable decision. If you do not offer this type of exit program, many of these leads with a high potential to purchase will get caught up in other matters, and your product will fall off their radar screens.

When exit marketing comes into play, a good lead has stalled. You know at this point the amount of time, money, and effort you have invested in this lead. Stay focused on this investment and opportunity. All you're doing with exit marketing is elongating the purchasing process and increasing the odds of a successful outcome.

The reason this program belongs to marketing is it is marketing's responsibility to work out the details and to supply them to sales. Sales must simply have the program available so it can be used when needed.

Exit programs should be counted as new marketing channels because they entail additional marketing expenses. The lead being offered the program, however, must still be tracked on the marketing channel that brought him or her to you in the first place. The exit program adds cost and a second source to the lead. For example, if national advertising was the original source and the client takes advantage of the exit program, the lead original source would remain national advertising with a second source consisting of the exit program. That way you can accurately track costs and not double your lead count. Think of this marketing channel as an add-on program to support the lead process.

I will use real estate as an example of how an exit program can work, but if your product is something different, look for ways to accomplish the same exit goals with your product. Put your plan together so you can convert more of these clients who are very close to purchasing.

Most real estate exit marketing programs work on the premise that if you can bring your clients back so they can experience what ownership would be like, you will succeed in making a sale. Even if clients agree to come back a second time to review the program but are not able to stay in the residence you are offering, that is still a very positive sign. The client is again spending more time in the sales process.

I have seen exit programs work when a product was in pre-sales. Offering clients some kind of value and charging them for coming back but also letting them know that, if they purchase, the stay up to a certain amount will be refunded through escrow can be a very successful strategy.

Just always keep in mind that an exit program is an opportunity to extend the commitment process. It keeps the client engaged in the offering, and if a client will invest more time in a second look, you have a great chance to convert the lead into a sale.

Key Notes to Exit Marketing Prospecting Program

1. Exit programs are not prospecting programs; they do not generate new leads for a site.

2. Exit programs are a sales tool to extend the commitment process for very qualified and interested clients.

3. Exit programs must be developed by marketing so that all processes go though marketing performance tracking for cost per lead and volume per lead.

4. All processes and procedures need to be developed and maintained by marketing and given to sales as a sales tool.

5. Since the goal is to extend the buying decision, it is important that these clients can, if possible, experience what it is like to be an owner. For example, return stays at a resort for two, three, or four nights, in which clients get to experience ownership and sales gets to make a presentation, can be an ideal strategy for this kind of program.

6. Make sure you have dual sources on these leads and that they are not counted twice.

7. Be sure that marketing has prepared all the processes so you can take this dual-sourced lead and track purely on the exit side with the additional cost and revenue.

8. Be sure you can give credit for the sale to the original marketing channel.

9. This is a program that takes training and coordination between marketing and sales.

10. Be sure to track exit leads and your results on monthly, quarterly, and annual bases to ensure this is a cost-effective program. Remember you are double investing in these leads.

Email Marketing Prospecting

Email marketing has become a very cost-effective way to market, and it is a great way to communicate with leads. Would you rather send a direct mail piece or an email if you could get the same response? I am sure you would pick email.

I am not convinced, however, that email is a great way to prospect for new leads. It reminds me of cold calling. With all the email that your clients receive on a regular basis, the notion that we can prospect for leads with email is highly dubious. But let's look at how email can really play a key role in your marketing. Rather than being a primary way to generate leads, email can function as a support to your current lead generation processes. It can be an excellent way of following up on leads with whom you have already established a relationship.

I do think there are opportunities for email to drive lead production. What I mean is email can increase the conversion of leads you have already generated into more presentations and sales. So let's take a look at how that can work:

1. Email is an outstanding way to communicate once you have established some kind of a relationship with the client.

2. Email works as a way of contacting clients you are having a tough time reaching on the phone.

3. Email works well for communicating a new message to potential clients.

4. Email may be a great way to reinforce a message you want to send your owners, especially in the owner referral process to help generate leads.

5. Email is the tool I recommend you use to invite broker agents to your referral seminars.

6. You will find that email is used a lot by your clients who respond to your website lead generation programs.

7. Email is used by clients responding to newspaper and magazine advertising.

8. Make your emails simple, easy to read, and right to the point. Remember that the delete key is going to be pushed if the client does not have a compelling reason to open the email or if the message in the email isn't clear and engaging.

I think email, because of its ability to enhance relationships that have already been established, is a very powerful tool for supporting the conversion of a lead to a presentation and then to a sale. We will talk more about the important role of email for sales teams in Part Four.

Key Notes to Email Marketing Prospecting

1. Email programs should go through the same image production as all your advertising programs.

2. Email becomes a great support tool for *all* your marketing channels.

3. Once you have established an owner base, email between the sales agents and clients can be very effective for developing relationships as well as generating referral leads and selling owners additional products.

4. Make sure any of your team that is going to use email as a form of communicating with clients is well trained as to what your company or brand will allow. Messages need to be well aligned with your company and or brand.

5. Emails with good text and videos can have a very powerful effect on lead production and conversions from leads to sales.

Part Three
Innovation and Execution

The Building of Your 21 Proven Strategies

It has taken over thirty years to develop these 21 proven strategies. After years of testing, refining, performance enhancing, and reporting on actual results with a variety of products and brands, we offer these proven strategies as opportunities to effectively improve the sales and marketing of your products. The boxes below show you the innovation and execution side of our proven strategies, which we will be covering in detail on the pages that follow.

Innovation and Execution

Innovation in sales—change
your growth curve.
Chapter 12

Great execution in
marketing and sales
Chapter 13

Chapter 12

Innovation

Train yourself to be a second curve thinker

INNOVATION IN SALES AND marketing is one of my favorite subjects. Through the years I have been involved in quite a few innovative sales and marketing programs. In today's world there is no doubt that innovation is a "must" for your sales and marketing culture if you want to be a leader in performance. Of course, after you innovate you must follow through, and that can be equally as fun and clearly is as important.

This important topic, which obviously applies to all spheres of human activity, can really be conceptualized in terms of what is called a sigmoid curve.

The sigmoid curve is an S-shaped curve that has intrigued people since the beginning of time. In a sense the sigmoid curve sums up the stories of life and civilization themselves. We start off our lives slowly, experimentally. Sometimes we slow down or fail along the way; other times we speed up and do well. That's also the story of the Roman Empire, the British Empire, the Soviet Union, and all empires that have ever existed. Your sales and marketing operations can learn a lot from this famous S-shaped curve as we will see in this chapter.

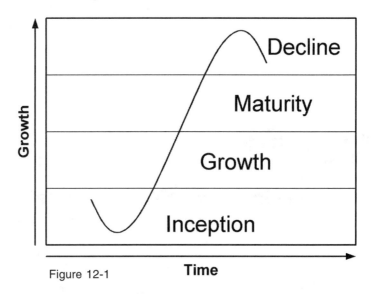

Figure 12-1

The Sigmoid Curve

Figure 12-1 shows how every new life, every new organization, project, sales and marketing program, initiative, or relationship starts out by faltering at inception. Then it grows, enters a mature stage, and finally declines and perishes. If that were all there was to this theory, it would be pretty depressing. But what makes the sigmoid curve interesting to all who study it is the fact that an organization can proactively restart its own new sigmoid curve in any focus area it wants rather than just watching the old curve go over the hill and die out.

Think of that for just a minute: The life cycle of most organizations follows a pattern of inception, growth, maturity, and decline. But what if a life cycle could be directed back to inception and did not go into decline? Think how innovative it would be to take decline out of the life cycle. Very few organizations have accomplished this feat, but the ones that do are clearly the innovative leaders in their fields.

Here is the innovative thought of this chapter. I would like everyone to take this one thought away from this chapter. *Are you or can you become a second-curve thinker?* At the end of this chapter I would like you to ask that question of yourself. Then I would like you to make a list of everything you can think of to become more of a second-curve thinker. The rest of this chapter will make the concept of second-curve thinking clearer to you.

Let's review each part of the life cycle of the sigmoid curve:

Life Cycle #1—Inception Stage

During the inception phase of a new life cycle, an organization almost always experiences a dip, an apparent setback. There's a temporary but real and sometimes alarming drop in resources and a sagging of energy and productivity on the part of work teams and individuals. It is all a very normal part for this life cycle.

For example, parents of newborn babies know from experience that as an infant begins to grow following birth it actually loses weight for a time. This can be alarming for new moms and dads unless they have been told to expect a normal dip in weight. Likewise, when an organization encounters life changes or embarks on new initiatives, it needs to recognize that in the inception phase of a life cycle it will experience a temporary dip. People throughout the organization will do well to remind one another that such a dip is normal, just like the newborn losing weight.

Every new growth plan, every new effort, and even each change in the goals or makeup of a group triggers another inception phase with its characteristic dip and its accompanying anxiety. On the positive side, that dip during the inception phase is akin to flexing your knees before you jump over a physical obstacle. By temporarily squatting or dipping, you can jump much higher and farther than you could with your knees straight.

Life Cycle #2—Growth Stage

As you leave the inception stage of your life cycle, you move into your growth stage, which is probably one of the most exciting times in a business. During this time you and your organization are growing, learning, and prospering together. It is a time of great confidence, enjoyed by most everyone who is in this stage of the sigmoid curve. Think again about human life: These are the years between five and twenty when you grow faster than you will ever grow as an adult. This is also probably the time when your business will grow faster than any other time during its life cycle.

Life Cycle #3—Maturity Stage

Maturity is a very interesting time in most life cycles of people and organizations. You have just come through your growth stage, which was quite prosperous and stimulating. You are now enjoying the success you earned during the growth stage of the curve. During this time most companies, organizations, teams, empires, and people have problems. All tend—and it is very natural—to be very comfortable during this maturity stage. Everyone wants to continue on with this phase like it will sustain itself forever. Why would you think of changing when things are going so well? If it's not broken, why fix it? But I promise you that as you sit back and enjoy the maturity stage right around the corner is the decline stage of your life cycle.

Truly innovative people, organizations, groups, and teams are ones that realize that when you are in the maturity stage of your life cycle, you must aim for renewal if you want to avoid the decline stage of every life cycle. It takes a real leader to recognize the

stage of life you are in and to do something to avoid the
one you are moving toward. It takes some real innovation and insight to combat the natural feeling that things
are going well and are extremely comfortable. Most
people will have the feeling that nothing needs to be
fixed or changed; they will just want to ride this maturity wave forever. They are not aware that the maturity wave is
going to crash for certain.

Innovators have to reinvigorate the team during this maturity
cycle while there is still the energy within the team to do so in a
productive manner. If you wait for the decline stage to set
in, it will be too late. Most organizations will not have
the energy or momentum to renew themselves at this
point. This renewal needs to be accomplished when the
maturity curve is still rising. If you can, you should try to
renew your life cycle just before it reaches the top of
the maturity phase. That would be ideal and allow your business
to avoid the entire decline cycle.

See figure 12-2.

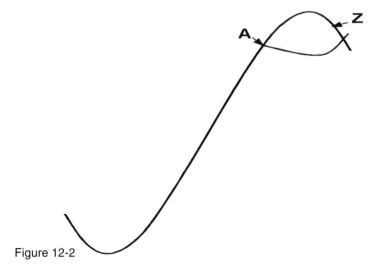

Figure 12-2

So the questions are: Where are you on the first life cycle curve? And when do you start the second curve? You will have to make your own assumptions to answer these questions, but in general you must constantly engage in second-curve thinking. We need to stay skeptical, curious, and inventive. We need to challenge ourselves and the assumptions underlying our current curve. We need to develop alternatives. We need to ask how we can reinvent ourselves and what that would look like. This is second-curve thinking, which is where real innovation takes place.

Can you start conditioning yourself to be a second-curve thinker? If you can, you will separate yourself from the competition and develop an organization that can sustain growth for much longer periods of time than is typical.

The message of the sigmoid curve is that we need the foresight to start making changes even when it is not yet obvious that change is necessary. We need the courage to switch from one curve to the next when the time has come.

To lead a team while things are going well into a change that starts the life cycle all over again requires vision. The person who can accomplish this is a true innovative leader in business, teams, organizations, or life.

Time of Great Confusion

Whenever an organization begins a new life curve, the new and the old curves must coexist for a time, which can create a challenging situation known as "the time of great confusion."

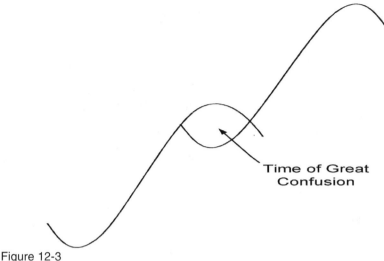

Time of Great
Confusion

Figure 12-3

The time of great confusion is indicated in figure 12-3. Organizations, teams, and groups need visionary, entrepreneurial leadership and an optimistic, courageous group spirit during this time. A new outlook is generated by a great leader of people—someone who understands what the future will bring and is willing to keep the future bright by changing what is going on today.

During this time of confusion you will have to manage the confusion, the denial, and the inevitable tension of sustaining two curves simultaneously. It can be a very traumatic time for those who have a stake in the old curve. They may strongly resist the new curve with its changes. You will have to remain open to constant questioning, learning, and adjusting as the group navigates its way through new, uncharted territory. You will need to summon the confidence and the discipline to allow resources to be pulled from old-curve ways of doing things and apply these resources to new unproven ways. You will need to develop totally new resources to support the new lifestyle curve.

Here are eight things to consider when changing your growth curve:

1. **Commitment to a compelling shared paradigm shift.** You really need to realign and re-focus your organization in terms of second-curve thinking. The situation will get better as the first curve disappears.

2. **Having the right people in the right roles.** Jim Collins's book *Good to Great* talks a lot about having the right people on the bus. You need to make sure you have the right people on your bus and that they are in the right seats. You will need to maximize individual strengths and minimize weaknesses.

3. **Broad, inclusive skilled participation.** Renewal is a time for effective communication and for making sure you inspire confidence about your group's ability to change. What this means is that sometimes you need to sell the people who are going to sell your products first. In this case you need to sell your people on why you are changing and the clear benefits of this change for them before you can move ahead with effective change.

4. **Developing a passion for the new process.** You will need to make the vision of the new curve come to life so the team can clearly see the light at the end of the tunnel. That light needs to be a bright light that everyone would like to bask in. If everyone sees it that way, it will drive the commitment and energy to move ahead. Spark creativity and sharper thinking in this new direction.

5. **Continual protesting against change.** You will find this is a time more than ever for one-on-one meetings with key employees. They need to know you care about this change and how it is going to affect them. Leaving the curve they are in and moving into the unknown second curve can be a frighten-

ing prospect for some. Strive to create a comfortable culture of openness, humility, and cooperation.

6. **Continual planning.** You need to map out the action steps toward your vision. Take small baby steps and celebrate the accomplishment of each of these steps.

7. **Early successful performance.** Build confidence and momentum and attract support. These goals will again entail one-on-one as well as group meetings. People need to have the sense that their team is moving toward the second curve and making real progress. This will ensure that the team members who thought they could just hang on to the first curve will let go!

8. **Frequent, optimistic, and encouraging performance feedback.** This is a time when you should let each team member know you are all in this together and that the change you are all seeking is much greater than just the salvaging of the business. Productive change is a way of life, and teams that can change in a positive way are clearly better teams. You need for everyone to realize that change can be difficult but necessary and deeply satisfying. Boost job-satisfaction and accountability and continue to make improvements.

Let's assume you are the leader and that you have determined you are somewhere in your maturity cycle but that now, while your movement is still upward, is the time to start the second curve for your sales and marketing team. I would recommend that you launch your new curve in phases. We will launch into a five-phase process to start to develop the new curve.

Phase I—The First Thirty Days

You need to plan your second curve carefully, taking into consideration how the team will have to adapt to this new situation, what your timeline is, who will be responsible for making the change, and what the organization will look like when it's all over. Be sure to list clearly the benefits of effecting this change.

You are the leader, so make sure you take the time you need to get everything straight in your own mind. Take all the time you need. If you need six months, then take it, but do not start a new curve unless you have a comprehensive and compelling plan of action for moving forward. Make sure that you begin with the end in mind. You need to articulate clearly what the end goal is going to be, and you need to be positive that this end result is worth the effort. Below is the second curve you have come up with.

The second curve will be all about driving cost-effective sales beyond what has ever been accomplished by this team before.

Phase II—The Next Thirty Days

The next thirty days are all about positioning. This is very important. How you position a second curve for your team is critical. You need to have a plan detailing who you need to talk to in order to make the transitional period really work. Speak with team members one at a time, and make sure all of them are on board with the plan, the processes, the concerns of implementation, the risks of not changing, and most importantly the end results. In particular, you need team leaders working with you and selling this important change to the team.

Try to position the idea of change as a great opportunity for the business, so that all employees are energized and focused on how the transition will benefit their own work and prosperity. Give them the encouragement they need to want to be part of the transition team. You need to convey the attitude that the company will not leave a single employee behind.

Phase III—The Next Sixty Days

You are ready now to roll your plan out to your teams. Here is an example of how a roll-out may look in a sales and marketing organization:

First, it is time for group presentations. You want to put some emotion into this. It's not just a standard presentation you are about to deliver. Craft a first-rate audio-visual presentation. It may be a great time to have a short emotional video about someone or some team that went through a big change and came out much better for it.

This presentation should be all about encouraging people to move ahead on a different path than they have ever followed before. The presentation also needs to provide an example of what would happen if the company does not change but instead stays on the first curve. The most important thing is selling the end result, which is: *The second curve will be all about driving cost-effective sales beyond what has ever been accomplished by this team before.*

Employees will need to get a taste of what it will feel like once the company has changed and become more successful.

Here are some guidelines for your presentation at this meeting:

1. Make separate presentations to your marketing and sales teams, focusing on the responsibilities of each. Make sure you have one of your fully-committed leaders on each of these teams.

2. State the new goal and let the teams start to tell you what they currently are doing to increase cost-effective sales revenue.

3. Each team should perform an assessment of all current sales and marketing activity. You really need to know where you are before you can understand where you need to go to expand your revenue.

4. Each team should create a booklet that explains its goals and philosophy for the transition. It should make a side-by-side comparison of old-curve strategies and new strategies.

Put a date on the completion of this booklet and appoint someone to present creative ideas for new-curve thinking to the entire staff. You will need to be at this meeting to answer questions about the new curve. The goal of this meeting will be to initiate the necessary changes and to create some very positive energy.

5. Create new goals for growth by drawing upon the ideas that came out of the above meeting.

6. Have team leaders prepare a draft of each plan, one for sales and one for marketing, within thirty days and present these second-curve plans to leadership.

7. Align project priorities for marketing and sales while defining expectations.

8. Determine where any barriers are to improving marketing and sales processes and categorize them in writing. Focus on the behavior of associates in your organization, which is driven by the expectations your business environment creates and the

rewards it offers. Barriers limit the individual associates and therefore also limit your ability to improve.

9. Eliminate non-value-added projects and activities so your focus can be on second-curve ideas.

10. Identify the key program drivers and issues involving marketing and sales processes that you deem most challenging.

11. Start program and process integration across your project. Make sure everyone understands the strategies, and have in place players who can execute the plan. Begin to adapt and improve various marketing and sales processes.

12. Leadership should update the second-curve plan to increase cost-effective revenue and lead flow.

13. Evaluate marketing and sales human resources needs and the depth of available associates. Match objectives with existing personnel or make recommendations for changes as needed. Recruit new talent, if necessary, with capabilities to implement complex marketing and sales strategies.

14. Critique project systems and financial accounting and reporting procedures. Ensure that the capabilities of project systems are sufficient to measure and quantify performance for programs and for personal associate achievement. If you do not measure it, it will not yield on an optimum basis.

15. Refine procedures for all aspects of customer processing and sales presentation activity. Try to prepare the team process for a molding of existing associate talent into the implementation plan for a new formalized, performance-driven, high-yield sales game plan. Failure to find consensus on this issue will doom the plan from the outset.

Phase IV—Leadership Rolls out the Final Plan to the Team

Create a booklet that synthesizes the activities of all your teams. Each activity should be described in terms of the following format: program description, objectives, benefits, processes, assumptions, lessons learned, and action items.

This will be the final presentation you make to the team about second-curve strategies, so make it as effective as possible by playing on emotions, using effective visuals and music, and focusing on how change will have a positive impact on the company and everyone involved.

At this presentation you should hand out the team game plan booklet. It should address the items below.

1. Key strategic issues that provide direction for moving ahead.

2. Develop individual and team capabilities while defining expectations.

3. Translate your project plan into all departments.

4. Ensure that your goals have consensus support and are specific and measurable. Make sure they are realistic and tied to a measurable target and a specific period of time.

5. This booklet should finalize your new curve plans and clearly delineate what, where, and when things are to be completed and by whom.

6. Create key measures for baseline performance in all sales and marketing associate performance areas.

7. Barriers that would keep individuals and teams from achieving objectives should be removed.

8. Rewards and recognition mechanisms should be aligned with marketing and sales goals under the new curve.

9. Embed the performance orientation strategy into the fabric of your plan.

10. Make sure recruitment is complete at this time of additional high-impact sales.

11. Start to identify and develop marketing and sales alliances.

12. Look carefully at your sales associate individual performance as this will help drive the plan. Look for areas where you can increase production.

13. Make sure you have the best tools for supporting your sales efforts beyond lead generation. Evaluate presentation and follow-up processes.

14. Review the best ways to drive more qualified marketing leads that will fully support the new curve plan. Look carefully at cost per lead and volume per lead comparisons.

Phase V—Launch the New Curve

Enjoy the new curve as it goes through its life cycles. This curve will have a lifespan like most, but this time you will have a team that understands exactly how a curve works. Enjoy and celebrate each new success along the way that results from the changes you have made. If there are lessons you learn about new strategies, positive or negative, be sure to record them. There will be a lot to learn and many adjustments that will need to be made as you move along a new curve.

You can expect to encounter setbacks during your inception and also appreciate that this is normal. Put your seatbelt on as the curve jumps into its growth cycle and enjoy the ride. Second curves that are planned well will have longer growth cycles than the originals curves had.

Then settle into your maturity cycle and let this raise the confidence levels of all team members involved in developing the second curve. A great learning experience will have been had by all, and everyone will be enjoying the great results. You and your team will have made this happen!

Of course, do not relax too long, as we all know that right around the corner is the bright strategic light called change. So off with the old and onto the new curve.

Key Notes for Innovation

1. Understand the life cycles of the sigmoid curve.
2. Train yourself to be a second-curve thinker.
3. Prepare yourself for the launch of a second curve.
4. Have a very solid plan as to when, where, why, and how you are going to launch your second curve.
5. Fully understand the "time of great confusion" and be prepared to lead your team through it.
6. Get your team involved in what you are doing. You cannot do this alone.
7. Follow carefully the five-part roll-out of your new curve. It will take at least four to six months to roll it out correctly.
8. Enjoy the experience of second-curve thinking.
9. Renewing your programs will demand time, effort, and commitment from your innovators and executors throughout the entire process.
10. Imagine never experiencing the decline life cycle in your business. It's like being forever young.

Let's hear from our characters about *innovation*.

Chapter 12: Innovation

Here is an action scene with our characters working on innovation.

If you want to dominate in lead management, innovation is a must. Make it a regular part of your business operations and review process.

World-Class Execution

One word makes the difference in how well you execute—Preparation

EXECUTION IS ONE OF the most important aspects of marketing and sales. No matter how well you do in planning and/or innovating, without great execution you have achieved nothing. Have you ever met people who are very smart and have great ideas but never get them off the ground? They know a lot but accomplish little. Some people are great with overall concepts but fail when it comes to implementation. These people need help with their execution skills. They usually do not like the preparation and organizational skills required to be a good executor. Put innovation and execution together, and you have the one-two punch of sales and marketing.

Innovators and executors do not always have to be the same people. Some companies have people who innovate and then turn their innovations over to someone else to perform the execution. That is perfectly fine as long as you have some system in place that promotes innovation and some team that ensure innovations are executed by your sales and marketing operations. Sales and marketing lead domination will be achieved by a company that on a regular basis can overhaul its sales and marketing programs and processes to make them fresh, new, exciting, more efficient, and more effective—and then follow through with flawless execution of these ideas.

In this chapter we will cover the characteristics of outstanding executors and examine how they think, what drives them, what they do with this drive, how they prepare, why their desire is so strong, why their commitment is so focused, and why their confidence in success is so sure. Show me a consistent top-performing sales agent, and I will show you someone who executes sales presentations in an outstanding manner.

We will put in writing the make-up or "DNA," if you will, of world-class executors and how that may differ from the average executor. We will find that world-class executors clearly think, feel, and act differently than average executors do. Average executors may not be willing or even able to do what world-class executors do, but by comparing these groups, we can arrive at significant conclusions that can be adopted and implemented to improve your own execution.

We will begin this process by outlining four key traits of a world-class executor:

1. Preparation—This is the number-one trait of world-class executors. Preparation is the foundation of their outstanding execution and what they draw their strength from. Preparation gives them confidence that their execution will be flawless and successful. An outstanding executor invests a great deal of time in preparation.

2. Belief—World-class executors have very focused minds that can visualize what the end result they hope to produce will be like. They believe they will succeed no matter what the circumstances are or what other people think or say.

3. Desire—Their desire to succeed in the execution of a task is so strong that it drives their preparation and reinforces their belief. This all-consuming desire dramatically increases their odds of successfully executing a given task.

4. Commitment—These world-class executors do not just think about doing something; they do it. Once they put their minds to a task, they follow it through with determination to the end.

By contrast, here are the traits of an average executor:

1. Preparation—This is the biggest difference between the two. Average executors don't invest the time necessary to set the stage for big success. If you want to increase your effectiveness in terms of execution, then increase your preparation significantly.

2. Belief—With better preparation, your belief in success will also increase. Want stronger belief? *Increase the amount of preparation you are doing.*

3. Desire—You need to have the desire to be an outstanding executor. If your desire is strong enough, then you can and will increase your preparation levels.

4. Commitment—If you desire to improve your execution, then make the commitment and follow through on it.

For this section I really wanted an example we can all recognize as a world-class executor so readers can grasp the preparation levels necessary for this kind of success. When I thought of extraordinary preparation, Tiger Woods' name came to mind, as did those of a variety of other athletes in professional sport. The problem was I really wanted to spend some time in person with the person I would select to understand better the way that person thinks and acts so that I could share that information with you.

I live in a wonderful small beach town in Southern California called San Clemente. To the south is the world-renowned Marine base, Camp Pendleton. It was there that I would discover my world-class executor. As you read these stories from my world-class executor, I think you will soon come to agree that the military has some of the best performers and executors in the world.

Camp Pendleton has an interesting saying; it goes like this:

> **It's only God that will truly judge the terrorists;**
> **It's the Marines' mission to arrange the meeting.**

There are always a few standout performers in every sport or business. They stand out because of the way they think and the way they are able to take their thoughts and turn them into action—action that produces world-class results. But the number-one factor for world-class executors is the way they prepare for their tasks.

I would like to share with you the story of one of the standout performers in the United States Marine Corps. I have had the privilege to hang out with him and learn about how he prepares, thinks, acts, and above all executes.

He is still serving and protecting our freedom like many in the military. His name is James Pell, petty officer first class. I met James because my wife, Susan, is a fashion designer in San Clemente and does quite a few wedding dresses in the Orange County area. People tend to come to Susan when they want a one-of-a-kind wedding dress. Because Susan does so many wedding dresses in Orange County, we get invited to quite a few weddings.

At one of these weddings I met James Pell. It was a full-dress Marine wedding with all the interesting Marine traditions. I noticed there was a young man dressed in a Navy uniform among all the highly-decorated Marines who were part of the ceremony. He had pinned to his chest the Bronze Star with Combat "V," two Purple Hearts, a Navy and Marine Corps Commendation Medal with Combat "V," an Army Commendation Medal, and a Navy and Marine Corps Achievement Medal with Combat "V." It looked like James had about a dozen medals on his chest. It seemed like a lot of medals for someone who was so young. It was very impressive to me, especially the Purple Hearts, which I recognized right away and was interested in knowing how he had gotten them.

When I first spoke to James, I was instantly taken with his confident manner and his great personality. He looks a bit like Tom Cruise but is taller. I simply asked him why a Navy guy was in a Marine wedding. I learned that the Marines are part of the Navy, and the conversation took an interesting direction. I decided to invite James to our house the next day; I was very interested in learning more about him. I really had no idea what was in store for me when we next met.

I ended up spending a great deal of time with James and found him to be a world-class thinker and executor when it came to the performance of his military duties. He is a humble person at times, and I had to encourage him to talk about some of the great things he has accomplished. I fully understood that some of his stories were difficult at best, as we talked about war and engagements in which lives were lost in battle. James is a medical man, and he also fought alongside the Marines. That meant he had been trained to fight like a Marine, but when someone got hurt he would lay down his gun and attend to the wounded.

It is very difficult to help someone else who needs medical attention and to defend yourself at the same time. These subjects were what made my meetings with James so extraordinary. His stories involved taking life in one minute and saving the lives of the wounded in the next. Sometimes the lives he was trying to save were ones he had previously tried to take! I have never had conversations that were so emotionally charged.

The situations James Pell had found himself in clearly had major consequences for poor execution. James had been shot in Iraq eleven times. Soldiers had died in his arms. His was the last face and voice they had known; the comfort he offered was the last thing they had experienced before leaving this earth. Many others he had managed to save despite terrible wounds. I was amazed how he never quit, never gave up hope. His desire, beliefs, commitment, and preparation were so strong that he had been successful in his extraordinary missions.

Here are James's stories in his own words:

I arrived at 3rd Battalion 5th Marines in August of 2002. Prior to showing up I spent six months being schooled by various Navy and Marine personnel in the art of battlefield medicine and light infantry. The training was mediocre at best, now that I can look back through everything I had to go through, but it was necessary to be where I am now.

I joined the Navy after exiting service with the Army, unhappy with both myself and the direction in which my life had taken me. Only later would I realize that these were ideas placed in my head by others with negative thinking and a poor outlook on life. My lesson learned was to think for myself and ignore those in misery looking for company. Better yet, I learned to feed off of their misery and convert it to push me harder to succeed.

Missing the training and camaraderie I had found in the Army, I went back to re-enlist for service. This time I had the voice of my father to guide me into the Navy. The two of us chose the medical profession because of its many secondary schools and employment opportunities in the civilian sector. I excelled at the academic portion of the Navy Hospital Corps School in Great Lakes, Illinois. I graduated with a 93 percent average.

During this time I met and dated my future wife. The two of us made a great team and pushed each other to study harder and to strive to be the best. When the time came to graduate our orders were not for the same locations, and the two of us decided to make the leap into marriage to stay together. She ended up at the hospital at Camp Pendleton, California, and I eventually earned a spot with the Marines as a line corpsman (medical).

I arrived ready for whatever it was I had to do. After a week of being in the clinic, I was referred to the Scout Sniper Platoon. I was asked whether I would like to be a Corpsman, to be an operator with one of the teams. A Corpsman represents the best of the best that the Marines have to offer on the battlefield. Since it was the opportunity of a lifetime, I gladly accepted and was given a list of gear and told where to be at 4:30 A.M. the next morning.

My Preparation

To become a Corpsman, you have to earn your way into the platoon—prove you have what it takes to prepare and execute at this elevated Marine level. The morning began with a physical fitness test that consisted of timed pull-ups and sit-ups. You had two minutes to do as many as possible in each category. After that was a timed three-mile run. To be accepted, you had to score 100 percent in all the events, so you had to give it everything you had. After the run, with lungs and legs failing, the leaders notified us that there was a cheater in our midst and that we'd have to perform the entire test again. The leaders reminded us that if we could not score 100 percent on the second attempt that we would not make the Corpsman platoon.

On the way back to the pull-up bars the first quitters walked away. They must have thought: Why play if I can't win?

The instructors yelled and jeered that we were too weak to make it and encouraged us just to quit. After returning from the timed run, for the second time, we headed out as a group for a "short run" with the instructors. More prospects quit, this time from overload and lack of faith in themselves. The instructors wanted to see who's willing to push themselves to their limit. Most people don't know what their limits are because they stop long before they are even close to reaching them. Most people stop running when they feel like vomiting or passing out or when their muscles cramp into a ball or when they start seeing stars. They are not Corpsmen. After vomiting, a Marine Corpsman would continue to run. When you pass out, they pick you up and wake you up, and you must keep running or you will fail your preparation training.

We then had five minutes to change into full uniforms and pick up our eighty-pound rucksacks for yet another run. This time it was up a very unforgiving 70-degree mountain. Halfway up there were more quitters. Your body is physically drained, energy reserves shot. Your muscles cramp, your lungs scream and burn. It is a breaking point that cuts the group in half. Over the next three days these grueling tests continued nonstop. We had to jump into water from towers bigger than you could dream of to prove we were fearless. We spent hours swimming. When someone cramped or vomited, there was no time out. Everyone was just watched closely to see how they reacted to the pain. This is how the Marines prepare their Corpsmen. As you can guess, not many make it. The ones who do are well-prepared for the future.

There were timed land navigation courses that took us across terrain with cliffs, thorns, and rivers while instructors hunted us near roads and open areas. If they found you while you ran from point to point, you were out. There were numerous timed rucksack runs, the shortest being nine miles. During this physical endeavor, the leaders made us stay awake all night to observe different areas and record everything that happens and everyone who passes into those areas. Anyone who fell asleep or missed something was out. Those who could handle all this and refused to quit or give in to their bodies' weakness were considered temporary members of the platoon or pledges in civilian terms. You remain a pledge until you attend the formal Scout Sniper School and graduate.

The attrition rate at this school is high, and most Corpsmen have attended twice or more before they graduate. After graduation, you are among the toughest, most dedicated, and most motivated Marines to face combat. It is a great feeling knowing the person next to you will never quit in the face of adversity. They will push their bodies to death to complete their missions and make sure they and their comrades will come home. No other job in the world could ask this kind of commitment from its employees. It takes a very select few to fill these ranks. I passed the training and preparation. I am thankful they gave me the chance to be among them.

After acceptance into the platoon, the days and nights were filled with learning new skills: moving without being seen, looking at an area one time and memorizing everything in it, judging how far away objects are by sight only, reading wind direction and speed, even following the vapor trail of a freshly shot bullet. We had to shoot from mountain tops and deep valleys, buildings, and worst of all wide-open fields with little to no cover. We were expected to make all our shots without being found by the experienced Marine snipers who watched for us through their binoculars.

I had to know and succeed at all these things in addition to completing my medical objectives. I had to carry the same gear as my Marines as well as medical gear to treat them for almost anything that can go wrong on a mission. I had to be stronger and faster than they were. Should they be injured, I would have to carry them and care for them. If they become sick, I am the one they will call at midnight for help. Because of all this, I earned a special place inside the teams.

In February of 2003 the rumors of the US deploying to Iraq turned out to be true. Excitement cannot begin to describe the feeling that flowed through all of us. We had trained day and night, wind, rain, and unbearable desert heat, all the while dreaming of doing our jobs in actual combat. For most of us, this deployment was a dream come true. For me, it sank in that I would undoubtedly end up with a bleeding, shot-up Marine in my arms expecting me to save his life. My mind was flooded with "what ifs." What if I don't know how to treat a specific gunshot wound and the person dies? What if we get gassed and I have to treat all my Marines for nerve gas exposure? What if I freeze up with fear? The panic settled in, and I convinced myself I wasn't ready. For the next month I read every trauma book I could get my hands on, every surgeon's book, and every chemical warfare manual I could find. I would not fail my marines in my duties.

The key to world-class execution is *preparation.* Are you starting to understand the level of preparation that James Pell and all world-class executors go through? What is your own preparation level? As you can see, you must have a strong desire and commitment to be a world-class executor. Many try, but few succeed. The lesson to learn in this chapter is: Review your preparation, belief, desire, and commitment. Can you see opportunities for improvement? How does your level of preparation compare to that of Corpsman James Pell? To increase your performance in the sales and marketing world and be an outstanding executor, you need:

1. James Pell Preparation levels
2. Belief
3. Desire
4. Commitment

I wanted to share with you what preparation meant to our friend James Pell. Sure, he was coached on his preparation, but it was James who made it happen. This preparation is so necessary if you want to succeed.

I must tell you that hearing the stories of James Pell's three deployments to Iraq first hand was indescribable. His tone of voice, his piercing eyes, and his facial expressions made it so real to me. It is something I will never forget.

Marine Corpsman James Pell was named Combat Medic of the Year in March of 2007. Here is what the Marines wrote about James Pell:

James Pell served his first Iraq combat deployment as the Scout Sniper Platoon Corpsman, H&S Company, 3rd Battalion, 5th Marines. During this period Petty Officer James Pell participated in 20 Scout Sniper Missions. He excelled during this deployment, becoming a valuable member of the platoon contributing to the tactical mission and prepared to provide the platoon life-saving treatment if necessary. His ability to provide quality care under fire resulted in the successful emergent treatment of active duty, enemy combatants, and Iraqi civilians. When Petty Officer James Pell returned from this first Iraq deployment, he was tireless in developing his combat casualty care skills in preparation for future deployments. As soon as the opportunity presented itself, he volunteered for a second deployment.

While serving on his second Iraq deployment as the Surveillance and Target Acquisition Platoon Corpsman (Scout Sniper), attached to Company I, 3rd Battalion, 5th Marines on the 15th November 2004 his assignment was combat duties in support of Operation Phantom Fury, Al Fallujah, Iraq. Early in the morning, Petty Officer James Pell assisted with capture of several suspected enemy insurgents. Upon inspection of the building, Petty Officer Pell realized that it contained not less than fifteen injured insurgents, and had been serving as an improvised "aid station." Once the building was secure, Petty Officer Pell began providing medical assistance to the wounded, regardless of their status as enemy combatants. As a result, all of the fifteen were properly stabilized and later transported to higher headquarters. Ten of the fifteen wounded were considered expectant to die; due to Petty Officer James Pell all survived.

Later in the day, India Company received contact from several hardened enemy positions. Unable to effectively engage the enemy with direct fires, Petty Officer Pell risked his life by braving withering small arms fire (AK-47) and relocating to an adjacent rooftop in order to employ hand grenades, allowing India Company's Marines to secure a foothold.

Petty Officer James Pell then laid down suppressive fire on a second enemy position, freeing one of his fellow Marine's who was pinned down by the enemy. James was able to move him to a securer position. He then relocated to a higher position in order to provide suppressive fire in support of an assault on an adjacent building that was much needed to secure the position. Another bout of intense small arms fire was directed at him while he moved. From his new position Petty Officer Pell was engaging hardened insurgents at distances of less than ten meters. As the assault progressed, Petty Officer Pell observed one of his Corporals suffer a severe gunshot wound to the head. Petty Officer Pell immediately moved into the enemy's cone of fire in an attempt to reach the wounded Marine and provide first aid. Petty Officer Pell moved without hesitation or regard for his own safety. He was hit eleven times by enemy fire and seriously wounded. Petty Officer James Pell maintained his composure and presence of mind, administering first aid to himself and continuing to provide suppressive fires as additional Marines arrived to evacuate the wounded Marine. When the day's fighting was over there were a total of 28 dead insurgents scattered through four mutually supporting buildings. None of the fighters had accepted when given the chance to surrender; they had fortified their positions and held on to the end. Petty Officer James Pell's actions were crucial to 1st Platoon's seizing of an initial foothold, and his subsequent fires surely prevented several more injuries. At the time when Petty Officer Pell was wounded, 1st Platoon and elements of the Company Headquarters had been fighting room to room and roof to roof for more than six hours. His composure and good spirits while being treated played a large part in keeping the Marines' morale from suffering. By the grace of God James Pell survived his second tour.

He has distinguished himself during his third combat tour by demonstrating remarkable proficiency, skill, and leadership in stressful combat situations. From 12 November 2005 to 11 November 2006 Petty Officer James Pell performed his duties in the most exemplary manner as an advisor to the Iraqi National Police. He was responsible for mentoring and advising the Iraqi National Police in the execution of their duties, including training for combat operations under extremely hazardous combat conditions.

On 28 February 2006, while the team was conducting training at the 1-4 Public Order Battalion compound, medium machine gun and small arms fire was heard near the location where 1-4 Public Order Battalion was conducting a siege operation with the rest of the 4th Public Order Brigade and the US Army's 2nd Battalion, 506th Infantry Regiment. A couple minutes after hearing the gunfire, it was passed over the tactical control net that one of their units participating in the siege was engaged with enemy forces.

As the closest coalition unit in the area, the team mounted up and moved to the location of the firefight. While getting an update from the senior Iraqi Special Police on scene it was pointed out that one of the Iraqi Special Police had been shot and might still be alive. Petty Officer James Pell immediately directed his team to move their position and use gunfire to provide him protection so he could reach the casualty. He grabbed the patient and dragged him to a safe position to assess and treat the injuries, but unfortunately the patient died due to the extent of his injuries.

Once back to safety the team leader and Petty Officer Pell were gathering information when Petty Officer Pell noticed one of the senior combat leaders on scene had received a gunshot wound to the leg. Petty Officer Pell grabbed a tourniquet from his med bag and applied it. It was clear that the round had severed his femoral artery. Petty Officer Pell worked to control the hemorrhage and prevent shock. If not for Petty Officer Pell's quick actions, the casualty would have bled out.

Upon completion of the MedEvac the team devised a plan to get the combat enemy personnel to lay down their weapons. The team leader was able to accomplish this and directed them to bring out their wounded to Petty Officer Pell. He worked on two casualties who had received head wounds. Petty Officer Pell worked feverishly to stabilize the casualties. Upon stabilization of the men he called for and directed the movement of all injured for MedEvac operations. Throughout the event Petty Officer Pell kept calm and reacted as trained. His mastery of battlefield first aid saved the lives of three people that day, and his ability to make quick decisions under fire helped the team to get the insurgents to lay their arms down, preventing further bloodshed.

On 13 June 2006, Petty Officer James Pell was designated as the National Police Transition Team Patrol Leader for a combined patrol that included a platoon of Iraqi National Police from 1st Battalion, 8th Brigade, and a squad from Alpha Company, 2-506th, and a squad of Iraqi Policemen. While conducting the patrol in Muhalla 822, in Al Doura, the combined patrol was engaged by anti-Iraqi forces at extremely close range. Three insurgent gunmen came around a corner approximately 40 yards away and opened fire at the patrol with AK-47 assault rifles and one PKC medium machinegun. Petty Officer James Pell acted immediately, directing the Iraqi element to drop, seek cover, and return fire. He intentionally exposed himself while moving from position to position ensuring the Iraqi element maintained proper cover and fire discipline.

At the same time he was directing the actions of the Iraqi forces, Petty Officer Pell passed via radio a situational report to the Army squad who had not yet turned the corner. This action alone prevented soldiers from unnecessarily exposing themselves to injury from anti-Iraqi forces. He quickly devised a plan that the Iraqis would pursue and try and pin the anti-Iraqi forces in place while the Army squad 3 would try to flank around to the west of the anti-Iraqi forces. His plan was immediately effective and started pushing the anti-Iraqi forces out of their position.

Throughout this event Petty Officer Pell maintained and displayed the finest discipline and leadership. If not for his quick actions and thinking, the Iraqi forces would have not reacted as a cohesive unit. His ability to focus their fire and actions took great tactical knowledge and exposed him to danger but saved many lives.

Petty Officer James Pell's administrative and organizational skills have also been highlighted during this deployment. Due to the relative detached nature of the National Police Transition Team and its mission, he almost single-handedly developed the Iraqi battalion medical program. Far before deploying to Iraq, Petty Officer Pell anticipated the needs of the Iraqi battalion to include all medical supplies, training aids, and manuals. He was instrumental in the acquisition of a medical site and assisted in construction and cleansing, storage of supplies, and the day-to-day operations. He supervised and treated approximately (25) Iraqi personnel on a daily basis to include medical issues ranging from E. coli to shrapnel and bullet wounds. He researched and acquired the necessary allocations to send Iraqi National Police to a national level medical class in Baghdad.

Over his three Iraq combat deployments Petty Officer Pell has been combat meritoriously promoted twice and has earned the Bronze Star with Combat "V," Purple Heart Medal, Navy and Marine Corps Commendation Medal with Combat "V," Army Commendation Medal, Navy and Marine Corps Achievement Medal with Combat "V," Combat Action, and numerous other campaign awards.

Time and time again Petty Officer Pell has proven himself to be the very best Combat Corpsmen. He possesses all the finest qualities of the Combat Corpsmen and truly understands the sacred duty of caring for his Marines and Sailors under the most extreme combat conditions and at any personal cost to himself. Petty Officer James Pell epitomizes the spirit of our sacred mission and his selection for this Combat Medic of the Year award will be a great honor to him and the combat corpsman who will and have given all.

This was what the Marine Corps wrote about James Pell, one of the most prepared individuals I have ever met. Think about the fact he was doing two full-time jobs: fighting for our country and saving lives as a medical man. He was fully prepared to execute these responsibilities to the best of his abilities. The consequences of not being prepared would have been permanent and everlasting for James Pell and his team. His preparation also included great belief, desire, and commitment to be the best he could be.

I will end this chapter by asking you this: How prepared are you in the responsibilities you have in sales and marketing and lead management? Whether you know it or not, your preparations will directly affect your future and the future of the teams you are on.

Chapter 13: World-Class Execution

Here is an action scene with our characters mind set on world-class execution.

If you are truly well prepared and practiced, you will perform to very high standards regardless of the conditions of the world around you. We see this over and over in life. It is also true in sales and marketing.

Music Break

Before We Start Sales
Our Rendition of the Guns 'n' Roses Song
"Welcome to the Jungle"

Welcome to the jungle; we have marketing 'n' sales.

The lions get all the leads you want; believe me, they won't fail.

We market with people that can find whatever you may need.

If you got the money, honey, we have your leads.

In the jungle—welcome to the jungle

Watch as we increase your client sales and fees;

With your black card you purchase with ease.

Welcome to the jungle—we take it day by day.

If you want a qualified lead, it's the price you have to pay.

We have a very sexy product—even if you are hard to please.

You can taste the bright lights, but you won't get them for free

In the jungle—welcome to the jungle.

Come meet my, my team; I, I wanna make you dream.

Welcome to the jungle—it gets better here every day.

Ya learn ta live like an animal—in the jungle where we play.

If you got a hunger for what you need, you'll get it eventually.

You can have anything you want,
but you have to purchase through me.

In the jungle—welcome to the jungle.

Come play sales and marketing with me;

Sit down and listen to my presenation; it's free.

And when your leads are qualified,
you never, ever want to come down—*yeah!*

You know where you are; you're in the jungle baby.

You're gonna learn—in the jungle—

Welcome to the jungle; watch it bring you your

Leads, leads;

In the jungle—

Welcome to the jungle

Meet my sales and marketing team;

In the jungle—

Welcome to the jungle;

Watch it bring you your

Leads, leads;

In the jungle—

Welcome to the jungle;

This book will bring you

All the lead management you need...*ha!*

Break Time

*Here is an action scene with our characters and Jamie taking
a break before they move on to the last section in the book
on converting leads to sales.*

Part Four
Sales

The Building of Your 21 Proven Strategies

It has taken over thirty years to develop these 21 proven strategies. After years of testing, refining, performance enhancing, and reporting on actual results with a variety of products and brands, we offer these proven strategies as opportunities to effectively improve the sales and marketing of your products. The boxes below show you the sales side of our proven strategies, which we will be covering in detail on the pages that follow.

Sales

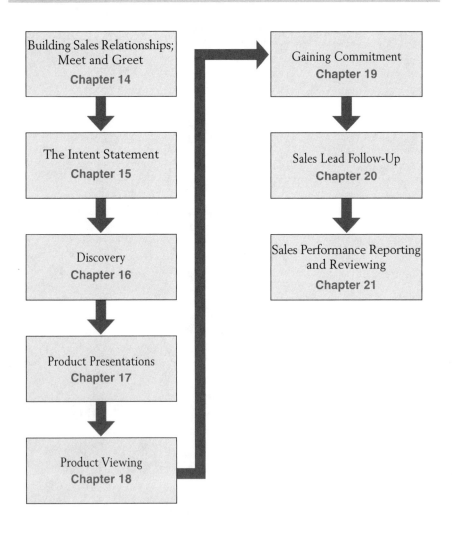

Introduction

Converting Leads into Sales

Hello! I am your personal sales guide through Part Four. I am very excited about sharing the best practices for converting leads into sales.

IF YOU STUDY AND act on the information provided in Part Two of this book, you will be well on your way toward lead domination from a marketing lead generation standpoint. You simply cannot dominate your market without performing exceptionally in the lead generation process. Next, it's essential that you be able to convert the leads you generate into sales. That is the focus of Part Four.

In the chapters that follow we will focus on the sales operation of your sales and marketing enterprise, with the goal of covering the best practices for taking marketing leads and converting them into sales. The key is to convert leads into sales revenues at a healthy sales pace and cost effectively. This type of sales revenue is what drives most everything we do in a sales and marketing enterprise.

Here are some key topics pertaining to the conversion of leads to sales. All of them will be developed in greater detail in the pages that follow.

1. What a sale is

2. Goods and services as opposed to money and its equivalents

3. Speaking in sales "love languages"[1]

4. Talent, training, desire, and commitment

5. Converting leads to presentations

6. Converting presentations to sales

7. Think, feel, act, then present

If you look up the word "sales" in *The American Heritage Dictionary of the English Language*, you will find:

> **The exchange of goods and/or services for an amount of money or its equivalent.**

Let's spend a minute on this definition. We start with the first part, the exchange of goods and/or services. For many products you are really offering both goods and services. You offer a physical product, which is your goods, as well as current and future

---

[1] The concept of "love languages" is adapted from Gary Chapman's *The Five Love Languages: How to Express Heartfelt Commitment to Your Mate;* LifeWay Christian Resources, August 2007.

experiences, which represent your services. An example is a second home that comes with a full maintenance plan. The physical second home would be the product, and the maintenance plan would be the service. The second part of the definition reads "for an amount of money or its equivalent." Customers need to feel they are getting their money's worth for what you have to offer, and making sales is mainly what this section is all about. This definition is something we really need to understand, as we will devote much of the sales portion of this book to elaborating it. In sales, the bigger the gap you can have between products and services versus money and/or its equivalent, the more sales you will produce.

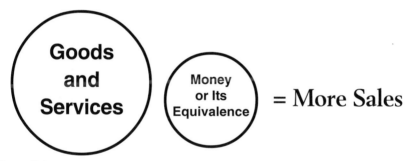

Figure 3-1

Figure 3-1 shows a situation in which the value created from goods and services far exceeds expense. This typically happens when you learn to speak your clients' "love language." Discovering your clients' needs and incorporating them into your presentation is what we mean by a sales love language. The more that goods and services are confirmed in your clients' love language, the larger the goods and services circle will become, and the smaller the expense circle will become. The result will be that customers make buying decisions in a quicker timeframe, which means you will produce more sales.

Figure 3-2

Figure 3-2 shows the value created from goods and services is equal to the expense. In this instance you will make some sales, but they will take longer and, therefore, fewer will be made. Knowing how much time it normally takes to make a sale and then working to reduce that timeframe is always part of the sales efficency equation.

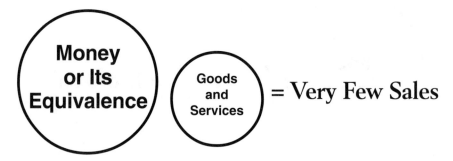

Figure 3-3

Figure 3-3 shows the cost far exceeding the value created from goods and services being offered. In this example the time it takes to make a buying decision will increase, and there will be very few people who move ahead with a purchase.

The most successful sales teams devote lots of time to creating strong value in goods and services in an effort to reduce the customer's perception of expense. This is easier said than done because in order to make your goods and services circle larger, you must deliver a sales presentation based on your customers' love language. Like anything else you do in life, if you spend the time practicing the right skills, you will improve.

Could you do something to make your goods and service circles bigger? How much time is it worth to invest in your presentation on a regular basis to ensure your goods and services circle becomes bigger? How big is your goods and services circle at the end of your sales presentation compared to your expense circle? Do you build your presentation around your customers' needs and make your presentation in your customers' love language? These are the questions top sales performers should be asking themselves. The sales agents who can make great presentations delivered in their clients' love language are the big producers when it comes to converting leads to sales.

All customers who have an interest in your product will respond to a love language that emphasizes how your product will make them feel. The better they think your product will make them feel, the smaller its expense will seem in their minds and the more readily they will purchase.

Here's an example of love language: In marriages we have learned—some of us the hard way—that if you want to have a good relationship, you need to speak to your spouse in his or her love language. What you say and how you say it in your relationship has everything to do with good communication. Here are four different ways to communicate to your spouse using themes of his or her love language:

1. Words of affirmation
2. Quality time
3. Giving gifts
4. Acts of service
5. Touch

Let's assume that your wife's love language is words of affirmation and the husband's is acts of service. The husband must understand that he needs to communicate in words of affirmation if he wants to speak in his wife's love language when he is communicating with her. If you do speak in her love language, watch to see the way she responds. I think you will be pleasantly surprised. The husband may like acts of service and because he likes this it may be natural for him to communicate his love language through acts of service. But for his wife he will not be speaking in her love language at all, and the relationship will not work as well. If he communicates through words of affirmation, the results will be outstanding because he is talking in her love language.

For a successful marriage, a husband and wife need to know the crucial aspects of each other's love language and act accordingly. The same principle applies to sales. If you do not know what your clients' love language is and are not presenting your product in those terms, then your sales presentations will not be as effective.

Think carefully about your last client and list the qualities of your product that would be part of his or her love language. After you have made the list, ask yourself how much of your sales presentation was couched in the person's love language. Did you waste time presenting things that are not part of the client's love language?

In the chapters that follow we will also focus on four variables that will dictate your success in converting leads to presentations and presentations to sales: talent, practice, desire, and commitment.

Talent in any field is something people possess in different levels. It's no different for sales. Sales talent is one's natural ability to communicate with people using their love language and building the goods and services proposition so that clients want to take action. Some people do this quite naturally, and others really need to work to accomplish it. Do you need sales talent to be successful? Talent isn't necessary, but it can really help. Each sales person you hire will have different sales talent levels, and these levels will be almost impossible to change. It's much easier to train someone who possesses a lot of innate sales talent, and that person will likely be much more successful with less effort than someone who has little natural talent for sales.

If your talent is mid-range to low range, you really need to compensate with training and working on your sales skills much harder. There is really no other alternative. If your talent levels are low and you are not willing to invest lots of time in perfecting your sales skills, then sales can be a very unfulfilling profession. Sales professionals who enjoy the profession usually have considerable selling skills, either innate or developed through hard work, and relate well to a specific product.

Selling is communicating in your client's love language, with a sincere desire to help fill a need your customers have for your product. Your sales presentation is a piece of verbal art that shows how the product and service you offer accomplishes this goal.

You have heard it said that *practice* makes perfect, but it is probably truer to say that perfect practice makes perfect. If you practice sales skills that are not correct, then maybe your practice will not be that effective. So make sure you practice the right skills and go through the right steps. The fundamental steps of the selling process are:

1. Greeting
2. Discovery
3. Presentation
4. Close
5. Follow-up

The more you practice these basic steps and apply the right skills to them, the better you will become as a sales professional. Your goal should be to make your presentations more comfortable for your clients and more productive for you.

Sales training could be compared to golfing. If you never practice, what happens? No matter how talented you are, you must practice if you want to get better at golf. And if you decided you wanted to play golf professionally, how much would you need to practice then? The difference between playing golf for fun and playing golf for a living would require much more practice. If you want to sell for a living, you need to practice often and continue to practice just like the golf professional if you want to earn a good living. In sales—no matter how talented you are and no matter how great the product is that you are selling—if you are not practicing your sales techniques on a consistent basis, you will never perform to your full potential.

Desire is the glue that holds it all together. If your desire to succeed in sales is strong, then the promise of success is imminent. How much do you desire to learn about your profession? How much do you desire to practice your sales profession? How strong is your desire to learn and work with top professionals? Having a very strong desire to succeed is essential if you want to be the best of the best or even the best you can be. If you have deficiencies in talent, you can make up for them with a strong desire and rigorous training. If your desire to invest time and be a better sales person is low, then there is not much hope for you in the sales profession—if you expect to earn a good living.

The last component is *commitment*, which requires that you focus your talent, practice, and desire with a clear plan of action. If you have a strong desire to become a better sales person but do nothing about it, nothing will improve. A committed person puts together a plan of action and follows it to make the most of his or her abilities. Once the commitment to take action kicks in, you will be surprised at how good you can really become.

With the correct training, a great desire to learn, and a commitment to take action, you will improve. I have never seen a sales person follow these principles and not improve his or her sales production.

The chapters you are about to read will guide you through what it takes to convert a lead to a sale. Each sales training chapter is designed to move your leads closer to a sale. You will see how to set up sales lead tracking performance reports and software systems to help sales and sales management track and convert leads.

The life cycle of a lead includes three categories:

1. A lead who has purchased
2. A lead who is not interested
3. A lead who is in progress

This is very simple because what I am saying is that a lead can only be in one of three statuses: purchased, not interested, and in progress. Each status has a prescribed follow-up.

As we move leads toward the sales finish line, there are intermediate steps that will be carefully tracked along the way to provide you with feedback on how well you and your sales teams are doing in converting the lead into a sale.

One of the key intermediate steps is how many leads you are able to convert to a sales presentation. This is one of the vital statistics you should track. Just divide the number of presentations an agent gives in a month by the number of leads he or she had been assigned. An agent who received forty leads for a given month and was able to deliver sixteen presentations would have a conversion rate of 40 percent. Each sales agent's numbers will be different, but the more the agents improve and are able to deliver a larger percent of presentations to their clients, the more likely they will be able to increase their sales. You cannot make a sale without giving a presentation, and the more presentations you are able to give and the more time you spend on perfecting your presentations, the more leads you will convert to sales. A quick note on what we call a presentation: A presentation is when your sales agent is able to deliver your product in a way that the client can make a buying decision.

Figure 3-4 shows the components of converting a lead to a presentation. This consists of lead processing, client preparation, and client sales presentation. These three steps can all be used for improving your ratio of leads to sales presentations. Figure 3-4 also shows the lead process. A qualified lead comes in, marketing accounts for and sources the lead and then assigns the lead to a sales agent, and sales puts the lead in its follow-up database. Sales next prepares the client presentation, which includes making initial and secondary contact with your client, building a relationship with your client, communicating to your client what the intent of a presentation is, and discovering your client's love language for the presentation.

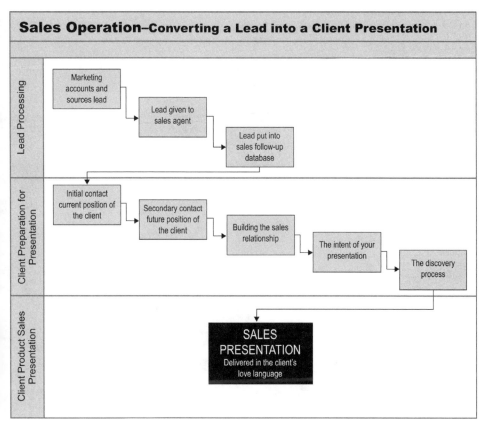

Figure 3-4

Figure 3-5 shows the steps necessary for bringing a lead closer to a sale after a presentation: custom benefits, confirmation of the best product to meet this client's needs, review of the value proposition, and asking for the purchase. When you ask the client to purchase, you will be in one of these three categories again:

1. Purchased

2. Not interested

3. In progress

After you ask clients to purchase—no matter what their response is or which of the three categories the clients are in—you will need to pursue a very important sales follow-up process.

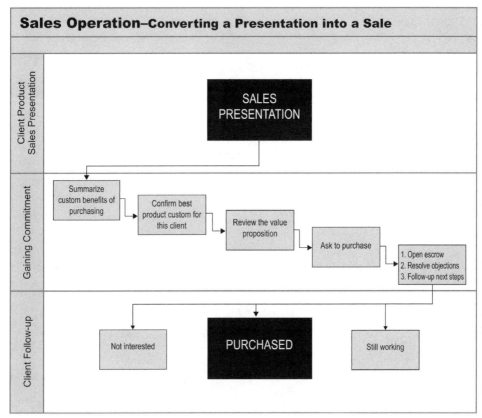

Figure 3-5

Another important topic is the mindset of your sales teams. In some selling environments there are so few sales people that one sales talent can account for as much as twenty-five percent of the production. Regardless of how many sales team members you have, you need your team to be in peak performance condition. It all starts with the way they think. The way they think has a lot to do with the way they feel, and the way they feel has a lot to do with the way they act. And the way they think, feel, and act has everything to do with the way they present, which is what they do for a living and what your company depends on.

If you are not managing the way sales people think, feel, and act, then you are not providing the leadership you should. There are many ways to keep an eye on these things. First, simply observe your employees' behavior. Second, look carefully at their quarterly team culture scores. These numbers are as important as any they produce, even as important as their main sales performance statistic—volume per lead. You will probably find that a sales person's culture scores correlate in significant ways with his or her volume per lead.

Below in figure 3-6 you can see the progression of a top-performing sales person. The way sales people present has everything to do with how well your sales team can convert leads to presentation. How well do they do in culture performance? How well do you track their culture performance? How many leads are converted to presentations? How many sales presentations are converted into sales? What is the quality of their follow-up? These questions are so important for creating the maximum number of leads that convert to presentations.

Most of us focus on sales performance, but let's make sure we focus equally on culture performance. Culture performance reports were shared with you under marketing reporting in chapter 10. These culture reports are very important in leading top sales performance. Figure 3-6 shows what these culture reports are really scoring:

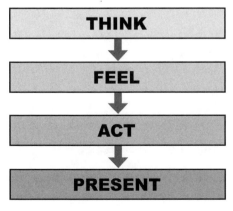

Figure 3-6

If you choose not to monitor culture performance by each member of the sales team, then you are at risk for poor workplace morale. Before you know it, you may have a sales team that is performing well below its optimal level. The bottom line is you cannot afford with sales teams not to make sure they understand their responsibility for the way they think, feel, and act. You have to establish processes to monitor performance in this area and hold each member of the team accountable for his or her team culture performance scores.

The two questions we use once a quarter to score sales agents on team culture are as follows:

1. Do I feel this employee is a positive influence in the business environment?

2. Do I feel this employee is a good team player?

As with marketing, each of the players on the entire sales, marketing, and administrative teams scores each of the other players. This is done in confidence, and no one knows who scored whom what, but all of your team members know their individual scores and how they scored relative to the rest of the team. If you have sales members who are scoring in the ninety percent or higher range, make sure you recognize this achievement some way through their compensation. If you do not recognize it, you will find scores will not be taken as seriously. If a sales person scores below seventy percent, you need to take proactive measures as this situation will be costing your company lost sales. The individual sales agent cannot perform at his or her true capacity with such low scores. It is important for sales people to understand that better scores mean greater success.

For more information about this culture performance report, please review the detailed information in chapter 10. There will also be a sales follow-up on this report in the sales chapters to come.

Lastly, let's consider lead domination from a sales standpoint. Listed below are areas you should try to improve if you want to convert more of your leads into sales:

Sales Domination

Nine Lead Conversions to Sales Success Strategies
(These are used in the sales domination ratings.)

1. *Building Relationships*—Start by creating a positive first impression and by developing trust on that foundation.

2. *The Intent Statement*—If you are going to ask your potential owners to purchase during the presentation, you should tell them that up front.

3. *Discovery*—How effective are you at discovering your potential owners' essential needs for your product? This is the key to a successful discovery.

4. *Product Presentation*—Explain how your product works, in terms of features, advantages, and benefits, using what you have discovered about your potential owners' essential needs.

5. *Product Viewing*—Show your product in a way that creates an emotional impact. Focus on how the product appeals to the senses and how it will make your prospective owner think and feel as an owner.

6. *Gaining Commitment*—Consider how best to ask your prospective owner for the sale and what to do if and when you receive objections.

7. *Sales Lead Follow-up*—Make sure all your leads are getting first-class follow-up from your sales teams.

8. *Sales Performance Reporting and Reviewing*—Implement monthly reviews and quarterly written sit-down reviews that provide feedback and future direction for each individual on the sales team.

9. *Innovation and Execution*— Have a process to implement, report, and review what you are going to innovate and execute from a sales standpoint.

Are you ready to get some proven strategies for converting leads to sales? Enjoy the chapters that follow.

Key Notes on Converting Leads into Sales

1. Work on making your goods and services circle as big as possible.

2. Make sure you understand how to deliver a presentation about your product in your prospective buyer's love language.

3. Hire, promote, and review based on employees' performance, talent, training, desire, and commitment.

4. One of your most important indicators is your conversion of a lead into a presentation. Make sure you are constantly trying to improve the percentage of leads who receive presentations.

5. Also crucial is the number of presentations that convert to sales. Constantly try to improve this percentage as well.

6. Always keep the vital sales performance numbers on each sale agent updated and reviewed.

7. You need to score team and individual culture just like you score team and individual sales performance. Make sure there is some reward for success in this area.

8. Keep a log on all the vital best practices of converting a lead to a sale.

Let's hear from our characters about getting ready to *convert leads into sales.*

Introduction: Converting Leads into Sales
Here are our characters in an action scene preparing to convert leads into sales.

To convert more leads into sales, you must be well practiced and prepared with strong selling and follow-up skills

Chapter 14

Building Your Sales Relationships

Try to be interested—not interesting; that builds trust

> Sales team, take a minute to write down the difference between a warm-up, a discovery, and a sales presentation.

IN THIS CHAPTER WE will focus on building sales relationships. You'll notice I didn't just say "building rela-tionships" but "building sales relationships." There is a difference. A normal relationship is about getting to know someone so you can develop a friendship and enhance each other's lives through sharing common interests. A sales relationship is about learning how your product can help solve a problem or satisfy a need or desire your client has. The only way you can consistently discover a client's need or desire for your product is by developing a strong sales relationship with that client in which he or she articulates those needs and desires. Strong sales relationships make your clients feel you care what is important to them, and that makes it easier for your clients to trust you and share their true needs and/ or desires for your product.

Because in this chapter we will focus on the sales process of converting a lead into a sale, we will use the term *prospective owner* rather than lead. I think this term best sets the tone for all leads who are given to the sales team.

The interesting thing about training to build sales relationships is that ninety percent of the time it is done without the owner being present, just as in football where lots of practice occurs without the opposing team being on the field. When the opposing team in football or the prospective owner in sales is in front of you, it is too late to practice your skills. It is time to execute. For some sales agents practicing alone can be a challenge, but to be the best you can, it's a must.

Sales success, which means converting leads to sales, depends heavily on good relationships with clients. Because of the way we generate leads, though, sales agents often have very little time to devote to building such relationships. You may have just minutes to start to develop your sales relationships. That's not much, but it is enough—provided you have practiced off the field and that you make every minute count.

No minutes count more than the very first ones spent with prospective owners. That's because the old saying "You never get a second chance to make a first impression" is true. We all make initial judgments based on people's voice, tone, appearance, and behavior. And once we form an opinion, we are far more likely to look for evidence that supports our opinion than to seek information that contradicts it.

Therefore, when you build a sales relationship, you need to focus on making the best possible use of the first precious moments with prospective owners. So in this chapter we will focus on the best practices for building sales relationships. There are three things that will help you convert leads into sales when you start to build sales relationships:

1. Preparation

2. Greeting your prospective owner

3. Your warm-up with your prospective owner

The greeting presentation to your prospective owner is very short—it should only take minutes. So if the presentation is so short, why is this chapter so many pages? That's because most sales relationship building should be done before you meet your prospective owner.

Preparation

Think of yourself as a sales athlete. The actual game (your sales presentation) may last only minutes. But you should be preparing for that live presentation for many hours. Preparing for a live presentation takes time, desire, and commitment. You need to polish the fundamentals of selling to stay in top condition, mentally and physically.

Start your conditioning for the live presentation by:

1. Knowing the product you are selling inside and out

2. Understanding your prospective owner

3. Building rapport

4. Learning how to motivate yourself

Knowing the Product You Are Selling Inside and Out

Your product enhances the prospective owner's lifestyle, health, family relationships, and overall quality of life. It is up to you to communicate these benefits to your prospective owner. To do this, whether you are giving a presentation over the phone or face-to-face, you must be well informed about the product you are selling. Your expertise makes your presentation credible. With this knowledge, you can individualize presentations and help prospective owners select the most appropriate ownership plan.

Learn about your competition second. Learn as much as you can about the different brands and products offered by your competitors. Understand the options out there for the consumer and why your product may be the best choice. Knowing your own product really means knowing how it stacks up against competitors' products.

You should also make sure you are representing the best available product in your market. If you are not, then you need to address that issue immediately. You should be representing the *ultimate* product, the best in the world. Never lose sight of this goal. There are many ways that your product can stack up as the best. Representing the best is very empowering!

Understanding Your Prospective Owner

Broadly speaking, there are four general personality types or social styles: assertive, expressive, analytical, and amiable. Being conversant with them will help you understand your prospective clients and make you a better sales professional.

If you learn how to relate to these different social styles, you will better understand your prospective owners and will be able to communicate with them more effectively since personality characteristics affect how we communicate and how we like others to communicate with us.

You may not know much about your prospective owners at the start of a presentation. But you can identify their likely social style and adjust your communication strategies appropriately. It is just as important to recognize a person's style and to adjust your communication in a phone presentation as in a face-to-face presentation.

Figure 14-1 shows the four social styles you should be aware of and two words that give you an idea as to how you would effectively deliver a presentation to these prospective owners. These two words give you your pace as well as the type of content you should use to present.

Assertive Fast Facts	**Expressive** Fast Emotion
Analytical Slow Facts	**Amiable** Slow Emotions

Figure 14-1

With a little practice you can become good at identifying the social style of your prospective owners. Mastering this skill can be very helpful for building your sales relationships.

Social Styles

- **Assertive** clients tend to be fast-paced and results-oriented. They enjoy making decisions and try to control situations. They place high value on results, relatively little on feelings and relationships. They like to have command of facts when making buying decisions.

- **Expressive** clients tend to be enthusiastic, extroverted, and fast-paced. They are responsive and emotional, uninhibited and creative. They get involved in many activities. They value social interaction, excitement, recognition, and prestige. They need to feel excited about something in order to buy it.

- **Analytical** clients tend to be logical, controlled, and focused on facts and details. Their pace is deliberate, and they value structure and discipline. Analytical types are reserved, slow to show feelings, and security conscious. They like predictability and need to understand and trust something before buying it.

- **Amiable** clients tend to be warm, open, "people-oriented," and slow paced. They value personal relationships, express emotions freely, and seek approval. They dislike interpersonal conflict so much that they may say what they think people want to hear rather than state their true opinions. Before buying something, they like to know others approve or have made the same decision. They need to believe that the sales person will be there with them.

So look for these traits that we have discussed, listen to how fast people talk and what they talk about, and you will become very good at identifying which social style characterizes your prospective owner. Once you have made that identification, the next step is to adjust your own communication style to mirror your prospective owner's social style.

Appropriate Communication Strategies

For assertive clients:

1. Provide facts quickly in a straightforward manner.

2. Ask for their opinions to engage them and appeal to their need for control.

3. Stress how your product will contribute to their goals to support their focus on results.

For expressive clients:

1. Provide information quickly and enthusiastically.

2. Get them emotionally involved in the excitement of your product.

3. Show them how your product will contribute to their prestige and offer an exciting way to entertain family and friends.

For analytical clients:

1. Provide information at a slow, deliberate pace in a clear and unemotional manner.

2. Back your claims up with evidence and proof.

3. Stress how your product is a logical and safe investment.

For amiable clients:

1. Provide information at a slow pace and in a warm, friendly manner.

2. Emphasize how happy other owners have been to show that the prospective owners are not alone in their decision to purchase.

3. Stress how your product will provide a good way to bring family and friends together.

Working on social styles is a fun exercise. The more observant you are, the better you will get at this skill. Focusing on your prospective owners really helps when you are building sales relationships. This practice is a great way to be just a little bit better at creating that all-important sales relationship.

Building Rapport

Mastering the art of building rapport is another essential part of preparing for any prospective owner interaction. Rapport is essential whether your presentation is face-to-face or not. When there's genuine rapport between two people, they trust each other, respect each other, value each other as people, and recognize each other's worth. Most importantly, they will listen to each other.

When you have developed a rapport with prospective owners, they trust that you are sincerely interested in helping them and not in selling them something that's inappropriate. They feel comfortable discussing their real needs. When prospective owners can freely discuss their needs, you can tailor your presentation especially for them. Your prospective owners will also be more likely to accept your recommendations. Thus, rapport is essential for sales success.

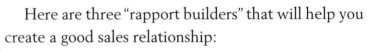

Here are three "rapport builders" that will help you create a good sales relationship:

1. Mirror the prospective owner
2. Speak effectively
3. Listen actively

Mirror the Prospective Owner

If you mirror the prospective owner in a few simple ways, that can help build rapport. That's because we feel more comfortable with people whose personal styles resemble our own. Mirroring only requires tuning in to a few obvious aspects of behavior and making small adjustments in your own style.

- Start with pace. The speed at which we speak and move is basic to our personality. You can recognize when a person's pace differs from your own. You need not match that pace exactly (which might be too obvious). But even a slight change in your pace can put a person more at ease.

- Then consider your vocabulary. Using industry slang, abbreviations, or jargon with prospective owners is not appropriate. Such language can be confusing and make people feel like outsiders. Work on developing clear explanations for technical terms and concepts. Your vocabulary should also reflect agreement with the client. Frequently using "yes," "certainly," and similar phrases shows you are "with" the person and thus builds rapport.

- You should also pay attention to a client's level of formality. Everything from the client's dress to his or her response to your greeting signals something about a preferred level of formality. Match the prospective owner as closely as is comfortable in this respect. An informal approach can offend a formal person whereas a formal manner can make an informal person feel out of place.

Speak Effectively

Using your voice effectively is one sure way to build rapport. Here are some tips:

- Be aware of the way you enunciate. Few people will feel comfortable or decide to purchase if they have difficulty understanding what you are saying. The pace of your speech also affects your clarity. When mirroring a fast-speaking prospective owner, don't speed up so much that you are hard to understand. Also check your volume. Speaking too softly or too loudly can make people uncomfortable.

- When you speak, be sure to do so in a way that projects confidence. Prospective owners expect you to be the expert on your product. Sounding sure and being sure of yourself puts them at ease. To project confidence, smile initially and maintain a pleasant expression throughout the conversation. You'll feel more confident, and that will be reflected in your voice. It is okay not to know all the answers. If you don't know something, be sure to write it down and find the correct answer. It is important for your confidence that you provide accurate information.

- Lastly, you should be energetic. When you greet prospective owners, in person or on the phone, sound eager to get started and maintain your enthusiasm throughout the presentation. If you are tired, make an extra effort to keep your voice warm. People should feel that you are enjoying presenting your product to them.

- If you aren't sure how well you are doing with your enunciation, volume, confidence, and energy levels, you need to have these things reviewed. Even if you think you are doing well, I would still advise you to have these things reviewed. Sales are made and lost based on communication skills. Have one of your colleagues review you in these four areas and provide feedback or tape yourself and listen critically to evaluate these four areas.

Listen Actively

Listening well is also one of the keys for converting a lead to a sale. It has been said that you can listen your way into a sale more easily than you can talk your way into a sale. If you ask the right question and listen carefully to the answers, you will be in a much better position to convert a lead to a sale than if you just keep on presenting. Listening may be the most important of all the rapport-building techniques.

First, you need to listen actively. You need to show you understand and care about the needs and/or problems of the prospective owner. If you do this, the prospective owner will gain trust in you and will speak to you more freely. The technique of active listening helps you absorb what is said and show that you are listening. That builds rapport, because people trust good listeners. Listening is just as important for phone presentations as for face-to-face presentations. In fact, listening carefully may be even more important on the phone, when it's especially easy to become distracted and to let your attention wander.

- Be sure to concentrate while the prospective owner is speaking. You may encounter distractions, such as other people talking, or you may create your own distractions by thinking about what you're going to do or say next. Such distractions make it hard to listen. It is often tempting to let your mind wander. Our minds tend to wander because we get bored. We get bored because people can talk at about eighty to one hundred words a minute, but the brain can listen at two to four hundred words a minute, so what happens is your brain gets bored and starts to wander.

- If any of these things happen to you, you are certain to miss important information about how and why this lead or prospective owner should convert to a sale. Even worse, because your inattention will probably show, you'll undermine rapport. To overcome not listening carefully, train yourself to listen just like you were going to be asked to give a biography on the people you are presenting to on national television. Listen with extreme focus and attention to all that is said.

- Focus on what the prospective owner is saying and not on what you will say or do next. Think about what is behind the person's statements. Then focus on listening for why they should own your product, because what they are saying is important to them. Try to be interested, not interesting. Don't start thinking about the next part of the presentation. When a prospective owner speaks, his or her words should be all that interests you.

- Listen actively and show that you are listening. Doing so builds rapport and encourages prospective owners to keep revealing information. Here are some ways to show you are listening. First, maintain eye contact. Eye contact says, "I'm interested. Tell me more." Maintaining eye contact can also help you block out distractions. Respond appropriately. Show your attention non-verbally by nodding or shaking your head, making a note, or smiling. Or give verbal signals, such as "Yes" or "Hmmm" or "Uh-huh."

- Respond if the person says something interesting or funny that calls for a reaction. Ask questions to clarify or confirm what the person has just said, but do not move to another topic unless the prospective owner is finished speaking. Paraphrase to show that you've heard and understood essential information. This shows that you've been listening and gives you important information for later on in the presentation. Don't interrupt. Make sure the person has finished speaking before you clarify, confirm, or paraphrase. Not interrupting is not only polite, but it also lets prospective buyers feel free to talk. Your interest in what the prospective owner has to say encourages him or her to talk more. The more the person talks and the more questions you ask, the more leads will be converted into sales.

Learn How to Motivate Yourself

The last part of your preparation in building sales relationships is to motivate yourself. Perhaps the most important element of all in sales success is your atti-tude. A positive attitude is a great asset in building sales relationships. All people, including your prospective owners, are attracted to positive attitudes. There are two primary ways to stay motivated and have a good attitude. One is to recognize attitude traps and respond accordingly, and the other is to work proactively with your team and to stay away from team members who are not positive.

Let's start with the well-known attitude traps. We all know that a positive outlook is one of the keys to your success. Yet we can all fall into negative moods and lose our motivation. Why? Because there are a few common attitude traps that can take us down. Let's talk about these traps and come up with some ideas that will help us avoid them.

Start with your own personal concerns. Financial worries, a slow week at work or a hectic one, health problems, family issues: All can erode a positive attitude. Self-image problems have a big impact. Everyone has times when self-confidence shrinks and self-doubt grows. Sometimes there are clear reasons, and sometimes the reason is not so clear. For no apparent reason you simply don't feel as attractive or competent or successful as usual.

This phenomenon is known as negative drift. Even when your self-image is fine and there are no negative personal concerns, a negative mood can descend on you. It could be the stress of working hard and fulfilling many other responsibilities. It could be the constant bombardment of negative stories from the news media. It could be just a human tendency to experience a cycle of negative and positive moods. Whatever the cause, it's important to be aware of when your attitude is turning negative. Like it or not, moods will affect your sales production. Maintaining a positive attitude takes work. But the work is worth it. People who make the effort to be positive feel less fatigued and more satisfied than do those who don't combat negativity. These positive sales people will put your team in a dominating lead position.

Here are a few things positive people do to maintain their positive attitudes:

1. Check daily to see whether their thoughts are positive. If not, they refocus their thinking, often by taking some of the other actions listed here.

2. Read inspirational books and listen to self-help tapes.

3. Attend motivational seminars.

4. Practice yoga or meditation and/or engage in hobbies to clear their minds.

5. Exercise frequently and vigorously.

6. Apply moderation to all aspects of their lives.

7. Get involved in religious, fraternal, or community service organizations.

8. Have written, measurable, and ambitious personal goals.

9. View themselves as successful, even though they may have failed at various times in their lives.

10. Enjoy their prospective owners. Prospective owners are usually interesting and successful. Focus on enjoying the experience of knowing them.

11. Build rapport with themselves. When they're feeling down, they treat themselves like a prospective owner or friend. They respect their own judgment, professionalism, and abilities, value their accomplishments, and listen to their emotions.

12. They take mini-breaks. They relax and refresh their minds by taking deep breaths, stretching while sitting, taking a short imaginary vacation to a favorite place, or walking during breaks.

We've talked so far in this chapter about program knowledge, understanding your prospective owners, mastering rapport, and keeping yourself motivated. These techniques are practiced by all true students of the sales profession, and most of this training is done on your own, away from your potential owners.

I would guess, though, that only perhaps twenty percent of sales professionals take these methods seriously and practice them. The rest just ad lib or hope they instinctively do what is necessary. That may be the reason twenty percent of sales agents make eighty percent of the commission dollars.

If you and your sales team want to dominate the competition and your market with the leads you are given, then developing these skills is a must. If you have good sales leadership and sales agents who want to perform to their full potential, then there will usually be no problem with making progress toward mastery.

Whatever your talent level is, the training you will receive in this section on converting a lead to a sale will enhance your performance. I have spent thirty years training teams on these principles. There were many, many more principles I threw out because they sounded good but did not work. What you are going to read about are sales tactics that have actually improved the ability of sales teams to convert leads into sales.

Meeting and Greeting Your Prospective Owners

A prospective owner's interaction with sales begins with a greeting. An effective greeting depends on instantly establishing good communication. Communication is the key to a good first impression, and a first impression is the key to building a relationship. This means that the greeting, though short, is the foundation of a successful sales presentation.

To deliver an effective greeting, keep the following in mind:

1. Understand the basis of first impressions.
2. Do a last-minute check to ensure a successful first impression.
3. Open effectively.
4. Develop your greeting.

Understand the Basis of First Impressions

Human beings communicate in three ways, with words, tone of voice, and non-verbal body language. Together, these are the major factors in determining a first impression. Which of the three do you think has the biggest impact with a prospective owner in forming a first impression of you? The answer is that words have only a 7 percent impact, tone has a 38 percent impact, and the biggest impact is body language at 55 percent. If the first encounter is not face-to-face, then only words and tone have an impact; however, if you talk to someone over the phone and have good body language while you do it, your words and tone will likely come out better.

What this means to you as a sales agent can be summed up with this quotation: "Who you are speaks so loudly I can't hear a word you're saying." The rapport-building skills you've learned, which include words, tone, and body language, help you convey to your prospective owners "who you are" so they can comfortably hear what you're saying. Other key factors to review in creating a first impression are your physical appearance, your thoughts and attitude, and your confidence in your initial greeting statement.

Do a Last-Minute Check to Ensure a Successful First Impression

To make sure you're ready to deliver an effective greeting and create a good first impression, do a quick check just before any face-to-face or non-face-to-face presentation. Here are some things to check:

First, check your thoughts and attitude. The correct mindset is essential to meeting and greeting prospective owners. This mindset enables you to think positively and make your words, tone, and body language effective. Zig Ziglar refers to this as "doing a check up from the neck up." Consider what you are thinking. What are your primary and secondary goals today? Write them down, see whether you accomplish them, and keep score if that keeps you more focused. How are you feeling overall? Focus on how confident and competent you are with the well-prepared presentation you are about to deliver. Think about how you are about to deliver a great presentation totally based on your prospective owner's needs.

Another thing you should focus on is getting your surroundings ready. Are your desk area and presentation materials organized? If they are organized, it will help you feel confident, deliver an excellent presentation, and reinforce your competence in the eyes of your prospective owners. You cannot afford to be scattered.

Make sure your physical appearance is appropriate. How you look affects the impression you make.

The words of your greeting, your tone, and your body language are important. Make sure you are confident about all these factors, which we will discuss in more detail in the following pages.

Lastly, you need to know the questions you will ask the clients in the greeting and warm-up. You must know the questions you'll ask, why you are asking them, what data you are looking for, and what you'll do with the answers. We'll spend a little more time on this subject in the chapters that follow.

Open Effectively

The opening moments of an interaction are critical. Your body language, tone, and words set the stage for the rest of the presentation. Be sure to smile and be yourself. You've practiced, trained, and prepared for this moment; now you can relax and enjoy the prospective owners and the satisfaction of selling your product. When you greet your prospective owner or owners, make good eye contact, greet and acknowledge everyone present with a firm handshake, exchange (sincere) pleasantries, and be enthusiastic.

Develop Your Greeting

The first words you speak to prospective owners are critical. Here are some models of effective greeting statements for face-to-face and non-face-to-face presentations. These were greetings used in selling a luxury real estate product in New York, but these same kinds of greetings can be adapted to the product you are selling.

Face-to-Face Presentations

Mr. and Mrs. Smith? Good Morning.

Welcome. I am excited to share our product with you today.

Thank you for taking the time out of your day to come see us.

My name is John Doe.

Please call me John. I'll be taking care of you today.

May I go by your first names? Is that what your friends call you?

I see you're dressed perfectly for the weather. It's another beautiful sunny day.

Have you been enjoying your time here in New York?

What do you enjoy doing most while you're in New York?

Oh, I see you're from Laguna Beach. How nice. Tell me what brought you to Laguna Beach.

Note that you should always inquire about the guests' stay. In addition, be sure to listen to what clients have to say, take notes if you need to, and respond to their needs if appropriate.

Non-Face-to-Face Presentations

Good morning/afternoon Mr. and Mrs._____.
Thank you for allowing me to spend some time on the phone with both of you.

I am extremely excited to share with you some of the outstanding luxury real estate opportunities that the St. Regis New York is now providing our clientele. I will answer any questions you may have, so, as I get started, feel free to stop me and ask questions about anything we discuss.

You actually have two items to sell in your sales presentation: yourself and your product, in that order. The warm-up is the time to concentrate on selling yourself.

Don't confuse the warm-up with the discovery sequence, in which you explore the prospective owner's product needs. If you ask in-depth questions too soon, the prospective owner may feel as if he or she is being interrogated. Why? Because you haven't sold yourself by building rapport, establishing credibility, eliciting trust, and reducing tension and anxiety.

If you start selling the features of your product before you have even discovered whether you client has a need for you product, you are making a mistake. I used to tell my sales teams that some sales people spend twenty percent of their time selling the product and eighty percent buying it back. If you start selling features, advantages, and benefits before you understand the prospective owners' needs, you are not selling your product; you are buying it back. We are only in the greeting sequence, so delivering your product presentation now is way too soon. You can never meet your full selling potential if you jump the gun.

Also, don't confuse the warm-up with the concept sequence or other parts of the presentation where you present product features and benefits. Some sales agents tend to lead with the product because they are so excited about it. But doing so before establishing rapport or understanding prospective owners' needs can make potential clients feel like you are giving a "canned" presentation and don't care about them. Instead, use the warm-up to focus on making friends with the clients, not on selling your product.

Since every prospective owner discussion is unique, you can't easily write down and practice your warm-up the way you can your greeting statement. Following communication points, though, will help ensure a successful warm-up.

All the techniques for building rapport and making a good first impression are essential in the warm-up. Remember to smile, mirror your prospective owner's body language, tone, and pace of speech, express a genuine interest in everyone in the party, and listen actively.

- All in all, a warm-up starts building a relationship. Clients will not buy from you until they are genuinely convinced that you are a friend or are at least acting in their best interests. To be a friend, you must build trust, and you must have empathy. Also keep in mind that the more questions you can ask and the more the prospective owners can talk, the better your relationship is likely to be.

- It helps to find common ground early in the presentation. Break the ice by finding something to talk about that you and your prospective owners have in common. Discovering such commonality has a bonding effect. It lessens sales resistance, reduces anxiety, and elicits trust. You can find common ground in many areas: a mutual hometown, a shared hobby or interest, similar values or concerns. Pay attention to logos on clothing that may suggest clients' interests. Notice jewelry or anything else that's unusual and might be turned into an enjoyable topic of conversation. Talk about anything but the program you want to sell, and remember that people never get bored talking about their interests and themselves.

Here are some quick reminders for doing your warm-up:

1. Let guests talk about themselves.

2. Find something you genuinely like about the person.

3. Establish commonality.

4. Do not sell, interrogate, or prejudge.

5. Take a "me too" rather than a "so what" approach.

6. Discuss hometown, family, recreation.

7. Let guests talk about themselves—"I like how you think."

8. Don't ask qualifying questions.

9. Pay sincere compliments.

10. Listen—listen—listen. Speak 33 percent of the time and listen 66 percent of the time.

11. When they say it, they believe it.

12. Reduce walls of sales resistance.

13. Don't prejudge.

14. Connect by active listening. Smile, lean forward, make eye contact when listening.

Here are some warm-up questions you can ask that are effective for starting a friendly conversation:

1. Where do you live?

2. What do you like best about living there?

3. What do you like to do most when you're not working?

4. Tell me a little about your family.

5. What activities do you like?

6. What type of work do you do?

7. How did you hear about us?

8. What was most interesting to you about our product?

9. What is planned for the rest of the day when we are done?

10. Do you use products similar to what we are going to talk about today?

Building a relationship at the beginning of a presentation takes relatively little time, but the preparation that goes into it can be quite time consuming. Nonetheless, it's worth it to make the effort because it will increase your conversion rate from leads to sales. In summary, work on your preparation, greeting skills, and your actual warm-up.

Key Notes for Building Your Sales Relationships

1. Building relationships requires a lot of preparation.

2. Know your product and those of your competition inside and out.

3. Master techniques for building rapport.

4. Learn how to best motivate yourself.

5. For your greeting make your best first impression.

6. Open effectively by developing and practicing your greeting.

7. Understand the difference between a warm-up, a discovery, and your product presentation.

8. Learn how to make conversations with good warm-up questions.

9. Ask questions. The one asking the question is controlling the presentation, not the one talking.

10. Talk about anything your prospective owner is interested in except the product you are selling.

Let's hear from our characters about *building your sales relationships.*

Chapter 14: Building Your Sales Relationships

Here is an action scene of our characters busy *building relationships.*

Building sales relationships takes a lot of preparation and practice before you get in front of your clients.

Chapter 15

The Intent Statement

These are the ground rules—what you can expect from your clients and what they can expect from you during a sales presentation

> If the intent of your presentation is to ask your potential owners to purchase, tell them that up front.

THE INTENT STATEMENT quite simply outlines the purpose of the presentation you are about to give. With the greeting and warm-up completed, the intent statement sets the tone for the business part of your meeting with prospective owners. The intent statement builds on the great sales relationship you are developing and therefore must be perfectly delivered in terms of words, tone, and body language.

An intent statement provides "full disclosure" about how your presentation and sales relationships are going to work. An intent statement establishes the ground rules about what you will

accomplish for your prospective owners and what you would like your prospective owners to provide for you. As you built the sales relationship, you really learned about the prospective owner. Here in the intent statement the prospective owner is now going to learn a little about you and how you will conduct your presentation.

You need to walk through the steps of this process and clearly let the prospective owner know how each step will progress based on the interest level he or she has expressed. This introduction is essential because there are really no secrets here. The prospective owner already knows that your job is to sell him or her. So laying out some guidelines about how you plan to present this selling process really adds to your credibility.

By removing any uncertainty about an unfamiliar process, the intent statement relieves anxiety and makes people comfortable with the presentation process. If you present your intent statement correctly, your prospective owners will be more able to hear and accept your message.

The intent statement also starts building excitement about your product and creates a sense of urgency about the opportunity to become owners. The intent statement directly reflects your positive attitude and your confidence in yourself, your presentation, and your product ownership program.

All in all, the intent statement is a small part of the total presentation—but a very powerful one. There are five critical components of a well-delivered intent statement:

1. Take away pressure.
2. Express empathy.
3. Address the agenda.
4. Set up the discovery.
5. Establish expectations.

You can remember these components quickly by focusing on the fact that the intent statement is meant to "TEASE." (See the beginning letters of the five important components above, which form the acronym "TEASE.")

These components need not be in this order in your intent statement. You may touch on more than one component at a time. For example, you may be able to express empathy as you make other points in your intent statement. You may also take away pressure just by the way you phrase and deliver the entire statement—as well as the rest of the presentation.

Let's take a closer look at each of these five components and your full intent statement.

Open and Close the Intent Statement

In addition to the five components discussed above, every intent statement should have a clear opening and closing.

To open an intent statement, say something like, "Let me explain how I would like to present our product to you and your family today." Such a positioning statement prepares the prospective owners for what you are going to say next. It also helps to put them at ease by demonstrating that you are going to make clear where the presentation is heading.

To close the intent statement, ask a simple question to determine whether your prospective owner feels comfortable with what you have said or has any questions or concerns. For example, "How does that sound?" or "Do you have any questions before we begin?" You can also ask similar questions during the intent statement to make sure your prospective owners are "with you."

Let's start with the "T" in TEASE:

Take Away Pressure

It's important early in the intent statement to take away pressure by reassuring your prospective owners you will be working with their timeframes for reviewing and purchasing the product. This direct, up front reassurance reduces your prospective owner's anxiety and puts people at ease. It also prevents them from keeping distance between themselves and the program opportunity, which they might do if they felt they had to "protect" themselves.

By your choice of words and your overall attitude, tone, and body language you can continue taking away pressure during the rest of the intent statement and throughout the entire presentation that follows the intent statement.

Now the first "E" in TEASE:

Express Empathy

Expressing empathy and showing that you understand and care about your prospective owner's feelings, needs, and concerns is another way to reduce anxiety and relax people. You express empathy by addressing basic concerns up front, often at the same time you first take away pressure. To do this, make statements that show you understand possible concerns and are prepared to address them.

During the warm-up you may pick up clues about specific concerns, which, of course, you should address as you express empathy. But you can also assume most prospective owners have a hesitant feeling about being involved in this type of discussion setting. The prospective owner knows he or she can make you happy by buying or sad by not buying. For some prospective owners this situation can create great anxieties.

Here are three ways to show empathy in your intent statement:

1. Let your prospective owner know you value his or her time and how long the presentation usually takes. Then get permission from your prospective owner to have that amount of his or her time.

2. Also let your prospective owner know that you will only recommend next steps based on his or her level of interest. If the person decides to become an owner, that is entirely his or her own choice.

3. Finally, let your prospective owner know you will be covering in the presentation only things that interest him or her about your product. If there is no interest in a particular subject, then you will skip it.

As with taking away pressure, you can express empathy throughout the presentation to show your attention to the comfort of your prospective owners.

Moving on to the "A" in TEASE:

Address the Agenda

A brief overview of the rest of the presentation goes a long way toward reducing apprehension and fear of the unknown. Hearing the agenda enables your prospective owners to understand what subjects and steps the presentation will be covering rather than wonder about what the next step will be.

To introduce the agenda, you might say, "Here's what we'll want to discuss today." Then you can briefly outline each step of the presentation, in the order in which you'll be doing it. As you go over the agenda, be sure to emphasize your views on the value of your product and to convey the pride and enthusiasm you feel for it.

Here is the "S" in TEASE:

Set Up the Discovery

During the intent statement you can begin to gain permission to ask the necessary questions that will help you identify your prospective owner's needs for your product.

People can resent questions if they do not expect them or understand their purpose. So use the intent statement to position the discovery and prepare your prospective owners to accept and answer your questions. The key to doing this is to make it clear how your questions and their answers will help you tailor the rest of the presentation to their specific interests and needs.

Last is the final "E" in TEASE:

Establish Expectations

Letting your prospective owners know the agenda helps establish their expectations for the discussion and presentation. Express empathy by assuring them that the presentation/discussion will be a comfortable experience.

In addition, a strong intent statement establishes expectations in terms of the direction, next steps, and the purchase process. You should make it clear that, if prospective owners like what they see or hear, you are going to make a recommendation on the best next steps in the purchase process.

Modern life is such that not to act on something only postpones the consideration to the point that your busy schedules will make it difficult to reconnect. If nothing else, at the conclusion of your discussions you should reach a mutual agreement about your prospective owner's interest level and next steps in the purchasing process.

By making it clear that, based on interest levels, you are likely to make a recommendation on the next steps toward purchasing, you ensure that there will be no surprises at the end of the presentation. Your frankness reinforces your prospective owner's impression of your honesty. After all, they know you have something to sell. It's up to you to be up front about that fact but also to convince him or her that you will recommend a purchase or take the next step only if your product seems right to the client. Stressing this provision in the intent statement is another way of reducing anxiety and preparing your prospective owner to receive your message.

Let's take a look at an ideal intent statement script. Keep in mind that you must practice this before you deliver it to your client. Practice with your fellow associates and/or tape your presentation. Review carefully your words, tone, and body language. Practice your intent statement—not just the words but also your tone of voice and body language. Without all these being correct your intent statement will not rise to its full potential as a way of helping you convert leads into sales.

Example of an Intent Statement

Here is a sample intent statement for a *face-to-face* presentation:

Mr. and Mrs._____, what I would like to do is explain what our product presentation consists of today.

But first, I want to let you know that it is very important to me that our discussion proceeds in a manner that focuses on your interests. I will need to ask you some questions to discover some information about you to do this. Is that okay with you? Also, the amount of time we spend together and the way we spend it is entirely up to you and your interests.

Before we start, is there anything of particular interest I should focus on or any information you want to share with me?

Good. Here's what we want to cover. First, I'll give you a little background and history about the product I will be sharing with you today, including why this product has become so popular for people and families like yours.

Next, I would like to ask you some questions to see whether our product and the concept of ownership can help you achieve a certain quality of life or help you meet some specific goals you and your family may have for owning our product. If it does, I will work with you to show you the steps involved in purchasing the product. We can then explore additional reasons you and your family might benefit through involvement in our product.

Likewise, we will visit one of our beautiful product models that best suits you. It is representative of what you can purchase.

After that, we can discuss various packages and prices and show you just how easy it is to become an owner with us if you are interested.

All this is about today is us making a personal evaluation of the way you are currently fulfilling needs and how that may change if you owned our product.

If you find our product and ownership concept can fulfill the needs you have or add value to your life or your portfolio, then we would like you to seriously consider the next steps toward purchasing one of our products. Today, the reasons that are favorable for purchasing are: (Insert your reasons. Also indicate inventory available, pricing, phase, and incentives.)

Any questions before we start?

Here is a sample intent statement for a *non-face-to-face* presentation:

Mr. and Mrs._____, what I would like to do is explain what our product presentation consists of.

But first, I want to let you know that it is very important to me that our discussion proceeds in a manner that focuses on your interests. I will need to discover some information about you to do this. Is that okay? Also, the amount of time we spend together and the way we spend it is entirely up to you and your interests.

Before we start, is there anything of particular interest I should focus on or information that you want to share with me of importance to you?

Good. Here's what we want to cover. First, I'll give you a little background and history about our product.

Next, I would like to ask some questions to see whether our product and the ownership concept can help you achieve your specific goals by owning the product. If it does, I will work with you to show you the value of your family owning our product. We can then explore together how you and your family might benefit through your involvement in this product.

Likewise, you can visit our website or I can email you one of our beautiful product brochures that best suits your needs. It shows what you can purchase.

After that, we can discuss various packages and prices and show just how easy it is to become an owner with us if you are interested.

If you find that owning our product could enhance the way you share time together or add value to your life or your portfolio, then we would like you to seriously consider the next steps toward purchasing. Today, the reasons that are favorable for purchasing are: (Insert your reasons. Also indicate inventory available, pricing, phase, and incentives.)

Any questions before we start?

Key Notes for the Intent Statement

1. Have a reason for delivering a presentation and then deliver that reason to your prospective owner.

2. An intent statement is your up-front plan of what your presentation will entail.

3. A properly delivered intent statement should relax your prospective owner.

4. A properly delivered intent statement will establish expectations for you and your potential owners.

5. You must carefully practice an intent statement. You do not want to try to ad lib it.

6. Intent statements must be delivered with the correct words, tone of voice, and body language to be effective

7. Intent statements take the surprise out of the sequences of a presentation.

8. Intent statement are always used by sales teams that want to dominate the conversion of leads to sales.

Let's hear from our characters about their *intent statements.*

Sales teams, if your intent is to discover what your prospective owners' needs are, then present your product based on those needs. A plan of action expressing what is going to happen in your presentation is good for you and your prospective owners.

My intent is to do the least amount of work and make the most amount of money. I just do not see any real benefit in practicing parts of my presentation.

Chapter 15: The Intent Statement

Here is an action scene with our characters working on their intent statement.

Your clients should have a clear direction for the intent and the steps of your sales presentation.

Chapter 16

Discovery

Sales success begins with discovering your client's essential needs

Sales team, let's make a list of all our clients' essential and incidental needs. Discover essential needs and you have the key for turning many more leads into sales.

THE SECRET OF SALES success can be summed up in one word: needs. "Needs," as it relates to your product, means simply what prospective owners want, the goals they hope to accomplish, or the problems they hope to solve. When their needs are met, prospective owners are motivated to purchase. The sales agent who uncovers a prospective owner's essential needs knows what lies behind them, understands their relative importance, and will convert the most leads to sales.

Clues about needs may surface at any point in a presentation, but the discovery sequence is when you focus most closely on uncovering and understanding a prospective owner's needs. Throughout this chapter I will use the word "needs," but what we are really looking for are essential needs. This understanding enables you not only to target needs but also to avoid providing information that does not interest the prospective owner. Unnecessary information can clutter the presentation and confuse the prospective owner.

These factors make the discovery sequence one of the most important steps in the sales presentation—perhaps the most important of all. The discovery sequence is the foundation upon which the success of the entire presentation rests. Success in a presentation means converting a lead to a sale. In the examples below I use one of the products we were selling, the St. Regis New York (both whole ownership and fractional ownership real estate). You can modify the examples to fit the product and or service that you are offering.

Let's review some of the elements of a successful discovery. Your product probably addresses some important human needs, including family togetherness, love, romance, relaxation, health, security, savings, and status.

Your objective in the discovery is to recognize and understand the prospective owner's unique set of needs, which are the keys for moving the prospective owner from a lead to a sale. After this step, you can focus the rest of the presentation on the specific features, advantages, and benefits of your product that meet the prospective owner's needs. That way your presentation will have emotional impact, which is precisely what moves prospective owners to make a purchase.

To conduct a successful discovery, you need to:

1. Understand open and closed questions

2. Get oriented

3. Explore needs—uncover needs—seek the need behind the need

4. Recognize the difference between essential and incidental needs

5. Ask discovery questions

6. Listen

7. Establish and start to focus on the product concept presentation coming next

The discovery, which usually takes place in your office or on the phone, should never feel like an interrogation. It should feel to the prospective owner like a comfortable conversation in which he or she learns more about what your product offers, with no pressure whatsoever.

Understand Open and Closed Questions

Uncovering what might move prospective owners to purchase requires asking more than one or two superficial questions. You need to dig deep to find and understand needs that will move prospective owners to become owners. That means using questions strategically to understand all of the prospective owner's product-related problems and needs. Developing a questioning strategy starts with understanding the basics about open and closed questions.

Closed Questions

A closed question limits answers to "yes" or "no" and elicits specific facts. It demonstrates your attention to detail, lets you control the conversation, and enables you to confirm you've understood what the prospective owner has said.

Examples of closed questions:

1. Are your familiar with [your product]? (yes/no)

2. How many grandchildren do you have? (fact)

3. Do you usually travel alone, or does your family come along? (choice of alternatives)

Closed questions need to be used with caution. If you ask too many closed questions, you risk missing important information that could help you discover needs and move the sale forward. Closed questions can also make prospective owners feel like they're getting the "third degree."

Open Questions

An open question encourages the client to speak freely, elicits a wide range of information, often in areas you couldn't anticipate, doesn't control the conversation as tightly as closed questions, and enables you to clarify something the prospective owner has said.

Examples of open questions:

1. Please tell me about your experience with [your product].

2. What does "luxury" mean to you?

3. How would you describe a perfect second home?

Open questions have many advantages, such as demonstrating your interest in the prospective owner, thus building trust and credibility, relaxing prospective owners so that they provide information freely, getting at needs you would miss if you didn't ask exactly the right closed question, and encouraging your prospective owners to express their needs with no parameters.

Many closed questions are good for gaining useful information. But sometimes an open question designed to get the same facts might yield more useful information.

For example, "Have you been to a fractional ownership presentation before?" is a closed question. If answered "Yes," it is often followed by other closed questions, such as "Which resorts?" "Do you own now?" You could pursue the same information by asking an open question, such as, "What's your experience with fractional ownership?" Prospective owners might answer at length and provide many clues to needs that you can explore further. This valuable information would come without a series of closed questions that might make some prospective owners feel like they are being "grilled." Deciding whether to use open or closed questions is a matter of judgment. Here are two guidelines:

First, consider the prospective owner. Is he or she talkative and/or outgoing? If so, the person will often respond well to open questions. Prospective owners who are less talkative and more reserved may need to be drawn out by closed questions.

Second, consider the information you're trying to get. If you are not getting what you need, think about which type of question you've been using most. Then try switching to the other type.

An effective discovery depends on a mix of open and closed questions. The choice is up to you and the client you have. To be a high performing sales agent, you should understand and practice these two questioning techniques off the field long before you deliver your discovery so you can efficiently and effectively use either questioning technique.

Get Oriented

The first step in an overall questioning strategy is to get up to speed on the prospective owner's current situation—in other words, get oriented. If you know where your prospective owners are today, it is much easier to create a plan and direct them where they may want to be tomorrow.

You may have gained some basic information during the warm-up and intent statement earlier, which you usually want to confirm at the start of the discovery. You may need to gather some basic information in order to begin exploring needs. In any case, you can use open or closed questions to verify facts and gather more information.

Answers to orientation questions provide a frame of reference to help you identify potential needs. These you can explore in more depth during the discovery sequence and then address in subsequent sequences.

At some point early in the discovery sequence you may want to confirm facts or understandings. You may have had some information about the prospective owner before the presentation. It's important to confirm that it is correct so that you can build on it. You may confirm some information gathered during the greeting, warm-up, intent statement, or discovery.

You will find that closed questions are especially useful for confirming facts or understandings. For example:

- "You're a golfer—is that right?"
- "Am I correct that you're staying in one of our villas now?"
- "You mentioned you're a financial consultant, I believe."

Note that you can confirm information by making a statement, such as the last example above, and wait for a reaction. You can confirm information at any time during the discovery or in other sequences when you need to be sure you have understood what the client has said.

You can also use questions to clarify points, to gather more information, or to update what you know. For example:

- "How often does your whole family get together?"
- "You mentioned that there were some problems with your second home ownerships in the past. Can you tell me a little more about that?"
- "When did you say you're planning on retiring?"

Open questions are especially useful for clarifying although closed questions can also be used, as in the last example above. You can ask for clarifications at any time during the presentation when you need more information.

Exploring Needs

When you get oriented, you uncover clues to the prospective owner's important product-related needs. For the rest of the discovery sequence you should focus on pursuing these clues to find out what your prospective owner's needs are.

To explore needs effectively, there are three things you should focus on:

1. Uncover needs.
2. Seek the need behind the need.
3. Recognize essential and incidental needs.

Uncover Needs

Less experienced sales agents are sometimes tempted to ask a few orientation questions and then immediately start to present product features, advantages, and benefits. But they don't yet know enough about the prospective owner's needs to be effective in their presentations. If you are not presenting to your prospective owner's needs, your presentation will sound canned or generic and will not produce the result you desire.

Successful sales agents ask questions to understand their prospective owners' needs in terms of product tastes, preferences, product-related problems, familiarity with your brand, and experience, if any, with your product. Such information and the needs you discover can drive your prospective owners to purchase your product if you make the most of these discoveries.

When I was selling New York real estate, my team posed questions designed to uncover needs. You can modify these questions to help sell your own product.

Why did you choose New York for last year's family reunion?

What is the number-one factor in your choice of purchasing a second home?

What are the greatest benefits you feel you get from having a second home in New York?

A need is something prospective owners want to take action on. For example, they want to play golf, they are eager to spend more time with their grandchildren, or they intend to choose a location with skiing opportunities close by.

Prospective owners often state what sounds like a need to you but what they themselves do not think of as a need. For example: "That resort didn't have much for kids to do." Or: "The restaurants in that hotel were not great." These are simply statements of fact, not needs. They do not express a desire to take any action based on these facts. Unless you discovered that having things for kids to do or a nice restaurant is important to them in purchasing, these are statements of fact not needs.

To build toward a sale, you must ask questions to get prospective owners to recognize both their own needs and how purchasing your product would meet those needs.

Prospective owners don't purchase your product on the basis of facts alone. The decision to purchase always has an emotional component, and it helps to gain insight into the prospective owner's feelings about your product. These feelings may be as straightforward as the desire for comfort and relaxation or as complicated as the need to refresh a marriage or reconnect with family. If you recognize such feelings, you'll be better able to show how your product meets the prospective owner's most important needs.

Seek the Need Behind the Need

The first need prospective owners express in response to a question from you can be called the presenting need. Sometimes prospective owners express this need in a straightforward, clear, and complete way.

> ## NEED
>
> *We like to vacation with our grandchildren.*

At other times, you may sense that behind the presenting need lies another one, not yet stated. Often, the unstated need is the more emotional and important one. If you can meet the emotional need in addition to the presenting need, your case will be much stronger. Besides, if you cannot meet the presenting need, you may be able to meet the hidden emotional need and thus offer an important benefit.

For example, a prospective owner might say, "We like to vacation with our grandchildren."

Perhaps your follow-up questions to this statement will uncover a related but different need. The prospective owners are from Chicago. Their son and daughter-in-law are both in graduate school in California and have little time for vacations. The prospective owners want to visit California and take the grandchildren for a week or two at a time, but they also want some free time for golf and tennis while they spend time with the grandchildren. If your product offers golf and tennis in California, you have discovered a hidden need behind spending time with the grandchildren that will help in converting a lead to a sale.

As another example, say the prospective owners tell you they really need "flexibility" in a second home purchase. What does that mean? Flexibility in timing? In types of homes? In choice of locations? You must explore to find out the need behind this presenting need before you can tailor your presentation to show how exactly your product can provide "flexibility."

Recognize Essential and Incidental Needs

Many needs prospective owners express are actually desires for specific features they want in your product. In this example we will use a second-home purchase. The needs below may become decision criteria needs, and they may include:

◆ Room size/comfort	◆ Price
◆ Beautiful facilities/décor	◆ Nearby attractions and activities
◆ Distinctive cuisine	◆ Flexibility
◆ Spa and exercise facilities	◆ Size of second home
◆ Sports facilities—golf, tennis, etc.	◆ Services—housekeeping, room service, etc.

It's important to learn the prospective owner's decision criteria needs. These are what we call "essential needs." Your product must be able to satisfy these essential needs for you to convert a lead to a sale. After the discovery you must focus your product presentation on the most relevant features, advantages, and benefits that speak to your prospective owner's essential needs—if you want to convert more of your leads to sales.

That means you need to understand how prospective owners rank their decision criteria needs. Some are essential whereas others are incidental, the "nice-to-haves" that are not absolutely necessary to a purchasing decision.

Less experienced sales agents may consider all criteria needs equally important, but more skillful agents ferret out the essential

needs and focus intensively on those. You can clarify the importance of these needs in your discovery by simply working with
clients to rank needs. This step is critically important to you as a
sales agent and to your prospective owner. Just get a pencil and a
piece of paper and write down something that looks like this:

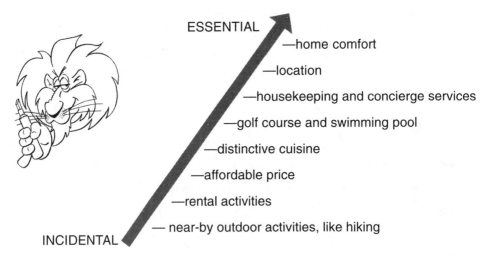

ESSENTIAL
—home comfort
—location
—housekeeping and concierge services
—golf course and swimming pool
—distinctive cuisine
—affordable price
—rental activities
— near-by outdoor activities, like hiking
INCIDENTAL

What we learn from this process is that prospective owners'
needs are not all the same. Some needs are essential, and you
must deal with those, but others are not deal breakers or deal
makers. Don't assume anything when it comes to discovering needs.
Find out which needs are essential and which are "nice-to-have"
but incidental.

A few sample questions aimed at helping prospective owners
rank their needs include:

1. Let's rank your specific second-home needs in the order of
   most to least important to you.

2. What are the most important factors to you in choosing a second home?

3. How important is having full spa facilities?

4. How important is rental activity for your second home?

Ask Discovery Questions

So far, we have been concentrating on the "how" of discovery (open and closed questions) and on the "why" of the critical importance of understanding needs. Now let's think about the "what," such as what specific questions will help you uncover the needs that will move prospective owners closer to becoming owners.

As you gain experience, you'll develop your own variations on these questions to elicit the information you need. When developing your own discovery questions, make sure you can answer these basic questions:

1. Why are you asking this question?

2. What is the information you are looking for?

3. How will you use the answer?

Remember that the questions you develop are only the beginning of the dialogue. Every prospective owner will answer questions differently, so your follow-up questions should always be tailored to the prospective owner's answers. Make sure when you ask a question that you know what you are looking for, and keep asking the appropriate questions until you get that information. In most cases you will probably be trying to discover the needs of your prospective owner and then determining whether those needs are essential or incidental needs.

Before you start asking questions, always ask permission. Your intent statement may end with asking permission to conduct the discovery. If it doesn't, be sure to "ask before asking." For example, "Would it be all right if I asked you a few questions? They'll help me focus our time together on things that are important to you and your family."

Discovery Questions

Below are some discovery questions we used in selling the second-home real estate product at the St. Regis New York. You will have to modify these questions to suit your product. Just be sure you have rehearsed the questions and carefully considered the data you are looking for in response to the questions well in advance of the presentation.

1. What kind of second-home experience do you really enjoy?

2. What do you use your second home for? Getaways? Vacations?

3. Over time, do you plan to increase the number of getaways and vacations you take annually?

4. Why are getaways and vacations important to you?

5. How do you feel when you don't get away or vacation?

6. What was your most memorable second-home getaway or vacation experience ever? And why?

7. Describe your ultimate dream second-home.

8. What other areas would you like to explore in getaways or vacations?

9. How do you envision the changing needs of your family influencing your second-home plans in the future?

10. What concerns or questions must we satisfy today in order for you to consider second-home ownership in New York?

Our sales team spent many hours looking at each question and reviewing what data we were looking to elicit with each one that would help us discover our potential owners' needs. You will find this sales training exercise has a significant impact on your sales team's performance.

The whole idea of this discovery sequence is to ascertain your prospective owners' needs. The better you are able to do that, the better you will be at converting leads to sales. A sales team that does not spend time on the discovery process will never achieve its full potential. Sales teams that not only become experts at discovering needs for their products but also take it a step further and discover which of these needs are essential and which incidental and adjust their presentations accordingly are the true selling pros.

Key Notes for Discovery

1. Write down your discovery questions.

2. Know why you are asking each question, what information you are looking for, and what you are going to do with that information.

3. Write down two open and two closed questions that would be helpful for selling your product.

4. Make sure you know where you are with needs before you start the discovery process. Get oriented.

5. Uncover needs, then explore needs, and always look for the need behind the need.

6. Write down some examples of essential and incidental needs and review how you would act accordingly in your presentation.

7. Ask discovery questions that you have practiced so many times you know them by heart. You should be able to ask them without even looking at a list.

8. Be sure to listen actively during your discovery.

9. Always ask how your prospective owners envision using your product and what they see as its benefits.

Let's hear from our characters about the important *discovery sequence*.

Chapter 16: Discovery

Here is an action scene with the characters doing their discoveries.

Sales teams that discover the essential needs of their clients and match these to the products they are selling will enjoy big success in converting leads into sales.

Chapter 17

Product Presentation

Your choice: Do you want to tell or sell?

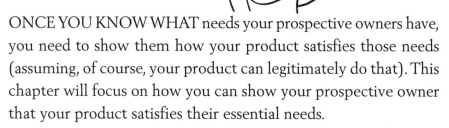

Okay, sales team, in this chapter you have a decision to make. Do you want to educate your clients or sell them your product? You cannot do both. Personally, I would like us to be selling not telling.

ONCE YOU KNOW WHAT needs your prospective owners have, you need to show them how your product satisfies those needs (assuming, of course, your product can legitimately do that). This chapter will focus on how you can show your prospective owner that your product satisfies their essential needs.

How well your product, with its features, advantages, and benefits, can truly satisfy the prospective owner's needs is the key to making a sale. You must know your prospective owner's needs; otherwise, you will not really be selling your product but merely talking about it. There is a big difference between telling and selling.

Sales agents have a choice in each presentation. Do they want to educate the prospective owner, or do they want to sell to the prospective owner? It is very difficult to do both. If you want someone to learn about your product, then go ahead and tell them all the wonderful things your product will do. But I will assure you the sales agent who does that will not be highly productive. If sales only required educating clients, then every school teacher who wanted to make some extra income would get into sales and be highly successful.

I think this distinction between telling and selling accounts for why twenty percent of sales people make eighty percent of the commissions. Most of the eighty percent of sales people who never live up to their full potential make this one big mistake: They educate their leads instead of selling them. Wherever you are in the lead generation process, you should be well aware of this important principle, because if you want to dominate in converting leads to sales, you have to have a sales team that sells, not educates.

Here is a great test to ensure your sales team is not only selling but is also getting better at selling all the time. On the lead slip that marketing turns over to sales, have the sales team fill out the sales section. Your sales team will write down the needs your prospective owner had for your product and how well your product matched those needs. You will see two different columns: one for essential needs and one for incidental needs. Any essential needs the prospective owner had that your product could or could not satisfy should to be noted on this lead slip. This is done not to keep tabs on the sales team but so the sales team really focuses on discovering needs and satisfying them instead of educating.

Sales teams, like all teams, can learn a lot from what they have done that either works or doesn't work. Think of the valuable information you can assemble if you take the essential needs of each of your prospective owners, review how well your product matched those needs, and share how your different agents presented your product based on these essential needs. Think of the productive sales team meetings you could have on this subject if you got together on a regular basis and reviewed the ideas, presentations, and scripts that other sales people have used with success to sell your product, based on essential needs that have been discovered. This exercise alone can move sales teams to the next performance level. Imagine having each sales agent report back to the entire sales team on each sale he or she has made. If all agents shared with the sales team what the essential needs their prospective owners had and how they presented their product to fully satisfy those needs, what a great meeting that would be.

I have waited until now to introduce the type of lead form I would recommend you use in your sales and marketing operation. I didn't introduce it earlier because I want you to think about this lead form as a sales tool, not as a marketing accounting tool. I want you to think of this lead form as more than a lead form for accounting and tracking lead performance; I want the sales team members to think of it as an opportunity to become better at presenting their product, which is what this chapter is all about. It provides an outstanding opportunity to learn more about sales and marketing.

Because we are focusing on sales in this chapter, we will look at the opportunities for using this lead generation document to increase the number of leads we are converting to sales.

The 𝕷ore Institute
of Shared Ownership
Lead Generation Document
Fax to 949-xxx-xxxx

MARKETING

Source _____

Name _____

Address _____ City _____

State_____ Zip _____ Phone _____

Email _____ Fax _____

Site _____

BROKER INFORMATION

Referring Real Estate Office _____

Referring Broker _____

Address _____

City _____ State_____ Zip _____

Email _____ Phone _____

Broker Client Protection Approval _____

By signing below, I give the Lore Institute permission to contact me about _____
I understand that this permission overrides my listing on any state and federal do not call list. I can opt out of future calls at any time by requesting to be placed on the company do not call list by calling xxx-xxx-xxxx.

_____
Client's Approval

SALES

Sales Agent Assisted to: _____

Essential Needs:	*Product Match:*
1. _____	1. _____
2. _____	2. _____
3. _____	3. _____
4. _____	4. _____

Incidental Needs:	*Product Match:*
1. _____	1. _____
2. _____	2. _____
3. _____	3. _____

From a sales standpoint this lead generation document can be used to do the following:

1. Record clients' essential needs and how you can match these to your product

2. Record clients' incidental needs and how you can match these to your product

3. Improve sales agents' performance in their discovery and product presentation sequences

4. Review what happened in the discovery and product presentation steps of each sale

5. Train all sales agents on these important subjects

6. Share valuable practices at your sales meetings or huddles

7. Further develop your training for new sales agents so they can have very strong discovery and product presentation sequences

We have not yet taken the product you are selling into account. That's fine, because you should complete your greeting, intent statement, and discovery before you get to your actual product presentation. Some sales people introduce the product sooner, but they are probably not your top performers. In this chapter we will start to focus on your product, especially how it integrates with your prospective owners' lifestyles and essential needs. You will focus on key features, advantages, and benefits of your product that can be used to demonstrate how your product can meet the essential needs of your clients. Presenting product features, advantages, and benefits correctly can make your sales team very effective in terms of converting leads to sales.

Relationship building and the intent statement will consume about twenty percent of the total time of a normal presentation. That means one fifth of your time is "officially" spent building rapport, establishing trust, putting the prospective owner at ease about the presentation, and making him or her feel comfortable with you. Discovery accounts for approximately thirty percent of a standard presentation, as you pose questions, listen carefully, try to identify the prospective owner's essential and incidental needs, and target product features, advantages, and benefits to focus on in the remainder of the presentation.

Thus, fifty percent of your presentation time should be spent before you start "selling" your product. Countless hours should have been invested by your sales agents off the field practicing the best techniques for building relationships and properly executing the warm-up, greeting, intent statement, and discovery. Only after you have completed these sequences can you focus your product presentation on what is truly meaningful to the prospective owner. The question that sales agents need to ask themselves for their own personal growth is this: How much time should I spend with prospective owners before I start my product presentation?

In the real world a client may ask you a question right at the beginning of your interaction about your product. He or she may ask what it costs or how it works or how big it is. So you should answer these questions the best you can—but keep in mind you are educating your clients when you answer these questions. You are not, at this point, doing your product presentation, which is a selling rather than an educational process. So when you are asked a question by your prospective owner, you may have to do some educating. Just make sure such a question does not lead you to launch into your product presentation.

Your actual product presentation should not start until you have completed your warm-up, greeting, intent statement, and discovery process.

I cannot begin to tell you how many times I have seen sales agents delivering their entire product presentations right when they first meet clients. Agents become so excited about their products that they begin to present way too early. If you do this, just remember you have decided for whatever reason that you will be an educator for this presentation. If you are educating, you are clearly not selling.

Let's assume you have done a good warm-up, greeting, intent statement, and discovery. Now you are ready to start your product presentation.

The process of presenting your product begins with a brief overview of your company and its history and the story of your product. You want to highlight the value and stability of your company along with the popularity and competitive advantage of your product.

The product presentation continues as you explain how your product is sold and how it works. At the end of your presentation you should strive to create a sense of urgency about the product and taking action on it in a reasonable timeframe. At every step, the success of the product presentation depends on your understanding of the prospective owner's needs and your ability to connect the features, advantages, and benefits of your product to the essential needs you have discovered.

Revisit Essential Needs from Discovery

As mentioned before, the foundation of the product presentation is the discovery sequence, during which you learn the prospective owner's essential needs. At that point you should start identifying relevant features, advantages, and benefits of your product to focus on. That means you must be as sure as possible that you have done a thorough discovery and have clearly identified the prospective owner's essential needs.

Before starting the product presentation, do a quick mental inventory of what you have learned in the discovery sequence or check your notes. You may feel you have not yet uncovered all your client's needs. Maybe you missed some hidden needs or did not explore a need in enough depth. If so, do not hesitate to ask a few more questions before continuing. You can do this "gracefully" by positioning your questions. Say something like, "Mr. and Mrs. Smith, I've been thinking about what you said a few minutes ago, and there are a few more things I'd like to ask you before we continue. Would that be all right with you?"

Then ask your questions, note the responses, discover any additional needs your client may have, and move on to the product presentation.

Of course, questioning does not end with the discovery sequence. In the course of discussing features, advantages, and related benefits, you will have many opportunities to confirm, clarify, or deepen your understanding of prospective owners' needs. Such questions help you continually sharpen your presentation focus. They are also useful for helping prospective owners see how your product's benefits meet their needs.

Turn Features and Advantages into Benefits

As you discover your prospective owners' needs, you should try to connect them with a feature or advantage of your product. During the product presentation and the sequences after it, when you focus on these features and advantages, it is essential to present them in terms of the benefits they provide that match client needs. Benefits let prospective owners know how they will feel when they use your product and how it will satisfy their needs. Always emphasize benefits that address needs. This strategy is one of the keys to sales success.

It's important to understand the differences between a feature, an advantage, and a benefit. An example should help clarify these differences. In our example we will use an ocean-front second-home real estate product. You should be able to discern how these categories apply to whatever product or service you are offering.

A *feature* is a characteristic of, or fact about, a product or service. For example, the ocean-front second home has four thousand square feet of living space, with an additional fifteen hundred square feet of outdoor living balcony space. The color of the house is tan. During a presentation, focus on features is a matter of educating rather than selling.

An *advantage* is how your product features stack up favorably against the competition in the marketplace. For example, the four-thousand-square-foot second home with the fifteen hundred square feet of outside balcony may represent the largest outdoor living space in the market. If you offer the only product with this exceptional outdoor living opportunity, that is your advantage in the marketplace. This feature with its advantage attached may separate your product from the competition, but focus on advantages is still a matter of education—unless the size of the balcony is part of the essential needs you have discovered from your prospective owner.

A *benefit* is how a feature and/or an advantage satisfies a specific need a prospective owner has expressed or how the feature and advantage will make the prospective owner feel as an owner of the product. For example, let's say you discovered your prospective owners have two children they bring along with them when they are using their second home so they can spend quality time together as a family.

The benefit of having a four-thousand-square-foot second home is that there is enough room for everyone in this family to relax in the home. Each family member will have a separate room, and if the children or the owners want to bring friends along, too, there is plenty of room in the home. Also, as the children grow up, the need for their own separate space becomes even more important.

On top of that, there is an additional fifteen hundred square feet of living space, offered exclusively by this product, where the entire family and friends together will have plenty of room to enjoy an exceptional outside living experience. The entire family along with friends could enjoy a barbeque out on the balcony with spectacular views of the ocean. Priceless memories and experiences would be remembered forever by your friends and family. This could be the real selling benefit.

Features and advantages are *product-centered*. Benefits are *owner-centered*. You should aim your presentation directly at the prospective owner's essential needs, which means focusing on benefits. Benefits will affect the way your prospective owner thinks, acts, and feels about owning your product.

A benefit is not a benefit unless it satisfies a need, meets a decision criterion, or solves a problem that's important to specific prospective owners. An ocean-front second home would probably not be a benefit to a couple who did not like the idea of being close to the ocean.

Features and advantages are mere facts unless you turn them into benefits that will make your prospective buyer think, feel, and act in a different way with respect to your product. Focus on benefits and then see how your prospective owners perceive them. Let them tell you how they feel after your benefits presentation.

Use questions to confirm, clarify, or deepen your understanding of prospective owners' needs. For example:

- "Mr. and Mrs. Smith, you mentioned earlier that use of the second home is important to you and that any second home ownership program you purchase would have to include certain activities for you and your family. Can you tell me more about this need for you?

- "Mr. and Mrs. Smith, you told me you would sometimes use your second home with your entire family, sometimes with friends as well, and at other times it might just be the two of you. Could you say a little more about how all that affects your choice of residences?"

- *Use the language of benefits* to link the features and advantages of your program to the prospective owner's important needs. Use verbs to show how features and advantages provide benefits that meet the prospective owner's needs or solve problems. Effective verbs include:
  1. Saves
  2. Assures
  3. Provides

Focus only on benefits related to needs or problems your prospective owners have stated and you have explored. Use language your prospective owner understands. Industry jargon and abbreviations unfamiliar to the client do not communicate the benefits of your product. Besides, using language prospective owners don't understand is impolite and does not provide the experience in the presentation you need to deliver.

Here's an example of benefits expressed in effective language:

"By purchasing this second home, you can enjoy the company of all your family and friends during your vacation experience both inside and outside this beautiful home. That ensures these special experiences will provide lifelong memories in this perfect vacation location, just as you told me you wanted."

Check the prospective owner's reaction once you've discussed a benefit. Checking your prospective owner's reactions helps you:

1. Test your understanding and make adjustments if necessary

2. Move directly to resolving concerns if there are any

3. Ask for prospective owner commitment if no concerns arise

How can you check the client's reaction without sounding pushy? Tie your question to the benefits the client wants, as in these examples:

"How does our second-home value fit in with your desire to spend more time with your friends and family?"

"Does the size of the residence meet your second-home needs?"

When you discuss features and advantages of your product, put yourself in the prospective owner's shoes and ask yourself, "So what does that mean to me?" The answer will be a benefit, and making it clear will help you build your successful presentation.

Prospective Owners' Time Constraints

All of this sounds great if you can get the time to deliver your presentation, but what do you do if the prospective owner has no time? With high-end customers, in particular, finding time may prove difficult. If time is an issue, the goal should be to earn the right with your selling skills to book another appointment for a presentation when the prospective owner has more time. Here is a way this can be accomplished:

Face-to-Face Presentations

Front Desk: Hi. We have guests out front here who would like to get some information but only have a few minutes. Their names are Mr. and Mrs. Smith.

Sales: Hello, Mr. and Mrs. Smith. My name is John. How are you both today?

Guests: We're fine. We heard you are building some second homes here, and we wanted to get some information about it, but we only have a few minutes since we have a tee time we need to make. Can you just give us a brochure?

Sales: I'd be happy to. When is your tee time?

Guests: In ten minutes.

Sales: No problem. I'll keep you on schedule. Let me notify my front desk so they can prepare a brochure for you. While they do that, if you'd allow me just five minutes, I'll give you a brief overview of why so many guests like yourself have taken the time while they are here to visit with us to learn about some of the unique features of our ownership plan. How does that sound?

Guests: Sounds fine.

Sales: Where do you both call home?

Guests: California.

Sales: Is this your first visit here, or do you come often?

Guests: We come a few times per year.

Sales: Do you already own a home here, or do you typically rent accommodations when you visit?

Guests: We stay here at the hotel.

Sales: What specifically keeps you coming back?

Guests: We love the weather and the golf courses.

Sales: You're not alone. With guests like you in mind, we have developed a real estate ownership plan that has all the features and advantages of second-home ownership without many of the concerns and headaches. We've discovered that many of the guests like yourselves reside out of state, so we've created an ownership plan that caters directly to you. Sound like something that may interest you?

Guests: Maybe.

Sales: Great. Well, I promised to keep you on schedule. Why don't we plan on spending a little more time together while you're here on-site to give you a complete overview of what we are developing here as well as to allow you both to take a look at our homes first hand? If you are like most guests, we'll spend about thirty minutes or so, depending on your interest, of course. If that sounds good to you, I have a couple of time options. How about just before dinner this evening or just after breakfast tomorrow?

Guests: Late this afternoon would work. We'll plan on coming back at 4:30.

Sales: Great. My contact info is here in the brochure. I look forward to seeing you this evening. If for some reason I get delayed, what is the best number I can reach you at?

Guests: My cell: XXX-XXX-XXXX.

Sales: Enjoy your golf.

Here is a second time constraint you may have to deal with. The prospective owner says, "We are leaving today and cannot come back. We just want to get the info, and if we're interested, we'll call you."

Sales: No problem. Most of our guests learn about us from our national advertising or from referral, and more than 70 percent of my owners I have not met face to face yet, since we did most everything over the phone and by email. Having stopped in today, you're ahead of the game. The brochure provides a solid foundation of basic info. What we can do as a next step is schedule a phone call together after you return home and review the brochure. You can let me know then what questions you might have. From there, I can fill in the blanks for you. If that works for you, I would be happy to call you at either your work or at home. Which would you prefer?

Guest: Work.

Sales: What are your work number and your email address? I'd like to send you some additional pieces of info not in the brochure for you to review.

Guest: XXX-XXX-XXXX and XXXXX@XXXXXX.com.

Sales: Thanks. I'll send the email to you today so it will be there when you return to work, and we'll touch base this week after your return to schedule a time to talk more. Thanks for visiting.

If you hear that a prospective owner just wants information and will call you if interested, then I'd recommend responding as follows:

Sales: Sure, that's why we created this brochure piece, but as you can imagine it really only scratches the surface. What I have found works best is for you to take this information and see if it piques your interest further. If you're like most guests, it will. You'll have a ton of questions—most importantly, how much does it cost. What I suggest is after you return home we can schedule a brief fifteen-minute call to review and make certain you have all the basic information to decide whether to pursue it further. I would hate for you to make a choice based on partial information. If that works for you, I'd be happy to call you at either your work or at home. Which would you prefer?

Guest: Work.

Sales: What is your work number and your email address? I'd like to send you some additional pieces of info not in the brochure for you to review.

Guest: XXX-XXX-XXXX and XXXXX@XXXXXX.com.

Sales: Thanks. I'll send the email to you today so it will be there when you return, and we'll touch base this week after your return to schedule a time to talk more. Thanks for visiting.

Time constraints are sometimes very legitimate objections and other times express the fact that your prospective owner is just not interested. You need to understand which is the situation with your prospective buyer. If the person is interested and just has legitimate time constraints, then the examples above should work well for setting up a strong follow-up program.

If the prospective owner is really not interested he or she will probably not accept a call from you in response to your entreaties. That is okay. At least you found out the person is not interested. The key is to assume everyone is interested and act accordingly until the prospective owner tells you something different.

The Key Steps of a Product Presentation

1. Company overview—emphasize the stability and commitment of your company

2. Product history as it relates to your industry—emphasize the stability and commitment of the industry

3. Product history as it relates to your company—emphasize the stability and commitment of your company to your product

4. Product Presentation—how your product works—features, advantages, and benefits tied to the discovery

5. Start to create urgency

6. Trial closing

Remember that the focus of your presentation must always be on the prospective owner's needs and interests. If any of the topics covered in steps 1 through 6 do not interest the prospective owners or relate to essential needs they have expressed, do not present the information or cover it quickly, without much detail. It makes sense, however, that everyone who purchases any product wants to feel that the product has good present and future value. That is why we recommend you make questions one to three standard in all presentations. Let's assume that value of some sort is an essential ingredient in all purchases.

The following is an example of a product presentation I used when I was working with Starwood in 2003, selling the company's fractional ownership private residence clubs. It will give you an overview of each of the six key steps of the product presentation. By reading this example, you will see how I set up my cue cards to present each of the steps in my product presentation. That will give you some guidelines for preparing the steps in your own product presentation. Then you can develop your own presentation, based on the product you are selling, and practice delivering it until it feels natural. As you gain experience, add to the content, hone the language to your own style, and change the emphasis to suit specific prospective owners you're working with.

Step 1: Company Overview

The Starwood Story

Starwood is one of the largest hospitably companies in the world, one of the largest owners of hospitality real estate in the world, and one of the largest and most successful hotel companies in the world. Those achievements are remarkable for a company that began in 1996. Here is the history of this exciting company:

- In 1996 Starwood purchased a few luxury hotels and started the Luxury Brand collection of high-end hotels.
- In September of 1997 Starwood purchased Westin Hotels for $1.8 billion. Westin had become a leader in its segment under the Starwood leadership with the introduction of the Heavenly Bed® and the first non-smoking hotel in the world.
- In October 1997 Starwood purchased ITT Sheraton Hotels for $14.8 billion. Sheraton had the largest number of hotels in the Starwood portfolio, with some of these hotels being one-of-a-kind luxury resorts in Europe.
- In February 1998 Starwood purchased St. Regis Hotels.
- In December of 1998 Starwood opened the first brand that it had created from scratch, the "W" hotel in New York City. This brand has become one of the most successful in hotel history because of the unique experiences and design that Starwood created.

- In July of 2002 Starwood created The Starwood Preferred Guest Program, which won the coveted Freddie Award for the best award redemption program in America and internationally. Starwood has won this award five years in a row.

- In January of 2003 Starwood opened its first residence club, the St. Regis Aspen, an innovative sales success that was at the top of the industry.

- In 2004 Starwood created the aloft brand inspired by "W" and the element brand inspired by Westin.

- In January of 2005 Starwood opened a second residence club resort at the St. Regis New York. This was Starwood's first urban resort. It sold so well that Starwood took sixteen additional whole ownership residences it had for sale in New York and converted them into its residence club product.

- In April of 2005 Starwood purchased the Le Meridien brand.

Today, Starwood is one of the leading hotel and leisure companies in the world, with more than nine hundred properties in eighty countries and nine different brands.

With a little work, you can develop the same kind of historical narrative about your own company.

Step 2: Product History As It Relates to Your Industry

Next, you need to spend some time explaining the history of your product, which will give your potential buyers a good feeling about how well accepted it is in your industry.

To return to our example, the residence club industry is a multibillion dollar business led by a well-known group of luxury hospitality companies. The industry first gained momentum in the late 1990s and has since grown from approximately $160 million in 1999 to more than $2.1 billion in 2006. Sales of this exciting new second-home product increased by more than 200 percent from 2003–2005. This popularity was due to the fact that purchasers for the first time had a viable alternative to a traditional second home purchase.

Second-home purchasers used to say they use their second home for only seventeen days every year. The popularity of this fractional ownership product stems from the value proposition of what you pay and what you are able to use. Second-home purchasers also liked the fact that their second home with fractional ownership was fully maintained for them. This fractional real estate can be purchased in great locations and is being offered by major luxury brands offering a multitude of amenities and luxury services that enhance the second-home experience.

Step 3: Product History As It Relates to Your Company

Then spend some time explaining the competitive edge of your product. That will give your potential buyers a good feeling about the relative quality of what you're offering. It will establish another reason to purchase your product.

The following is an example of a statement about Starwood Residence Club Ownership. You can adapt it to suit your own product history as it relates to your brand.

Many people are quite surprised to learn that Starwood is in the second-home residence club business. Actually, we've been in that industry for close to eight years. For the first four, we strove to understand the industry and to perfect our second-home residence club product and concept so it would be the *best consumer product* in the industry. We call it *the perfect second home.*

In terms of the industry, we recognized that the residence club business needed a developer who would not only pay special attention to the physical quality of the product but would also offer an outstanding level of service, for added value to the real estate. Most important to Starwood was providing the best value proposition in the second-home residence club industry. Starwood's reputation as a world-class provider of luxury service and Starwood's unsurpassed family of resorts made the second-home residence club industry a great opportunity for us. We could combine our flexibility in different luxury experiences with our legendary Starwood service and be the leader in the luxury second-home residence club industry.

What we will talk about today is luxury second-home ownership by Starwood. It is truly state-of-the-art living, offering a gracious and luxurious lifestyle that exemplifies the good life. After perfecting our residence club concept, which we will talk about more in a moment, we opened our first product in Aspen, the St. Regis Residence Club, in 2003. It is absolutely gorgeous and set records as one of the fastest selling resorts of its time. We sold more than 250 residence club ownerships! Soon after Aspen opened, we opened our second residence club in New York, the St. Regis Residence Club New York on 5th and 55th. This resort has again set sales records in the industry. This second resort far exceeded all expectations for sales within our company, so much so that we converted sixteen residences that were scheduled to be sold as whole ownership into residence club products. Today we opened our third residence club resort, The Phoenician in Arizona. We also have potential plans to possibly open the St. Regis Punta Mita in Mexico and the St. Regis Bal Harbour in Miami.

As I explain the perfect second-home concept, I'm sure you will understand why it is so popular and why people who are

looking for second homes in luxury real estate markets are purchasing our product at a record pace.

Before I show you our residence club product, I would like to
introduce you to one of the fastest luxury second-home concepts
in the world today, Starwood Residence Clubs.

Step 4: Product Presentation

The key is to customize your presentation to fit the individual
needs of the customer. Review each point with prospective owners and make sure they understand the benefits of the
product to them, especially in terms of their essential
needs. At all points, keep your presentation simple to
avoid confusing your prospective owner. Visual aids
can also enhance a presentation. If you do make a presentation with some sort of brochure, be sure to know all
you tell, but do not tell all you know. Try to focus your presentation on the client's essential needs

In our Starwood presentations, we used a company-generated
tri-fold to present the product, which allowed sales agents to write
down part of their presentation next to some great pictures showing how the product worked. This tri-fold had sections in it that
highlighted the obvious benefits of the product.

The great thing about the tri-fold was that at the end of the
presentation you could give it to the prospective buyer and keep
a copy to do additional follow-ups if needed. Sales agents should
always keep a copy for their follow-up activities.

Do not give a brochure like this one to your prospective owner
until the presentation is over. You will be gaining commitment
toward a purchase as the presentation continues, and you do not
want to do anything that would indicate the client should not
purchase while he or she is there with you. Giving a brochure

away before you ask the prospective purchaser whether he or she would like to become an owner may lead the person to believe that not many people have purchased on the basis of this initial presentation. That's not the impression you want to create because you want to make a sale then and there.

If you use a tri-fold brochure or other visual aid for your presentations, keep the following in mind:

1. Keep it simple and focus on what is important to the prospective owner.

2. Remember to address any essential needs or needs behind needs that the prospective owners have expressed and you feel are relevant.

3. Get excited—deliver your presentation with passion. If you're not excited, how do you expect your prospective buyers to be?

Step 5: Start to Create Urgency

Urgency or getting your clients to take action is usually accomplished by having potential buyers feel you have satisfied their essential buying needs. When all or at least many of their needs have been satisfied, they become emotionally attached to your product and are more likely to act. There are two things you can do to create a sense of urgency. First, give your clients something special that they will view as getting more than what is normal. Second, do something that will create some fear of loss. Those things will certainly enhance a sense of urgency.

Remember to address needs and, when appropriate, needs behind needs. By this point you should have discovered needs they want satisfied and demonstrated how your product will satisfy them. Finish by asking whether prospective owners have any questions.

Step 6: Trial Closing

Once you have presented the features, advantages, and benefits of your product, it's time to "test the waters" with a trial close. For example, you might say: "Now I would like to show you the actual residence. But first, let me say that, based on what you've heard so far, it looks like you and your family could benefit from this offering. Do you agree, given what you've seen and heard so far? What parts of the offering do you like the best?"

If you take the six steps of this product presentation and mold them to fit the product you are selling, I am sure you can create a very effective presentation. Script it out, study it, practice it, tape it, and listen to it. Invest the time, training, and commitment on this part of your sales presentation, and I promise the rewards will be well worth the efforts, and you will be turning more leads into sales.

Key Notes for Product Presentation

1. Understand the difference between telling and selling.

2. Use the lead document form as a training tool for your sales team.

3. Don't start your product presentation too soon. Spend an appropriate amount of time on the initial steps—warm-up greeting, intent statement, and discovery—before you start presenting your product.

4. Know the difference between a feature, an advantage, and a benefit and how best to use them in your product presentation.

5. Keep in mind that benefits are what sell, especially if the benefits are tied to essential needs. Use verbs like "saves," "assures," and "provides" when presenting benefits.

6. Write out your product presentation and practice it until it goes smoothly and naturally.

Let's hear some tips from our characters about the *product presentation*.

Here is an action scene with our characters doing their product presentations.

Without knowing what your client's essential needs are and delivering your product to these needs, the product presentation will not reach its full potential. It's the difference between telling and selling.

Chapter 18

Product Viewing

The emotional side of ALL sales

Sales team, in this chapter I want you to focus on building an emotional connection between your product and your prospective owner.

THE PRODUCT VIEWING should be independent from the product presentation whenever possible. The product presentation is about taking the prospective owner's essential needs and explaining how your product satisfies those needs. Once that's accomplished, you'll need your prospective owner's full attention with no distractions when you are presenting the physical product. A beautiful product viewing can actually distract your prospective owner from learning how the features, advantages, and benefits of your product can satisfy his or her needs. So to maximize the conversion percentage of leads to sales, I highly recommend making the product viewing a separate event.

The product viewing is a great presentation after the prospective owner fully understands how your product satisfies his or her needs. The product viewing is the emotional side of your presentation. How your product looks, smells, and feels has everything to do with the emotional side of your selling process. Do not let the logical side of selling, which is focusing on your product's features and advantages, interfere with the emotional side of your selling. Let your prospective owner view your product without any distractions.

Because you will have gathered good information during the discovery and product presentation, you can customize your product viewing session by addressing at least two of the prospective owner's essential needs. You will find many needs related to the product are emotional, like the personal desires to own and use a beautiful, luxurious product. But your product will have many other benefits that appeal to other needs as well. Addressing your prospective owner's important needs while demonstrating the product model has a strong emotional impact, and it prepares the prospective owner to commit to owning the product.

During the product viewing, make sure you demonstrate the features, advantages, and benefits of your product in a way that involves the prospective owner's senses of sight and (if appropriate) touch, smell, taste, and/or hearing. Sensory engagement has a powerful emotional impact that will help you convert many more leads into sales.

Make sure you understand the prospective owner's needs by asking simple questions. For example, "Mr. and Mrs. Brown, you said before that you both like to cook when on vacation and especially bake. Is that correct?" If the answer is yes, get them in the kitchen and let them see each other cooking and baking in that kitchen. Let them imagine the experience. Use the language of benefits to link this feature of cooking in the kitchen to the prospective owners' important needs. Use verbs such as "saves," "provides," and "assures" to make your points. Like all other presentations in this book, it will take some time and practice to perfect your technique, but the rewards of success will be well worth the effort.

Here are the basic components of a product viewing presentation:

1. **Product knowledge**—You need to fully understand all the details pertaining to your product, including, where applicable, services, amenities, exclusivity, special attractions, and so on.

2. **Showing the product**—There needs to be someone on your team who ensures that samples or models are in perfect shape for viewing all the time.

3. **Trial closing while showing the product**—There is no better time for a trial close than when the emotional side of the sales process is peaking.

4. **Transition from product viewing to discussing pricing and terms**—While showing your product there will be an ideal time to start moving toward the next step of your presentation, which is gaining commitment. That next sequence is initiated with a simple question.

Make sure you understand how and why each of these components should be presented. Keep your product viewing presentation simple, focus on benefits that meet the prospective owners' needs, and remember to know all you tell but not to tell all you know.

Product Knowledge

It is essential to be thoroughly familiar with all aspects of your product. With that knowledge, you can focus on the features, advantages, and related benefits that interest your prospective owners and provide them with value. You'll focus on aspects of product knowledge that relate to the product's look, touch, smell, and feel. All of these are emotionally stimulating to the prospective owner.

As with all other aspects of your sales presentation, you must be scripted and practice your product viewing presentations. Make sure you are an expert when it comes to connecting your product knowledge to the prospective owner's essential needs, and only highlight features that do relate to those needs. Focus on the way your product looks, feels, and so on to stimulate the prospective owner emotionally.

Showing the Product

This should be the fun part and the emotional highpoint of the presentation. Keep in mind that there is no second chance for a first impression. Once you show your product, that part of your presentation is gone forever.

I believe you can only deliver a great first impression after you have built some kind of a sales relationship, explained how the sales process works though the intent statement, discovered the client's needs, and shown the prospective owner how your product satisfies his or her needs. At this point you have enough knowledge to show your product and make a great first impression.

Make sure your prospective owners experience what it will be like to be an owner of your product and can see their friends and family enjoying this product with them, if appropriate. If you put prospective owners in the picture, you will undoubtedly produce additional sales.

Trial Closing While Showing the Product

Here are three simple but very effective trial closing questions you can use:

1. Which of the products I have shown you so far do you believe best fits your and your family's needs?
2. What features of our product will you and your family enjoy most?
3. Based on what you have seen so far, do you believe this product is something that will benefit you and your family?

If the answer is yes to the last question, move on. If the answer is no, it is just an objection. We will review handling objections in the next chapter.

Transition from Product Viewing to Discussing Pricing and Terms

When you are done with your product viewing, say, "Let's go back to my office where we can review pricing." (Or wherever you think it would be best to review pricing.) You are now ready to move into the gaining commitment sequence.

Key Notes for Product Viewing

1. See whether you can become an expert as a sales agent, presenting the sensory attractions of your product.

2. The product viewing is all about creating emotions. If you are not excited about this part of the presentation, neither will your prospective owner be. Get excited.

3. Connect features, advantages, and benefits to sensory aspects of your product.

4. You need to write out and practice the four components of this presentation: product knowledge, showing the product, trial closing, and transition into gaining commitment.

5. Make sure that someone every day is looking at your product samples or models and making sure they are in five-diamond condition for viewing.

6. It is a great sales training exercise to get with your sales agents and review all the opportunities you have for getting prospective owners involved in the sensory aspects of your product. Be creative here.

Let's hear from our characters about *product viewing.*

Chapter 18: Product Viewing

Here is an action scene with our characters showing leads the physical product.

On top of addressing your clients' essential needs, if you can present your product so your clients feel better through touch, smell, look, and sound, you will convert many more leads into sales.

#### Chapter 19

Gaining Commitment

When you ask your clients to purchase, be well prepared for a yes or a no answer

Sales team, I want you to learn one perfect closing question and have a pre-set plan on how to handle all objections and/or questions in response to that question.

AFTER BUILDING A SALES relationship and delivering your scripted, well-rehearsed intent statement, discovery, product presentation, and product previewing, you should feel confident about asking prospective owners for their commitment. The highest form of commitment, but not the only one, is a purchasing agreement, followed by completion of the escrow agreements and closing in real estate or whatever you need to do with your product to count a sale as sales revenue for your company. Chapter 19 focuses on gaining this level of commitment. Then chapter twenty will discuss your follow-up processes and other commitments you might obtain.

Gaining commitment serves as your report card on your entire sales presentation. We understand that not everyone purchases, and not everyone should. But some sales agents gain commitment in a higher percentage of presentations than others. The sales agents with the highest closing percentages are our top paid and most productive, and every sales agent's goal should be to become part of that group.

What do top sales agents do to maintain their high closing percentages? They provide outstanding prospective owner experiences during the sales process, execute strong pre- and post-prospective owner follow-up, are committed in all the sales sequences, and have the desire to master a variety of selling techniques.

These techniques include summarizing benefits the prospective owners have accepted, agreeing on the best packaging and pricing for the prospective owner, reviewing the logical and emotional reasons to purchase, building urgency, asking the prospective owners to purchase, and resolving objections. If you do not gain commitment with these techniques, you can identify why you did not gain commitment and develop a plan of action to follow up.

There are seven steps toward gaining commitment:

1. Summarize the benefits of purchasing
2. Confirm the best package and price for the prospective owner
3. Explain the economics of price and package
4. Create product urgency
5. Ask for the purchase
6. Resolve objections
7. Complete lead documentation recap forms

Try to gain commitment in a quiet place where you can control the environment. An ideal area would be your sales office, where the tools you need to gain commitment are close at hand. In today's world, though, do not rule out over-the-phone sales.

Step One—Summarize the Benefits of Purchasing

Start moving toward commitment by summarizing the benefits the prospective owners would receive if they purchased. When you do this, be sure only to summarize benefits that relate to the prospective owner's essential needs and needs behind the needs that the prospective owners have expressed to you.

Summarizing benefits gives you an opportunity to see how the prospective owner feels about your offering and your ability to satisfy key essential buying needs. Your summary is, in fact, an effective trial close. Here is an example of how you might begin your summary:

"Mr. and Mrs. Smith, before we consider which ownership package seems best for you and your family and discuss purchase prices, let's quickly review some of the benefits that you and your family will enjoy if you own our product."

You can then reiterate the benefits, saying something like: "First, it seems to me that you and your family would enjoy [benefit]. Do you agree? Let's review why this is important to you and your family?"

If you can summarize three or four of these benefits, you will be in good shape.

Step Two—Confirm the Package and Pricing

You need to focus on two distinct considerations when presenting package and pricing options. Determine what would work best for the prospective owner, a high-range package or a middle-to low-range package.

To confirm package and pricing, start by presenting no more than two options. Doing this makes it easy for the prospective owner to choose. It is always easier for people to make a choice between two alternatives than a choice among many, but it is important, too, that customers have a choice so that they do not feel boxed in or powerless. That can happen if prospective clients have only one alternative.

If possible, the two packages and pricing options should be quite different in price. All packages must fit the prospective owner's needs. This makes the options quite different. Give the prospective owners options for their financial commitment and product type, and they will feel more comfortable making a commitment.

Then make a recommendation for one of the options and explain why you are making it. But always let prospective owners make the final decision without facing any pressure.

Here is an example of how you might confirm the package and pricing:

"Based on what you've shared with me about how you like to use our product, I think the [product package] would be best for you and your family. I will show you two options, [number one] and [number two], and I will let you choose the one that seems to meet your needs best. Then I'll show you the purchase terms on the package you choose."

Then write up two product packages, the prices, and other costs. Make sure there is a reasonable difference in price and product. You want the prospective buyer to feel good no matter which package and price he or she picks.

Take out your product materials and say something like: "Let me explain why I think this is the best ownership package for your family."

Make the explanation very simple, referring to the prospective owner's essential needs, the benefits the package offers, and why the option you recommend will satisfy the client.

Write down the packages, the price and other costs. With your product materials still out, say something like: "Let me explain why I favor option number two and think it will work well for you and your family—even though I really like option number one also." Explain why option number two is a good option for the prospective owner and why you favor option two over option number one. Then ask your prospective owner, "Which one of these would you like for me to show you our purchase terms on?"

Step Three: Explain the Economics of Price and Package

You should go through this step because it will help you gain commitment. Remember, your product sale is primarily an emotional one. People will purchase your product because it satisfies essential purchasing decision needs. Economics is on the more logical side of the sale. Most people buy for emotional reasons, but they justify why they made a purchase with logical reasons. I would not cover economics in all cases. Gauge what your clients needs are and adjust your presentation accordingly in terms of applying more logic or more emotional appeal.

Here is one of my favorite examples of a logical appeal, which we used in the fractional real estate market. Fractional ownership is sold as an alternative to second-home ownership. You should take the time to develop a logical statement like this one for your product.

"It is a fact that average second-home purchasers use their second home seventeen days a year and pay for it 365 days of the year. If you divide the number of days they use the product into the number of days they pay for the product, you get the value proposition. In this case it is a 5 percent value proposition, which means you pay for this second home all year but only use it 5 percent of the time. People spend more time thinking about the fact that they do not use their second home than they spend using their second home. Interesting, isn't it?

"A very popular alternative to purchasing a second home full-time is fractional second-home ownership. This fractional ownership program is called a smart-money purchase. It's what I call a perfect second home. Fully maintained for you, it has an average of a 60 to 90 percent use factor, which is a much better value proposition than the traditional 5 percent second-home usage. This means that because of the flexibility of the use plan this product can be used on average 75 percent of the time.

"Purchasing fractional ownership over the past years has been very popular as sales went from $160 million in 1999 to $2.1 billion in 2006."

At this point, you can review the economics of a second-home purchase, but only go there if you need to because the client wants more logic and/or value in the proposition. If not, do not go into this detail. This is your decision at this point. If your prospective owners have a second home and have expressed some concerns about its cost, present information, using figures the prospective owners themselves have supplied, if possible. I will not at this point give you an example, but I will recommend that you have prepared a simple, well-rehearsed economic presentation as well as a more detailed one, both ready to go depending on your clients' needs.

Step Four: Create Product Urgency

Now it is time to create product urgency. There are many different ways to do this, and your approach will depend on the product you are selling. Here are categories you should review. Then, with your product in mind, create your own scripted presentation for each topic.

If you want to be exceptional at creating a sense of urgency, you need to focus on special value and fear of loss. Urgency can make a big difference in terms of the amount of time it takes for your prospective owners to move ahead with their purchases. You should keep track of that time as part of your vital sales numbers. Knowing what the average time is between sales presentation dates and purchase dates will really help guide you. The shorter this time is, the more sales you will be able to make. Be careful here that you don't condense the decision-making process so much that clients feel so pressured that they do not take action. One of the best ways to reduce the amount of time it takes is to work on the urgency of your presentation. Let's review some of the tools we all have to do this.

Here are ten opportunities for creating a little more fear of loss and conveying the sense of the special opportunity. Both of these when used correctly create urgency. Always keep in mind that the longer a decision takes to be made, the more a prospective owner's regular life takes over and the more your product will start to fade from the person's consciousness.

1. First availability—The amount of inventory that is left for you to sell is sometimes a great fear-of-loss urgency tool. Mentioning how little remains will only be effective if your product provides compelling essential needs to the prospective owner.

2. Price phasing—If you have pricing that increases as you sell, this phasing can be a great tool for creating fear of loss.

3. Founder ownerships—When you first sell a new product, you may have a very special and limited opportunity for purchasers to become founding owners. This program will appeal both to a client's fear of loss and desire for special benefits.

4. Premium products that are limited—A superior product manufactured in limited quantities will likewise appeal both to a client's fear of loss and desire for special benefits.

5. Premium experiences for purchasing—If you can create a very limited experience that a prospective owner would love to have and tie it to the purchase of your product, you can again hit both urgency factors. For example: In the fractional real estate business, if your clients are golfers or spa clients, you could create their account with a one thousand dollar credit in either of these areas for use when they arrive.

6. Incentives for purchasing—This is the most commonly used means for creating urgency. An example in fractional ownership would be covering the owners' maintenance fees for the first year.

7. Special product benefits for purchasing—A big benefit that is limited to only so many buyers.

8. Liquidation—For some products you are selling, the ability to liquidate your product if and when the prospective owner wants it is an important key to making clients more comfortable about moving ahead.

9. More privileges of what they are purchasing—If you can temperately give a buyer a little more of what they are purchasing for a specific period of time, that can help create urgency, too.

10. Terms for purchasing—If you can provide some very interesting limited terms for purchasing, that can be very helpful also for your urgency proposition.

If you experiment with these ideas and see which ones work for you, you can increase your conversion of leads to sales. These sales will happen more quickly than normal, and because of this shorter period of time, you will make sales that you would have lost if the sales process had taken more time.

Step Five: Ask for the Purchase

By this point, asking for the sale should be almost automatic. Still, I have seen very good sales presentations that did not have any final closing question in them. After all the work these sales agents had done, they just did not ask the prospective owner to buy. Most of the time these were sales presentations that were ad-libbed rather than scripted and rehearsed.

Here is an example of a closing question we used at the St. Regis New York when selling both our whole and fractional real estate products:

"Let me summarize what we are talking about today. We have been discussing a lifestyle choice, not just a second or vacation home. We have been discussing St. Regis's perfect second home gracious living for successful people like you who are very particular about how they spend their time and who are seeking additional ways to access this good life.

"People purchase from us because they understand and enjoy the good life, and they see that this is the way they can own the special well-located piece of New York real estate on 5th Avenue.

This is truly a piece of the good life for their lifetime and their family's.

"Would you like to be part of the good life with us here in New York?"

Step Six: Resolve Objections

When you ask prospective clients to purchase, they can only do one of two things: purchase or object. Just remember that every objection represents an unmet need, which means each one is an opportunity to move the sale forward. If you can address the unmet need, you will be closer to a commitment.

To resolve objections, you need to:

1. Clarify the unmet need
2. Classify the objection
3. Respond appropriately

Clarify the Unmet Need

As prospective owners get close to a purchase decision, their feelings of risk may increase. They worry about the consequences of their decision. These concerns may be objections to some aspect of your product in general. Also, the concerns may be intangible worries, more like personal fears about this major decision. Whatever the objection, you must understand the unmet need behind it. Once you understand the unmet need behind the objection, you can again get back on track toward gaining commitment with your prospective owner.

To explore the unmet need, you have to:

1. Recognize the signs
2. Confirm the objection
3. Clarify the unmet need

You need to be able to recognize the signs. Sometimes prospective owners state objections directly, and you can immediately begin exploring the unmet needs behind them. At other times, prospective owners don't clearly express their objections, but the concerns remain under the surface, undermining the sale. You must recognize that an objection is lingering, try to bring it to the surface, and explore it before the sale can move forward.

How can you tell if prospective owners have unspoken objections? Be aware if, at any point during the presentation, a prospective owner:

1. Questions everything you say

2. Holds unrealistic views on such issues as price, terms, privileges, and so on

3. Keeps bringing up issues that have already been discussed and that you think are settled

4. Is argumentative or passively resistant

5. Hesitates or is reluctant to respond to a trial close or your closing statement

At any time during a presentation when you suspect a concern has arisen, the best thing to do is just ask the prospective owner. Ask in a non-threatening way and don't use loaded words like "worried" or "fearful" but instead choose neutral words. For example:

1. "Is there something you're uncertain about here?"

2. "Do you have any questions that we haven't addressed yet?"

3. "How will your children feel about this?"

In addition, you should ask about objections or concerns when you are getting close to asking for commitment. For example:

1. "Do you have any concerns at all about the program we've been discussing?"

2. "Is there anything that might cause you or your family to be hesitant about ownership?"

By asking such questions when you sense a hidden concern or as you near closing, you can get a reading of where things stand. It is important that you understand at this point how close your prospective owners are to purchasing. You need to understand how much additional work needs to be done so that these prospective owners can be comfortable in making their decisions. You need to uncover hidden objections and immediately address them.

Once you suspect an unspoken objection, ask confirming questions to verify that your impression is correct. For example:

1. "I have the impression that you have some hesitation about owning with us. Am I right?"

2. "You had expressed some uncertainty about whether our program is flexible enough to meet your needs. Do you still feel that way?"

Understanding an objection and the need behind it enables you to handle it appropriately. More importantly, taking time to hear the prospective owner's concerns demonstrates your owner-centered approach.

Classify the Objection

Once you have explored the need behind an objection, the next step is to identify the precise type of objection. Identifying the objection will let you know how to handle it. We'll look at four types of objections:

1. Doubt

2. Misunderstanding

3. Drawback

4. Hidden obstacle

Doubt—Prospective owners may be skeptical about any benefit you offer. This attitude of doubt does not mean that the prospective owner thinks you're being untruthful or deliberately exaggerating. Rather, doubt is part of many people's approach to buying anything. Skeptical prospective owners, for the most part, are simply being good consumers.

Here are examples of statements indicating prospective owner doubt:

1. "Really? We'd save that much? That seems like a very high figure."

2. "I find it hard to believe that we'd really get all the services you've described for that price."

Misunderstanding—Prospective owners often raise objections that are based on misunderstandings. They believe we cannot meet an important need when, in fact, we can. A misunderstanding convinces prospective owners, wrongly, that your product cannot provide something they need.

Here are examples of misunderstandings that arise in the fractional real estate business:

1. "I will be completely dependent on a reservation agent or system."

2. "We don't want to be locked into a second home at the same location every year."

In these cases, you just need to present the facts to counter the objection.

Drawback—Unlike the previous two, these objections are based on facts. In other words, they are true drawbacks. For instance, your product might not be able to meet one of the prospective owner's important needs.

Drawbacks might sound like this:

1. "This simply does not make financial sense for us right now."
2. "Frankly, we do not like the way your product works. It is too restrictive for our family."

Hidden obstacle—When prospective owners reject your closing question, the problem may be none of the objections discussed above. Instead, prospective owners may have a hidden obstacle that only surfaces late in the sale, such as marital problems, financial concerns, or job insecurity. Perhaps the client has seemed interested just to be polite but actually prefers other options.

Hidden obstacles might sound like this:

1. "That's interesting. But frankly, we're just not ready to make a decision."
2. "Thanks for the presentation. But we need to talk about this with our lawyer."

How can you deal with these unexpected roadblocks? The best strategy is to avoid them by asking good, focused questions up front. Learn as much as possible about clients and their preferences and needs so that you won't be "blindsided" at the last minute.

If an obstacle does take you by surprise, your best approach is a direct one. Ask the prospective owner what it will take to get him or her to choose in favor of your product. Then do whatever it takes, so long as it's consistent with your standards and policies.

Respond Appropriately

Throughout the presentation, you have built rapport and mutual respect. You need to create a perfect atmosphere in which to resolve objections and even capitalize on them by showing how your product can meet underlying needs.

If you cannot meet these needs, your skill in responding to objections will still help you maintain rapport and continue to build good will for your company and product. And you'll keep the door open for possible interest in the future.

To respond appropriately to objections:

1. Choose the appropriate strategy
2. Check for acceptance

First, demonstrate respect for your prospective owner. When you uncover an objection, it's tempting to jump right in and "fix it." Only the prospective owner, though, can truly resolve an objection. The prospective owner owns the concern, and only he or she can let go of it. To show that you respect and value prospective owners, do not prescribe what the prospective owners should do. Prescribing is controlling, and it raises the prospective owner's resistance. Do not pressure a prospective owner to make a decision. Trying to force a decision heightens anxieties and can push a person into not buying. Do not argue with prospective owners. It goes without saying that even when you know prospective owners are completely wrong, you must be very respectful when correcting them.

Inexperienced sales agents may respond to objections in these ways in hopes of getting prospective owners to move forward, but these strategies seldom work and often backfire. Sometimes a prospective owner may cave in and make the decision the sales person seeks. But bad feelings remain, and if anything should go wrong, the sales person will be blamed. These tactics clearly do not fit in with the experience we want our prospective owners to enjoy throughout the sales process.

Choose the Appropriate Strategy

Each type of objection calls for a somewhat different response, and each response enables you to demonstrate respect for the prospective owner, respond to an objection without arguing, and still handle the objection.

In the case of doubt, provide information and proof. It is usually fairly easy to resolve doubt about your product. You can explain verbally and demonstrate how your product can meet the need behind the prospective owner's objection. Some prospective owners, however, may not be satisfied with verbal explanations. Provide proof, in the form of brochures, articles, fact sheets, testimonials from owners, or anything else that supports what you are saying.

For misunderstandings, provide information to clear up the prospective owner's faulty impression. It is often effective to offer proof in this instance, too.

For drawbacks, first understand the needs that your product cannot meet and then deal with the situation. You can outweigh drawbacks by citing your product's benefits without arguing. Remind the prospective owner of needs you've discussed that your product does meet. You may also be able to uncover needs you haven't discussed before and address them with benefits your product can provide. Then remind the prospective owners of all these benefits and suggest they outweigh the fact that your product cannot meet just one need. Lastly, you may be able to get the prospective owner to re-define a need or criterion to better suit the strengths of your product.

Check for acceptance—When you've addressed an objection, check that the prospective owners have accepted what you've said and that the objection has been resolved.

For example, you might say:

1. "How does your family feel about the world-class experiences offered through our product?"
2. "Does that make sense now?"
3. "Do you still have any concerns about our ability to do that?"

If the objection has been resolved, then you can continue with the sales process. If some objection remains, you can involve the prospective owner in a discussion about how to resolve it. The prospective owner might be able to suggest a simple way to approach the objections. For example, you might say:

1. "What would it take to set your mind at rest on this?"
2. "How could we eliminate these doubts?"

At the end of this gaining commitment sequence you should record your data on your lead documentation form. You will use this for follow-up and put it in whatever lead accounting and performance reports you have within your organization.

As you can see, gaining commitment, like all other sales sequences we have covered, requires sales skill but most of all practice, desire, and commitment on the part of sales agents. My experience tells me that one in five sales agents will follow through with what it takes to be the best of the best. If you are that one in five, the time spent will be well worth the accomplishments you will be able to achieve.

Gaining commitment is your report card sequence on your sales presentation. Extra time spent covering the areas mentioned in this chapter will help you understand where your sales presentation performance is currently and where you need to improve. If you follow this improvement process, you will be able to convert more leads into sales.

Key Notes for Gaining Commitment

1. Follow the seven steps for gaining commitment.

2. Write down, practice, and make sure you are comfortable delivering your final closing question.

3. During the gaining commitment sequence, try to give your prospective owner more than one choice to pick from.

4. Try to create a sense of urgency in your gaining commitment presentation.

5. Resolve objections and address unmet needs. To be the best you can be in gaining commitment, you need to be well-rehearsed and schooled in handling all prospective clients' objections.

Let's hear from our characters about *gaining commitment.*

Chapter 19: Gaining Commitment

Here is an action scene with our characters gaining commitments with their products.

Gaining commitment means summarizing your potential owner's essential needs, asking them to purchase, and being world-class at handling all objections.

Chapter 20

Sales Lead Follow-up

Research shows that 80% of the leads companies generate are not followed up on effectively

MAKE NO MISTAKE: YOU cannot succeed in lead production without great follow-up processes and execution of these processes. For successful sales lead follow-up performance, you need people, processes, systems, training, a follow-up review, sales materials, and performance reports.

In my experience, sales lead follow-up is the area that can most often be improved in sales and marketing operations. Research shows that sales agents can fail to follow up effectively on upward of eighty percent of the leads they get—an astounding figure if it's even close to being accurate.

Some of your biggest lead conversion to sales production gains will likely come through improving follow-up processes. If you and your sales and marketing team put the following ideas into action, I promise that you will have a much more efficient conversion of leads to sales. Let's face it: What good is it to be effective in lead generation programs if you are not equally effective in converting the leads you generate into sales?

The question you should ask yourself is: How many of your potential prospects purchase after the very first conversation and/or presentation and how many purchase after subsequent conversations and/or presentations? The answers will help you gauge the importance of sales lead follow-up.

Here are the people you need for lead follow-up:

Lead Support People—The Lead Bank Team

First, you need a small dedicated team of professionals who account for your leads by marketing channel, account for the lead cost per marketing channel, provide sales volume per lead by marketing channel and by sales agent, provide timely lead information updates, and accurately deliver performance reports on all leads. The group providing all this information is what I call the lead bank team. You cannot dominate your market without these systems and this team in place. In fact, I will be so bold to say that you cannot survive or at least live up to your true potential without a good lead accounting system and process in place. This lead team must be able to provide vital sales metrics, updated daily, weekly, monthly, quarterly, and annually, on all leads. These statistics need to be tracked on all three lead categories:

assigned, unassigned, and unregistered. We will cover each of these in a minute.

The lead bank makes sure that guidelines for what you call a lead are followed and accounted for. Earlier in the book we had recommended that the sales and marketing teams along with leadership agree as to what an assignable lead is. The lead bank enforces this agreement, keeps track of the number of leads in each category, and starts the conversation with sales and marketing about what strategies to adopt with respect to each category.

The lead bank also makes sure that every assignable lead has sales agents assigned to it and that each lead assigned to a sales agent falls into one of three categories: sold, not interested, or in progress. The lead bank then works very closely with the sales teams to make sure every lead in progress is updated once a week in the system. This is very important as you will discover that people may not do what's expected but they will do what's inspected. If you inspect your leads once a week, you will get more and better follow-up on your leads overall.

Whether you are processing leads for one sales agent or one hundred, it does not matter. You need to have these processes and systems in play. Otherwise, the large amounts of money you spend generating leads will be wasted. Think again about full articles that have been written saying that 80 percent of the leads you generate are not followed up on effectively.

If you need help putting these processes and systems in play or would like to have your current system reviewed for its effectiveness, please contact us at leaddomination@loreinstitue.com. We would be happy to see whether we can help you create highly effective lead accounting and reporting systems.

In figure 20-1 you can see the cycle of leads as they flow around the lead bank. The lead bank is not only in the middle of all these processes but for the most part controls them, ensures consistency, handles accounting, and reports on all the processes.

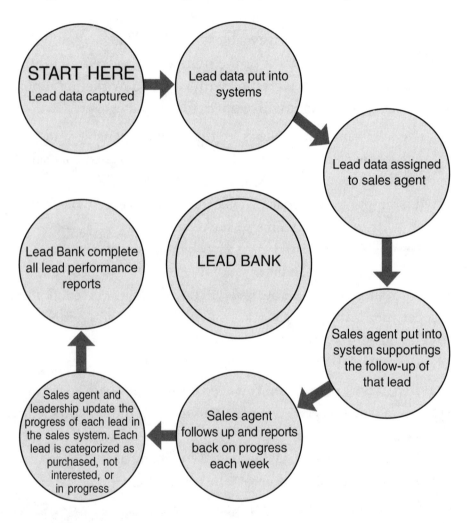

Figure 20-1

Lead Support People—On-site Administration

If you have multiple sites operating and receiving leads, you will probably need an on-site administrator to help account for leads generated. Also, if leads need to get to your sales team as soon as possible, it is good to have this administrator on-site. An on-site administrator is particularly important if you are receiving lead information from different time zones. The on-site administrator reports to the lead bank on all lead activity, and together they reconcile the lead count and distribution reports at the end of each day. If you do not have multiple sites receiving leads, then the lead bank might be able to perform all these tasks.

Lead Support People—Director of Sales

Depending on your budget parameters, you may have a director of sales as part of your lead follow-up team. This director will have a team of sales agents who report to him or her. The director's role is to help sales agents with all of their leads in progress. Each and every lead that has been generated should be contacted and updated at least once a week. If you have a director of sales, this job is one of the person's major responsibilities. The director should provide support and direction and make sure each and every lead is being followed up on. In addition, the director ensures that the quality of follow-up on every lead is such as to create the best opportunity for converting the lead into a sale.

Lead Support People—Sales Agents

Finally, your sales agents themselves play an important part in the follow-up process. Effective selling usually involves outstanding follow-up. Here are the responsibilities of a sales agent in the lead follow-up process:

1. Sales agents must be trained in their sales follow-up process. Your lead processes must be written down, simple to understand, and followed carefully. They also must be productive; if they aren't, they need to be evaluated and revised.

2. Sales agents must be fully trained on the software or whatever you are using to account and update the progress of each assigned lead. This software program should be something that helps sales agents with their follow-up organization, which supports converting leads to sales. The software should be easy to use, and you should have a trainer who not only trains but can give guidance to your agents. If you need help, let us know by emailing us at leaddomination@loreinstitue.com.

3. Sales agents must have a lead software support staff to provide support, answer questions, and make sure that the software is functioning correctly.

4. Sales agents should have someone to ensure that each assignable lead is tracked and updated each week in the software system. But remember sales agents are doing the follow-up.

5. Sales agents must agree to and sign off on the definition of an assignable lead. It is important that sales, marketing, and leadership are on the same page here.

6. Sales agents must have the best updated sales materials to use for follow-up, including brochures, videos, email sales support items, specialized letters to meet the current lead situation, as well as phone scripts and presentation to support the conversion of leads to sales.

7. Sales agents need to understand what their lead follow-up and sales goals are. I use pure sales volume and volume per lead as targets and goals. Sales agents need to be aiming for these kinds

of targets. How they measure up against them will provide all-important feedback on how they are doing. This is an important part of lead follow-up, so let me explain. If you take the number of leads given to a sales agent and divide it by the sales volume the agent produces, you will receive the volume per lead. For example: You give a sales agent 40 leads for the month and the person produces $30,000 in sales, then the volume per lead is $750. This $750 volume per lead is compared to the target you have for that sales agent as well as the average produced by the entire sales team, which will clearly show you the performance levels of the sales agent, especially when you compare the agent's year-to-date numbers the same way.

8. Sales agents should be learning team follow-up techniques all the time from your top-volume-per-lead sales agents. Learning opportunities support the sales team, create best practices for all sales personnel, and aid the sales teams in hitting its targets and goals.

9. Sales agents should be recognized and rewarded for their follow-up achievements.

10. Make sure you have a plan of action to help sales agents who are not hitting their targeted follow-up goals.

Process Needed for Lead Follow-up

There will be a huge difference in your success based on how well you are able to execute your lead follow-up processes. If there are no processes in place concerning how you are going to do your follow-up as a team, then there will be no consistent follow-up, and you cannot expect to reach your full potential. There must be a process for lead follow-up that is understood and followed by all who are involved in lead follow-up. Usually, lead production is the most expensive part of your sales and marketing budget.

If you want an acceptable return on your investment, then you must have well-defined lead follow-up processes and policies that are followed.

You must have a well-thought-out set of standard operating procedures (SOPs) for lead processing, especially follow-up. Your SOPs should be thorough and cover all that is best for the sales agent, prospective purchaser, and the company on lead follow-up. These SOPs can be modified at any time, but once they are written down and completed everyone, especially the sales agents, must sign off on them, indicating that they have read, understood, and will follow the procedures. Then your leadership must make sure these SOPs are consistently followed. I cannot emphasize how important this is. If you want to dominate in lead management, you must have a well-written and enforced set of SOPs. If you do not have them or if they are not enforced consistently, you will not and indeed cannot perform to your full potential.

Here is a checklist of the processes that should be well-defined and also understood and followed conscientiously by all who are involved in lead follow-ups. These steps are essential if you would like to have a highly effective sales and marketing lead generation and sales process.

1. Process to manage lead accounting complexity
2. Process with each step of follow-up that is expected from your sales agents
3. Process for handling "do-not-call" regulations
4. Process for handling unregistered leads
5. Process for handling unassigned leads

6. Process to make sure sales agents are not given leads that cannot be followed up on

7. Process for tracking leads by sales agent and by volume per lead

8. Process to track lead sales production by marketing channel

9. Process for supporting the sales agents with software programs

10. Process for certifying all sales agents in the software being used and to update the software

11. Process to secure your database of leads

12. Process that clearly outlines statutory and regulatory compliance requirements

13. Process for all lead data hygiene (Lead hygiene can mean many things, but from a sales standpoint it indicates that sales agents have confirmed the information they have been supplied with about leads.)

14. Process for broker protection of referred leads

15. Process for lead duplication

16. Process for delivering, reviewing, and acting on lead performance reports

I am sure there are many others you could come up with and add to your processes as you move along with your sales lead management programs. But at least the above will get you started in developing your processes.

Training Needed for Follow-up

We should take a minute and look back at the people who are involved in sales lead follow-up. Make sure all of these people have the correct training. This is a team of people working together on lead follow-up. If you want this team to work well together, then they must have clear guidelines for training, and these guidelines should be understood by all. You cannot afford for people in this lead follow-up process not to be well aligned.

Lead bank training—I see the lead bank as the heart of policies and process direction and enforcement. The lead bank needs to be trained and become experts on how to account, protect, distribute, enforce, update, reconcile, and report on all lead production. Its members should also be experts in training all sales agents and other support personnel on the software systems that are used to follow up and report on lead progressions. If you would like to use us for your lead bank, email us at leaddomination@loreinstitue.com.

On-site administration training—The lead bank usually trains this staff on how to account, distribute, and reconcile daily leads with the lead bank.

Director of sales training—The director should be trained on the very best lead follow-up processes and support and direct the sales agents with their follow-up programs.

Sales agents training—The sales team must be able to input accurate information on each lead in a timely manner in order to have an effective follow-up program. Make sure they are trained and understand the commission dollars that are linked to a strong follow-up program. They need the software training to follow up and update their leads in progress once a week and the best plan of action for converting these leads to sales.

Some of the best sales agents I know have issues with computer software follow-up programs. If a sales person is good enough, you may want to have an assistant for him or her, but only if the person can reach a targeted volume amount without help. If you give assistants to all your sales agents, their follow-up skills will deteriorate because they will become dependent on their support staff to do follow-ups for them. You must be certain that they can follow-up and that the reason they need assistance is they have so many sales and positive leads to follow up on that they can't find the time to follow-up on all their leads in a timely manner. You can have a support person who does all the mailing out of sales material for all the sales agents, but direct communication of the follow-up with the potential owner should be done by the sales agents themselves.

You need thorough training that walks the sales agents through the software program so they can do it on their own. Figure 20-2 provides an example of a page from our training manual, which supports sales agents learning our software program.

Section One—Add a Contact Record

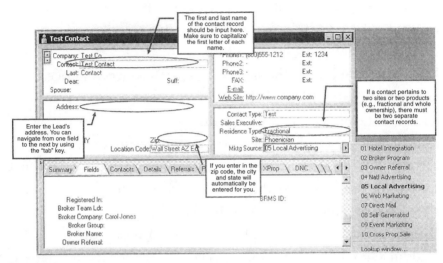

Figure 20-2

Reviewing the Sales Agent Follow-up Process

This is probably one of the most important processes that you have. Your leadership should be involved in some capacity with the review and analysis of your leads in progress. This is where your major monetary investment is, and if your return on investment is going to be favorable, it will probably be because of this process. You have invested money to generate the leads, so you should get a return on your investment, and you should have good indicators as to how your lead investment is going. The best indicator, besides the vital statistics of cost per lead and volume per lead, is the actual potential of the leads in progress. With the right programs and processes in play, you should be able to forecast the sales value of your current leads in progress. This is not only important to the sales team; it is also equally important to the marketing team. If leads in progress are progressing well, you will want to continue with your investment in that marketing channel. If the leads are not progressing well, you will want to adjust how you are investing your resources, moving funds from an unproductive channel to a more productive one.

Figure 20-3 shows the report we use for reviewing sales follow-up of leads with sales agents. This report is critical to your success. It has two sections. One is called the "leads in progress performance report," and the other is the "lead in progress performance report details." Both are important and will drive your lead return on investment. When you review the examples in this book, remember that each month stands alone. That means if you generate forty leads for John Smith in the month of January, that report is only for the month of January. This January reports stands alone until all the forty leads that were generated for John Smith are either sold or not interested. When you start to generate leads for John Smith in February, those will be recorded on a separate lead-in-progress performance report that is only for John Smith in February. So keep in mind that these reports should be separated by month and by individual sales agent.

The lead bank can generate all kinds of statistical lead performance reports from this data, but from a pure leads-in-progress performance standpoint these reports should be separated by each individual month and each individual sales agent.

I am going to spend a few pages in this book reviewing the reasons leads end up still being in progress, but you or your leaders will spend hours reviewing these reasons. I wish there were an easier way, but that is the price you pay to be effective in your lead follow-up program.

Leads in Progress Performance Report

Month	January
Sales Agent	John Smith
Date Updated	2/15/2009

Lead Received	40
Purchased	2
Not Interested	3
In-Progress	35
In-Progress Accounted for	35

Reason for Not Purchasing	JAN	FEB	MAR	APR	MAY	JUN	JUL	AUG	SEP	OCT	NOV	DEC
Contact Pending	6											
Needs More Information	3											
Timing Issues	3											
Not Sold on Concept	2											
Price Concerns	2											
Competing Product Interest	5											
Location Issues	1											
Other Cost Issues—Not Price	2											
Third-Party Approval	5											
Affordability / Price	1											
Product Visit Pending	2											
Contract Pending	1											
Documents Out	2											
Total	35	0	0	0	0	0	0	0	0	0	0	0

Figure 20-3

Figure 20-3 shows our leads-in-progress performance report. It lists the month, in this case January, the sales agent's name, John Smith, the number of leads he received in the month of January, 40, and the date this report was updated, 15 February 2009.

This report for January will be active until all forty leads that were given to John Smith are either in the "not interested" or "purchased" categories. Each month stands alone in its progress, so by July John Smith could have as many as seven separate reports to look at for his leads-in-progress follow-up performance.

The next box on this report contains the following information: how many leads John Smith received for the month, how many of John Smith's leads purchased, how many were not interested, and how many are still in progress. Remember that *all* leads fall into only these three categories: purchased, not interested, and in progress. This makes lead accounting a lot more simplified. So in this report these three categories should add up to the total number of leads you gave John Smith this month.

Figure 20-4 shows a section pulled out of our report. You can see in this report there are thirty-five leads still in progress and thirty-five leads accounted for. This report is perfect, but that will not be the case all the time. You will find many times that the number of leads in progress and the number of leads accounted for do not match. If they do not match, you need to start your review of the leads in progress with John Smith, see his follow-up notes, and see why in your software system the number of leads John Smith received that remain in progress do not match the number of leads accounted for in progress. This will help both John Smith and the company improve follow-up performance.

Lead Received	40
Purchased	2
Not Interested	3
In-Progress	35
In-Progress Accounted for	35

Figure 20-4

The next step in this report is to review the reasons all the leads in progress have not yet purchased. Figure 20-5 shows all of John Smith's thirty-five remaining leads in progress for the month, the status of each, and why they have not purchased. The only time you get leads off this leads-in-progress list is when they become not interested or purchase. This part of the leads-in-progress performance report is an outstanding way to forecast upcoming sales, to gauge the effectiveness of programs, and to help your sales agents with follow-up strategies. It can help make sure every lead that was assigned for the month is accounted for, that all leads have received the best possible follow-up process, and that all leads for this month will eventually either end up in either the purchased or not interested categories. Do keep in mind that leads in the "purchased" or "not interested" categories have their own very specific follow-up processes, but for now we will focus on the leads in progress since I feel you can make your biggest gains in this area.

Reason for Not Purchasing	Jan
Contact Pending	6
Needs More Information	3
Timing Issues	3
Not Sold on Concept	2
Price Concerns	2
Competing Product Interest	5
Location Issues	1
Other Cost Issues—Not Price	2
Third-Party Approval	5
Affordability / Price	1
Product Visit Pending	2
Contract Pending	1
Documents Out	2
Total	35

Figure 20-5

Let's take a look at the different reasons leads have not purchased so far in the month and how you might work with the sales agents to move as many into the sales category as possible. If you work together as a team on the leads in progress, then the sales agents can earn more commissions, the company can make more sales, and the prospective owners can enjoy your product.

Contact pending—This means that the sales agent has received the lead but has not yet contacted the prospective owner. So leads in this category are really un-worked leads. It is important that a strategy be put in place to contact these leads. If after a certain period of time and a certain number of attempts you are not able to reach this lead, then you should have in your standard written polices and procedures that this lead has been transferred to "not interested" status. Keep in mind that your policies and procedures on lead processing must be followed or you will lose all consistency in your process. If you lose consistency, you lose belief, and if you lose belief, you lose the program. The bottom line is: Enforce your lead SOPs with consistency. If a policy change is made, be sure it is communicated to the entire team.

Leads in the "not interested" category should not be protected as far as commissions are concerned. All other leads in progress—as long as the sales agents are making progress and moving the lead forward—should have protection for your sales team. Again, all of this should be covered in your SOPs.

Needs more information—If a prospective owner requests information, you should get it to him or her as soon as possible and move the lead out of this category. If this leads stays in this state for over a week, there is something wrong with your the follow-up process. Leads should never be kept in neutral; they are either moving toward a sale or away from a sale. When working with your sales agents, you need to evaluate which way each particular lead is moving.

Timing issues—Make sure your sales agents and leadership have defined what the timing issues are. There could be many different timing issues, and each needs to be handled differently. The best timing issue concerns clients who are interested but have requested some time to determine which one of your products they are going to purchase. If your product definitely satisfies some of their essential needs but something is holding them back from purchasing, then you need to discover what that is. Make sure sales agents do not have a lot of leads this category. If there are some, make sure they do not stay there long.

Not sold on concept—This is an interesting one. You may wonder why this category is not simply regarded as a "not interested" lead. The answer is that there are many sales that are made with a lead who is interested in your product, has a need for it, and can afford it, but your concept is new to them, and they need to become comfortable with the concept. A lead should not stay in this category over an extended period of time. The product concept concerns that leads have need to be resolved quickly; the longer the leads are out there with this concern, the less likely you will be able to move them forward.

Price concerns—This is a value proposition concern. Remember the two balls we showed you in the beginning of this sales lead conversion section. The bigger the value you create with the product and services, the easier it will be for the prospective owner to purchase. For leads in this category you need to create more value in terms of the goods and services you are offering.

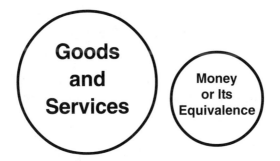

Competing products—Many things compete for the dollars your prospective owners have, and many products compete against yours in the marketplace. You need to know what your competition is and make sure you can compete. Again, it's a matter of creating a value proposition strong enough so that perspective owners vote for your product with their dollars rather than for the competition.

Other cost issues (not price)—These issues usually relate to ongoing costs such as special fees, upkeep, taxes, association fees, and so on. These extra cost issues need to be presented to your potential owner in the right light as things they should be happy to pay for because of what they will get in return.

Third-party approval—In today's world, depending on the price of your product and the financial worth of your client, the need for approval from a third party can be a fairly common situation. When you deal with third-party approvals, it is always best to get the name and number of the third party. Call the person, introduce yourself, and ask how you can help with the client. The bottom line is to get involved with the third party and to try to stay in control of the information, presentation, and progress of the sale.

Affordability—This is different from price concerns. A price concern means the prospective owner can afford your product but is not convinced the value justifies the cost. An affordability issue means the prospective owner likes your product and considers it to have good value but has difficulty being able to purchase it. If the value proposition is large enough, though, sometimes people find ways to purchase your product even if it is not affordable.

Product visit pending—Sometimes prospective owners need to see your product before they are comfortable about purchasing it. Your sales agents should set up a time for prospective owners to see the products they are considering purchasing. This is especially important in the real estate world, in which prospective owners often gather information over the phone but need to be reassured by actually viewing the product. Product visits allow prospective owners to determine whether they want to move forward in the purchasing process.

Contract pending—This is one you love to see, and you can use it to forecast future sales. "Contract pending" means a prospective owner has agreed to purchase your product; however, the purchase agreement has not yet been completed. Many times the reason that the purchase agreement has not been completed is there are product types or terms that still have to be decided or maybe financing or title issues are still pending.

Documents out—This is the best in-progress category for prospective owners. These prospective owners have agreed to purchase, and the purchase agreements are out. You are just waiting for the documents to be returned and for payment so you can move this lead in progress into the "purchased" category. "Documents out" is another category that is used for forecasting future sales revenues. I will say that contract pending and documents out leads in progress needs as much follow-up and attention as any of the categories. As always, the quicker you get these moved over to a sale the better.

Great lead follow-up teams will carefully review all the different statuses that leads in progress can be in. They have solid and effective sales follow-up processes that move *all* leads in progress forward. If your team isn't doing these things, you need to start formulating processes for following up your leads.

Let's now take a look at the leads-in-progress performance report details that accompany your leads-in-progress report. The report can be reviewed in figure 20-6. Let's focus again on John Smith for the month of January and on the thirty-five leads he has in progress. This report provides some details that lie behind the numbers. Here is the information on this detail follow-up report that you need to have at a minimum on each lead in progress:

1. Lead's name

2. Current status

3. When the lead was assigned to the sales agent

4. When the sales agent first made contact with the lead

5. When the next contact with this lead will be

6. What the next step is when you make contact with this client

This detail report will give you a good feel as to how many of the leads in progress are moving closer to sales and how many are moving away, which is very important for future forecasting of sales.

Figure 20-6 shows first the names of clients, used just to identify leads for follow-up. Next comes the current status, indicating why the prospective owner has not purchased. This information can be used for determining appropriate follow-up strategies.

The next column shows when the lead was assigned. Once you record this information, the lead aging process begins. Track how long a lead is in your system and the average time per sales agent it takes to get a lead from first contact to a sale. The more productive sales agents have shorter sales timeframes, so anything you can do to shorten the timeframe is good for sales. The next thing you need to track is when sales agents finally talk with prospective owners. This information is important because leads become cold if they remain too long in the system. The time from when prospective owners ask for information or make an inquiry to when sales agent actually talks to them is important to everyone involved.

Next, you need to track the number of leads that the sales agents have given presentations to. This is one of the important statistics that drive sales production. Top sales agents create enough excitement when they talk to prospective owners that they drive a high percentage of their leads to a presentation. Also record the date of the next communication with the prospective owner and the subject matter of that contact. All of this information is important to have updated each and every week, and you need to review it with your sales agents. If you are not consistent, agents will conclude this lead follow-up process is not that important to leadership. Sales agents and leadership need to be very comfortable with the review process as it should drive more sales. The most important things are that you use these two reports and review your sales agents once a week. If you do that, you will see results, and you will get the best return on your lead investment. Remember through this process your return on investment could mean working with less productive sales agents, getting tips from the most productive sales agents, accelerating more leads from top-selling marketing channels, and reducing leads on the non-performing marketing channels. All of these actions improve performance, and through this lead performance weekly reporting you can take this type of performance-driven action.

Now let's look at the report in figure 20-6:

Leads in Progress Performance Report Details

January
John Smith
Updated 2/15/09

Leads	Current Status	Lead Assigned	Lead Contacted	Lead Pres	Scheduled Contact	Next Step
Lee O. Gilconi	Contact Pending	11-Jan				Call at different hours of the day
Daniel Adams	Contact Pending	14-Jan				Call at different hours of the day
Charles Feitel	Contact Pending	16-Jan				Call at different hours of the day
Eli Dadouche	Contact Pending	5-Jan				Call at different hours of the day
Eugenio Villanueva	Contact Pending	1-Jan				Send email to set up a call
Farooq Tirmizi	Contact Pending	22-Jan				Send email to set up a call
Cansev Sanli	Needs More Info.	18-Jan	18-Jan	Yes	21-Jan	Saving article and phone call
Britisha Hardin	Needs More Info.	5-Jan	5-Jan	Yes	10-Jan	Send new floor plans
Brad Brown	Needs More Info.	12-Jan	12-Jan	Yes	15-Jan	Email present more value
Anoj Malhorta	Timing Issues	11-Jan	11-Jan	No	15-Jan	To deliver presentation
John Porter	Timing Issues	9-Jan	9-Jan	Yes	11-Jan	Set a visit to see product in April
Cyrano Bergerac	Timing Issues	9-Jan	9-Jan	Yes	13-Jan	Deliver my follow-up more value
Katherine Lee	Not Sold on Concept	26-Jan	26-Jan	Yes	27-Jan	Present to essential needs
Ioannis Farinis	Not Sold on Concept	28-Jan	28-Jan	Yes	30-Jan	Present history of purchasers
Luis Soto	Price Concerns	18-Jan	19-Jan	Yes	22-Jan	Show less expensive plan
Michael Napolitano	Price Concerns	7-Jan	7-Jan	No	15-Jan	Need to present the product to him
Peter Rock	Competing Product	12-Jan	12-Jan	Yes	15-Jan	Looking at a different location
Philippe Watteaux	Competing Product	17-Jan	17-Jan	No	18-Jan	Looking at a different product
Rajeev Godha	Competing Product	19-Jan	19-Jan	No	22-Jan	More benefits presented
Andrew Baren	Competing Product	20-Jan	20-Jan	Yes	22-Jan	More benefits presented
Adrian Rabinovici	Competing Product	22-Jan	22-Jan	Yes	26-Jan	Looking at a different product
Sagar Bhimavarapu	Location Issues	23-Jan	23-Jan	Yes	25-Jan	Wants ski area
Stanley Pomerantz	Other Cost Issues	30-Jan	30-Jan	Yes	5-Feb	HOA concerns
Jose Jardim	Other Cost Issues	17-Jan	17-Jan	No	19-Jan	Product and service presentation
Robert Schiffer	Third-Party Approval	19-Jan	19-Jan	Yes	21-Jan	Talking to financial adviser
Fay Gronski	Third-Party Approval	11-Jan	11-Jan	Yes	15-Jan	Talking to financial adviser
Richard Parker	Third-Party Approval	15-Jan	15-Jan	Yes	15-Jan	Talking to tax advisor
Jeffrey Harvey	Third-Party Approval	2-Jan	2-Jan	Yes	15-Jan	Talking to partners
Bruce McCashin	Third-Party Approval	4-Jan	4-Jan	Yes	15-Jan	Talking to legal
David Smith	Affordable Price	10-Jan	10-Jan	Yes	15-Jan	Saving article and phone call
Adolphe Aguera	Product Visit Pending	13-Jan	13-Jan	Yes	15-Jan	Will be out in March
Steven Huish	Product Visit Pending	14-Jan	14-Jan	No	15-Jan	Will be out in April
John Mirenda	Contract Pending	15-Jan	15-Jan	Yes	20-Jan	Checking on getting DOC out
Robert LeBron	Documents Out	25-Jan	25-Jan	Yes	27-Jan	Should be back by Feb 15th
Phil Klein	Documents Out	28-Jan	28-Jan	Yes	30-Jan	Should be back by Feb 1st

Figure 20-6

In this report you can see all the important information you need to improve your follow-up processes. Also, the information in this report will give you a very good idea about the quality of leads in the system and the follow-up that each lead is receiving from your sales agents. If you keep up with this type of leads-in-progress follow-up reviewing, your sales agents will get better and stronger at follow-up. Most importantly, you will always have a good idea as to what needs to be improved from a company, systems, process, and sales agent standpoint as it relates to lead generation and sales follow-up.

Figure 20-7 shows the leads-in-process performance report with a marketing source code included.

Leads in Progress Performance Report Details—Marketing

January
John Smith
Updated 2/15/09

LEADS	CURRENT STATUS	MARKETING SOURCE	LEAD PRES.
Lee O. Gilconi	Contact Pending	Hotel	
Daniel Adams	Contact Pending	Web	
Charles Feitel	Contact Pending	Local	
Eli Dadouche	Contact Pending	National	
Eugenio Villanueva	Contact Pending	Broker	
Farooq Tirmizi	Contact Pending	Broker	
Cansev Sanli	Needs More Info.	Broker	Yes
Britisha Hardin	Needs More Info.	Broker	Yes
Brad Brown	Needs More Info.	Broker	Yes
Anoj Malhorta	Timing Issues	Hotel	No
John Porter	Timing Issues	Local	Yes
Cyrano Bergerac	Timing Issues	Local	Yes
Katherine Lee	Not Sold on Concept	Hotel	Yes
Ioannis Farinis	Not Sold on Concept	Owner	Yes
Luis Soto	Price Concerns	Owner	Yes
Michael Napolitano	Price Concerns	Local	No
Peter Rock	Competeting Product	Hotel	Yes
Philippe Watteaux	Competing Product	Hotel	No
Rajeev Godha	Competing Product	Web	No
Andrew Baren	Competing Product	Hotel	Yes
Adrian Rabinovici	Competing Product	Broker	Yes
Sagar Bhimavarapu	Location Issues	National	Yes
Stanley Pomerantz	Other Cost Issues	Hotel	Yes
Jose Jardim	Other Cost Issues	Web	No
Robert Schiffer	Third-Party Approval	Hotel	Yes
Fay Gronski	Third-Party Approval	National	Yes
Richard Parker	Third-Pary Approval	National	Yes
Jeffrey Harvey	Third-Party Approval	Referral	Yes
Bruce McCashin	Third-Party Approval	Referral	Yes
David Smith	Affordable Price	Web	Yes
Adolphe Aguera	Product Visit Pending	Broker	Yes
Steven Huish	Product Visit Pending	Event	No
John Mirenda	Contract Pending	National	Yes
Robert LeBron	Documents Out	Broker	Yes
Phil Klein	Documents Out	Web	Yes

Figure 20-7

This report provides an outstanding way for marketing to look at pending business by marketing source codes. This report can allow you to do some great analysis and forecasting by source code on leads that are in progress for the month or quarter.

Also, if you are on the marketing side of a broker program, this report provides a great way to track the progress of your broker leads. Hotel integration marketing personnel can also review the clients they have generated. Both broker and hotel marketing personnel compensation is usually driven by leads progressing in the system. This report also allows marketing to forecast the effectiveness of particular marketing channels.

Sales Materials

Work with your agents to develop sales materials that can help you convert leads into sales. Someone will need to be responsible for getting the materials printed up and then worked into your follow-up processes.

Performance Reports

These reports are essential if you want to dominate performance in lead management and production. These reports must be completed accurately, in a timely fashion, and most importantly reviewed so that you can take action on what the report indicates.

These reports relate to sales lead follow-up performance. Leadership and sales agents need to get together once a week to review the status of all leads in progress. Large amounts of marketing dollars are probably invested in your leads in progress. These large amounts of marketing dollars are one of the main sources of future sales. Leads in progress being converted into sales will drive much of the future success of your sales and marketing enterprise.

Finally, let's examine the weekly lead review report shown in figure 20-8. As you review this final performance report and all performance reports in this chapter, always keep in mind that your leads are never in neutral; they are either moving closer to a sale or further away from a sale. If you use the strategies recommended in this chapter, you can start to move more of your leads toward sales just by consistently following up on all leads.

This report shows the progress of all the leads assigned to John Smith. As of August 1ˢᵗ, you can see he has one hundred and seventy-four leads in progress. If this operation was yours, and you were paying $500 per lead, you would have close to $90,000 invested in leads in progress that have the potential to be converted into sales. And that's just the leads assigned to one agent.

If I were reviewing this lead review report weekly, I would work with John Smith on the following:

1. Twenty percent of his leads have not been contacted.

2. Fifteen percent of his leads are still in need of information.

3. Fifteen percent of his leads require third-party approval, which means those third parties should be contacted.

4. He should update his three contracts pending and his three document out sales.

If you did not have reports like this one for reviewing John Smith, what would you do? I can assure you that your leadership and your company become very much at risk in getting the return on their investments that they need without this type of reporting. As you can see from this report, there is a lot more that you could work on with John, but you want to stay focused on the most important matters. The following week you would want to see progress on the items that were discussed this week.

Weekly Lead Review Report

Sales Agent   John Smith

Date Updated   8/01/2009

Total YTD Leads Received	320
Purchased	21
Not Interested	125
Total YTD In-Progress	174
In Progress Accounted for	174

Reason for Not Purchasing	Week 1	Week 2	Week 3	Week 4	Week 5	Week 6	Week 7	Week 8	Week 9	Week 10	Week 11	Week 12
Contact Pending	44	38	42	38	34							
Needs More Information	28	25	24	17	26							
Timing Issues	12	15	21	17	18							
Not Sold on Concept	8	12	8	10	12							
Price Concerns	4	4	4	5	3							
Competing Product Interest	22	18	16	14	17							
Location Issues	2	4	3	4	4							
Other Cost Issues—Not Price	18	19	16	12	15							
Third-Party Approval	20	27	30	23	27							
Affordability / Price	7	6	2	1	5							
Product Visit Pending	6	6	8	8	7							
Contract Pending	4	3	2	2	3							
Documents Out	1	2	1	2	3							
Total	176	179	177	153	174	0	0	0	0	0	0	0

Items to focus on this week:

1. _____

2. _____

3. _____

4. _____

Figure 20-8

There is a lot in this chapter to digest and put in play, but these are the things it takes to dominate lead production in your market. Best of success moving ahead with all you have learned in this chapter. Because this chapter is so important to your sales and marketing success, if there is anything I can do to help explain or support your sales lead follow-up or if you have comments and or suggestions on this material, please contact me at leaddomination@loreinstitue.com.

Key Notes for Sales Lead Follow-up

1. Be as consistent as you possibly can in updating *all* leads in progress at least *once a week*.

2. The training done by sales and the lead bank on your software program is very important. Try to make sure your software is simple to use but effective.

3. Support your sales team with the best visual follow-up materials for their prospective owners.

4. Leadership and sales need to continue to look for best practices on moving a lead forward in the sales process.

5. Make sure you recognize and reward sales agents who are the best at their follow-up process and are producing the results that go with top lead follow-up.

Let's hear from our characters about *sales lead follow-up.*

Chapter 20: Sales Lead Follow-up

Here is an action scene with our characters doing their sales lead follow-up.

National averages tell us only 20 percent of leads given to sales are followed up on effectively. Make sure this national average is not part of your sales lead operation.

#### Chapter 21

Sales Performance Reporting and Reviewing

Sales teams and agents are never neutral; they're either getting better or getting worse

These sales performance reports are report cards showing how well you are doing as a sales agent for the enterprise.

THE GENERATION OF cost-effective quality leads is only half of the success equation in sales and marketing. The other half is converting those leads into sales. To do that, you need effective reports and reviewing opportunities for managing, supporting, and directing your sales teams.

The sales teams I have managed have always included performers of varying abilities. If you gave the same one hundred leads to four different sales agents, you would get four different results, even if the leads were exactly the same. This variation has to do with sales talent, sales training, performance reviewing, coaching, and the desire and commitment of the sales agents on your team. Each agent has to be reviewed, coached, and directed on a consistent basis if you want to run an effective sales operation.

I believe the precise level of sales talent is something your sales agents possess when you hire them. Leaders cannot change this component very much. Sales talent has something to do with sales performance, so it makes sense to hire the most talented agents you can. All of us know of sales agents who have a high degree of sales talent. These are some of the sales agents who are seemingly effortlessly on top in sales performance. You do not necessarily need to be a highly talented sales person to be one of the top performers, though. In this chapter we are going to focus on reviewing, directing, and coaching your sales agents because these are important things leadership and sales agents can control to drive better sales performance.

All levels of performers need direction and a plan of action. It's a big mistake to spend time coaching and directing only the low performers. You should have a plan of action created also for your high performers. The things you focus on, review, report, and compensate for are for the most part what you can expect your sales teams to be most aware of. I would like to challenge all sales leadership to focus on the following:

1. Sales production
2. Team culture
3. Sales follow-up processes and performance

We compensate sales agents for sales production, and that is great. Some kind of compensation plan, however, needs to be in place for team culture and lead follow-up. Both of these can be quantified and reviewed just like sales performance. I would highly recommend that you add some kind of a compensation factor to these two areas as you really need them both to be first-rate if you are going to put together a top performing sales team.

There are only four reports you need for reviewing performance, directing the sales team, coaching the individual sales agents, and increasing sales performance. Each of these reports will help guide you and your sales teams to ensure the best possible conversion of leads to sales. Each report has its specific purpose, each is important, and each needs to be reviewed with the sales team on a consistent basis.

The four reports are:

1. Sales agents volume per lead performance reports
2. Sales agents team culture reports
3. Monthly sales performance updates
4. Quarterly written sales performance reviews

Figure 21-1 shows the sales agent volume per lead performance report.

Sales Agent—Volume per Lead Performance

All Marketing Sources
From January to April 2009

Sales Agent #1

	Jan	Feb	Mar	Apr	YTD
Leads	45	38	37	40	160
Volume	$550,000	$425,000	$650,000	$150,000	$1,775,000
VPL	$12,222	$11,184	$17,568	$3,750	$11,094

Sales Agent #2

	Jan	Feb	Mar	Apr	YTD
Leads	49	39	38	38	164
Volume	$500,000	$375,000	$395,000	$135,000	$1,405,000
VPL	$10,204	$9,615	$10,395	$3,553	$8,567

Sales Agent #3

	Jan	Feb	Mar	Apr	YTD
Leads	40	33	55	39	167
Volume	$300,000	$250,000	$275,000	$220,000	$1,045,000
VPL	$7,500	$7,576	$5,000	$5,641	$6,257

Sales Agent #4

	Jan	Feb	Mar	Apr	YTD
Leads	55	42	45	42	184
Volume	$150,000	$50,000	$290,000	$320,000	$810,000
VPL	$2,727	$1,190	$6,444	$7,619	$4,402

Totals

	Jan	Feb	Mar	Apr	YTD
Leads	189	152	175	159	675
Volume	$1,500,000	$1,100,000	$1,610,000	$825,000	$5,035,000
VPL	$7,937	$7,237	$9,200	$5,189	$7,459

YTD 2008—Entire Year	Agent #1	Agent #2	Agent #3	Agent #4
Leads	480	395	510	550
Volume	$5,760,000	$3,752,500	$3,060,000	$2,310,000
VPL	$12,000	$9,500	$6,000	$4,200

Figure 21-1

Volume per lead produced is calculated by dividing the sales volume that the sales agent produced by the number of leads assigned to this agent.

First, take a quick peek at what your agents' volume per lead performance was last year by comparison with this year, so you know who your high, medium, and low performers are.

Agent # 1 = High Performance
Produced an $11,094 VPL in 2009 and $12,000 VPL in 2008

Agent # 2 = Medium Performance
Produced an $8,567 VPL in 2009 and $9,500 VPL in 2008

Agent # 3 = Medium Performance
Produced a $6,257 VPL in 2009 and $6,000 VPL in 2008

Agent # 4 = Low Performance
Produced a $4,402 VPL in 2009 and $4,200 VPL in 2008.

This information is important to start with, but you want to help each and every sales agent to improve his or her current level of sales production. The volume per lead in this report becomes the target for increasing sales production.

The next step is to look at all the different marketing channels that make up the lead flow these sales agents received. Focus on the sales agents' volume per lead production by individual marketing channel, which will show you any specific marketing channels your agents perform well or not so well in.

Figure 21-2 below is the same report as figure 21-1, only in this case it's showing your different agents' performances for national advertising. In the first chart we will show you how the overall National Advertising Channel did in performance, and then we show you how the individual sales agents did in performance on this channel. If you have ten different marketing channels producing assignable leads for your sales teams, you would need ten reports like this one, one for each marketing channel. Look at these reports carefully and note which sales agents have the highest and lowest volumes per lead production by marketing channel. This is so helpful in directing your sales agents toward higher performance. If they are very low in a particular marketing channel, you can work with them to help them improve. If they are particularly high in a particular marketing channel, you can review and use what you have learned to help others.

Sales Agent Volume per Lead Performance by Marketing Source

National Advertising From January to April 2009

2009 YTD			
Marketing Leads		Sales Volume	
Budget	224	Budget	$4,031,071
Actual	210	Actual	$4,483,497
Last YR	310	Last YR	$2,247,840
Cost per Lead		Volume per Lead	
Budget	$1,427	Budget	$17,996
Actual	$1,401	Actual	$21,350
Last YR	$1,241	Last YR	$7,251

2009 April			
Marketing Leads		Sales Volume	
Budget	64	Budget	$1,151,935
Actual	85	Actual	$763,920
Last YR	82	Last YR	$1,585,880
Cost per Lead		Volume per Lead	
Budget	$1,438	Budget	$17,999
Actual	$957	Actual	$8,987
Last YR	$1,706	Last YR	$19,340

Figure 21-2

Sales Agent #1

	Jan	Feb	Mar	Apr	YTD
Leads	9	10	10	19	48
Volume	$164,577	$195,000	$320,000	$150,000	$829,577
VPL	$18,286	$19,500	$32,000	$7,895	$17,283

Sales Agent #2

	Jan	Feb	Mar	Apr	YTD
Leads	10	8	7	22	47
Volume	$250,000	$320,000	$250,000	$135,000	$955,000
VPL	$25,000	$40,000	$35,714	$6,136	$20,319

Sales Agent #3

	Jan	Feb	Mar	Apr	YTD
Leads	12	12	10	20	54
Volume	$510,000	$135,000	$275,000	$220,000	$1,140,000
VPL	$42,500	$11,250	$27,500	$11,000	$21,111

Sales Agent #4

	Jan	Feb	Mar	Apr	YTD
Leads	9	12	16	24	61
Volume	$450,000	$500,000	$350,000	$258,920	$1,558,920
VPL	$50,000	$41,667	$21,875	$10,788	$25,556

Totals

	Jan	Feb	Mar	Apr	YTD
Leads	40	42	43	85	210
Volume	$1,374,577	$1,150,000	$1,195,000	$763,920	$4,483,497
VPL	$34,364	$27,381	$27,791	$8,987	$21,350

Figure 21-2 (continued)

 Look next at each sales agent's team culture scores.

I feel this employee is a positive influence in the business environment.

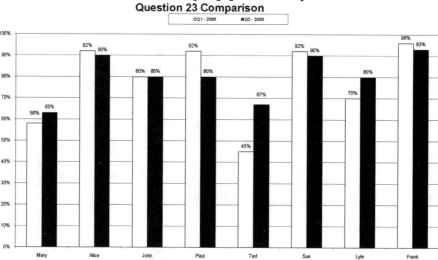

Figure 21-3

We reviewed this report in the marketing section, but let's look at it again with a focus this time on your sales agents. This report in figure 21-3 asks how positive each sales agent is in the working environment. This report includes everyone in the work environment, so you will need to focus on each sales person and how he or she scored in this report. This report can make a huge difference to your success. It will also help you and your leadership teams understand how to and who to manage on an individual team culture basis. The bottom line is that sales people who are positive in their team environment tend to be the most productive and clearly very good for the overall environment. If sales agents are not positive in the work environment, then even if they are productive themselves, they can be very destructive to the overall team.

Remember when we said that people may not do what is expected but tend to focus on what is inspected? How important do you think it is to be able to report on everyone on your team and their influence on creating a positive business environment, especially given that these are the people who create your sales revenue? Do you think if you could get good information on this subject it would help you manage a more positive working environment among your team? Do you think a more positive working environment leads to better production overall? If so, you'll want to use this report.

Each employee on your team, including all leaders, gets to rate all others at the end of each quarter on this question.

You rate each person on a one to five scale, one being the lowest score and five being the highest. Each employee rates everyone else in private, with no names appearing on the scoring sheet. The sheets are then sent off-site to a neutral party for compilation of the results. Employees will get to know at the end of the process their individual overall score only and how that compares to the overall team.

How important is it that each of the team members works hard in creating a positive work environment? I say it is essential, and like everything else, you have to work on it; it just does not happen on its own.

So everyone scores everyone else including you and any leaders who work with the team. The results are computed, and leadership only gets something back like what you see in figure 21-3. After you've gone through the scores with everyone, you should formulate a plan of action to try to help everyone improve their scores no matter how good or bad they were. Remember that we do not share everyone's score with everyone else; only management knows them all. All you show each individual sales agent is his or her own score and how it compares to the average score.

The people who do well need to be rewarded. You should figure out how to best do this. If you reward the top scorers, everyone on the team will strive for top scores. The people on the bottom need to be coached and counseled on how to increase their positive influence on the team. Give them support and direction and really have them work on improving their scores for the next quarter. You will be surprised at how many people who score low had no idea they were not a positive influence on the team. Just the fact that they know will make a big difference. Make this report part of their performance review. Do you really want someone on your team who is not a positive influence even if that person can perform well? Eventually, people who are not positive will affect the overall efficiencies of the team. Do this report once a quarter, and you will see progress in this area, which is so essential to your results.

Quarterly Team Culture Performance Report—Report # 2

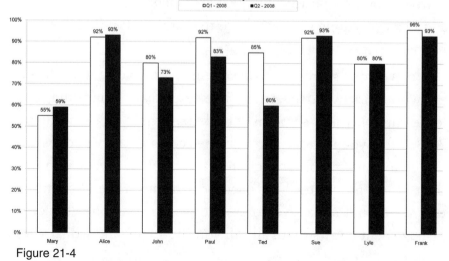

Figure 21-4

The same process applies with this question, which is very different than the positive influence question. Ideally, you really want people who are team players and who have a positive influence of the business environment. These are the outstanding performing team culture employees. They should be recognized as such. We score and rate performance on everything else: sales, number of leads, and so on. Team culture is every bit as important for a successful sales team.

Look at Mary's score. What should you do? How about Ted's score? Also, what are you going to do to support the three employees who scored over 90 percent? All of this, if followed up on, can have big results in terms of overall sales performance. The report is completed at the end of each quarter. As you can see, each employee's scores are compared to his or her scores from the prior quarterly review.

You should also do a monthly update with each sales agent, which is just a progress report so leadership and sales agents can sit down once a month and update individual sales agents' performance. The big written sales performance reviews are done every quarter, but you want to make sure that you sit down with your sales team members at least once a month to look at some of their vital performance indicators. In figure 21-5 you see an example of this monthly report.

This focus should be on reviewing the following items to see whether the sales agent's trends are improving or declining:

1. Volume per lead

2. Sales volume

3. Assigned leads

4. Presentation percentages

5. Lead follow-up

6. The sales agent's positive environment ratings

7. The sales agent's team player ratings

Sales Agent's Monthly Update

Sales Agent _____

Month Review _____

1. Volume per Lead

   a. Current YTD VPL _____   Current Month's VPL _____

   Updates _____

2. Sales Volume

   a. Current YTD Volume _____   Current Month's Volume _____

   Updates _____

3. Assigned Leads

   a. Current YTD Leads _____   Current Month's Leads _____

   Updates _____

4. Presentation Percentage

   a. Current YTD Presentation % _____   Current Month's Presentation % _____

   Updates _____

5. Lead Follow-up   Rating (1–5) _____

6. Positive Environment   Rating (1–5) _____

7. Team Player   Rating (1–5) _____

      Reviewed by _____

Monthly Comments:

_____

_____

_____

Figure 21-5

Finally, one of the most important future direction reports you have is the quarterly written sales agent review. This is the only report for which you need to sit down with every sales agent each quarter and review sales performance in a variety of categories and get comments from the sales agents, as well as from sales leadership, that will provide direction for moving forward.

Sales Agent Quarterly Reviews

This review is a must if you want to convert more leads into sales. If leadership really focuses on sales performance on a consistent basis, so will sales agents. If leadership doesn't, the sales agents will not be as focused. I like to go into lots of detail and really review all different levels of sales performance when completing these quarterly reviews. I find the more you show the sales team your comments about their performance and provide them with clear direction based on the performance, the more productive the team will be. If you want less performance detail than what I show, that is fine, but be certain that you have this review consistently with your sales agents and that you are well-rehearsed and prepared for this important time of review and future leadership direction.

Take a look at the review in figure 21-6, which is a complete detailed sales agent quarterly review. It continues on over several pages as we review with you an example of a complete sales agent quarterly written review. The numbers tht are used in this quarterly sales agent review are supplied to you and for you by the lead bank.

Sales Agents—Quarterly Review

Dates Reviewed—June 1 through August 31, 2009

Next Review—September 1 through December 31, 2009

Sales Agent Performance Being Reviewed—John Smith

Lead Performance Volume Produced per Lead Review

For the three months reviewed John Smith's sales volume per lead was $15,424 while the average performance by the sales team for this period of time was $10,220 in net volume per lead, which means Smith produced an extra $5,204 for each lead over what the average sales agent produced. Smith's performance over this period of time was outstanding. It should be noted that this volume includes only the new sales produced by Smith. The reservations that were converted over this period of time were not counted in this calculation. If you have pre-sales, where you made reservations before you were ready to do documentation to sell, you need to separate these because they were made in prior months rather than the current one.

John Smith received 109 leads for the three months with an average cost per lead of $978 dollars. That means marketing invested $106,602 in lead costs for Smith for the three months, and the company received $1,681,174 in net sales volume from the investment. The average marketing percentages for the sales team during the three-month period was 8.1 percent (which is the marketing total cost per leads divided by the total net sales volume). Smith's was 6.3 percent, which means that for every lead given to Smith over this period of time he saved the company 1.8 percent in marketing costs over the average. Again, his performance was outstanding.

Lead Performance Results Review

Smith's lead performance results are as follows:

Figure 21-6

Leads Not Contacted

Smith has 59 leads who have not been contacted, or 54 percent of his total leads. The average was 61 percent. These are exceptionally high numbers of leads not contacted by Smith and the rest of the team. Leadership needs to determine why so many leads have not been contacted this quarter. Leadership needs to review each of Smith's 59 leads to put together a plan for moving forward.

Leads in Progress

Smith has 17 leads in progress for the quarter, or 16 percent of his total leads. The average was 11 percent. Leadership needs to review each of these 17 leads to determine what follow-up strategies might promote results.

Leads for Site Inspections

Smith had none for the quarter, and there were none booked by the entire sales team for the quarter. The lack of results in this area was mostly driven by the fact that there was no place to house site visits because the residences and the hotel were completely booked for most of the quarter.

Leads Who Have Purchased

Smith has 4 leads who have purchased, or 3 percent of his total leads. The average was 1 percent. Smith's score was the best on the team.

Smith also has 2 sales with documents out, which is 2 percent of his total leads. Overall, the team was at .5 percent. Smith's score in this area was the second best on the team.

Smith has 3 pending sales, which is 3 percent of his total leads. The overall average of the team was 2 percent. Smith's score was the second best on the team. Smith's pending sales and sales with documents out should give him good momentum moving ahead into the next quarter.

Leads Who Are Not Interested

Smith has 30 leads who are not interested, or 28 percent of his total leads. The average was 26 percent.

Figure 21-6 (continued)

Sales Performance Review

As of the end of August Smith had $17,766,150 in reservations sales volume converted, which ranks him first out of four sales agents. His $1,681,175 in new sales for the quarter also ranks him first. His performance was truly remarkable.

Smith received 109 leads for this quarter. Over this period of time that ranks him third out of four sales agents.

Smith's leads to presentations were converted at 32 percent of the time, which ranks him tied for second out of the four membership executives.

Smith's closing percentage was 11.4, which ranks him first out of the four membership executives.

Smith's lead aging performance was 48 days whereas the team average was 65 days. This figure is measured from the date a lead is assigned to a sales agent until the time a sale is counted by the company. A sale is counted only when all documents to purchase have been completed and payment has been received. John was first out of four sales agents in fewest days between leads assigned and sales counted.

Lead Software Review

Smith can use some improvement here as we find that on the weekly review he is for the most part behind in updating his leads in progress. Most of this problem relates to his input into the system, not his actual follow-up on the lead. In other words, it seems he is doing the follow-up, just not recording the results. This must be corrected moving ahead. He is ranked third out of four sales agents. A plan of action should be recommended to improve his performance in this area before the next quarterly review.

Team Culture Review

Smith ranks third out of our four sales agents in team culture. He is at 65 percent in helping to create a positive work environment for his teammates and is in the 70-percent range in his team play ratings. Both of these scores could be greatly improved. Leadership needs to offer guidance to Smith about how he could improve in these areas.

Figure 21-6 (continued)

Vital Statistics Rankings

Item	Ranking #1	Ranking #2	Ranking #3	Ranking #4
VPL	#1			
Marketing Percentage	#1			
Reservation Volume	#1			
New Sales Volume	#1			
Number of Leads	#3			
Presentation Percentage	#2			
Closing Percentage	#1			
Lead Aging	#1			
Lead Software Usage	#3			
Positive Environment	#3			
Team Player	#3			

Smith Performance Management Comments and Direction

Smith needs to work with the lead bank to ensure he meets or exceeds software follow-up performance. The trainer of the lead bank should set up one-on-one training with Smith once a week until he improves in this area.

Smith has been scheduled to meet with leadership on the best strategies for improving his team culture scores. It is the responsibility of Smith and leadership working together to improve both of these percentages in the next quarterly review.

Smith needs to follow these recommendations to help support his performance and the team's in the future:

1. Reduce the number of leads that have not been contacted.

2. Work with leadership to put on a sales presentation and gaining commitment training for the rest of the sales agents. Leadership to take notes and reward John for the training.

3. Outstanding sales performances for the quarter! Leadership is going to invest in a five-day paid vacation for Smith and his family at a date and time that he chooses. Leadership cannot thank Smith enough for the great sales performance he produced for the quarter.

Figure 21-6 (continued)

```
┌─────────────────────────────────────────────────┐
│ Smith's Comments:                               │
│                                                 │
│                                                 │
│                                                 │
│                                                 │
│                                                 │
│                                                 │
│                                                 │
└─────────────────────────────────────────────────┘
```

_____   _____
John Smith   Date

_____   _____
Director of Sales   Date

Figure 21-6 (continued)

Let take a look at this review together. Smith was the best sales agent in this hypothetical example for the quarter. There is, however, room for improvement even if you are the best. Each review should have rewards and recognition for top performance and clear direction on areas that need improvement. John's improvement areas for the quarter will be in lead follow-up, focused on making sure he is inputting all his leads into the program and improving his team culture ratings.

But because he did so well with his sales performance here is what would be done for Smith.

1. Flowers would be sent to his wife thanking her for supporting him and letting her know that because of her support he was able to be the number one producing sales agent of the quarter. These flowers being sent are important, in my view.

2. John should be scheduled to do training for the rest of the sales agents, which will be good for the team and usually good

for the ego of the sales agent who is being asked to help the others. It is up to leadership to make sure best practices are shared with the whole team.

Again, as an important review, let's look one more time at the areas that this top sales performer can improve on. If you do not give your top performers areas to improve on, you are making a mistake. The areas in which Smith has opportunities to improve, leadership needs again to take control and give direction on the plan of action. Most sales agents who are top performers like Smith do not feel there is any need for them to improve. They were hired to convert leads into sales, and that is what Smith has done for the quarter. He was the best on the team! As a leader, though, it is up to you to move Smith to the next level of performance. Here is what should be done to help Smith improve:

1. Make sure there are specific, measurable ways to train and review the results on Smith using his software programs. Put your software trainer and Smith together to get this done. This may not be Smith's favorite part of his responsibilities. If you lead Smith to be better here, though, he will be a more valuable sales agent to your company and will be a better agent. Leadership must get this message across to Smith in a positive manner. If leadership sent flowers to his wife and is sponsoring a vacation for his whole family, it is in a great position to get Smith's attention to improve. Leadership should always be looking for ways to support and improve the team.

2. Leadership needs to invest one-on-one time with Smith to improve his positive environment and team player contributions. Understand that sometimes a top sales performer will not be the most popular with the rest of the sales team; but things don't have to remain that way. Good leadership can

really put Smith back on track here. This will be a big benefit for Smith and for the entire sales and marketing organization.

These four sales agents reports give you the information you need to drive sales performance by reviewing, directing, and coaching your sales teams. These reviews are important to your success in lead management. If you have any questions or need some support on these processes, feel free to email your comments to leaddomination@loreinstitue.com.

Key Notes for Sales Performance Reporting and Reviewing

1. Inspections and compensation motivate sales teams; make sure you provide both.

2. Have your four sales agent performance reports done on time and accurately. Also make sure reviews with sales agents are done consistently and on time. Make sure sales agents understand how important these reviews are to leadership.

3. Sales agents need direction to improve. Agents are either getting better or worse. Leadership needs to have a plan of action to improve agents' performances no matter what their current performance levels are.

4. Leadership should be well-rehearsed and prepared for these reviews and give constructive direction to sales agents for their quarterly written reviews.

Let's hear from our characters about
sales performance reporting and reviewing.

Chapter 21: Sales Performance Reporting and Reviewing

Here is an action scene with our characters doing their sales reviews.

Sales teams are never in neutral; they are either getting better or getting worse. Give them the leadership to improve and the direction to know how to improve, and you are well on your way to lead domination.

Conclusion

NOW THAT YOU'VE COME to the end of this overview of *lead domination* and you have an understanding of the 21 proven strategies, I would like to leave you with some final thoughts that will help you review the key concepts of this book.

When working on these strategies, you need to remember three things: *get started* then *get better* and *get it done*. I have found there is no simpler and more effective way of using these 21 strategies than those three steps.

Also know that lead domination is not a destination; it is a journey. We will continue to update and perfect these 21 sales and marketing strategies and, if you choose, we can share new information with you through our monthly newsletters. Once you get started, we will help you get better, and together we can get it done. Email us to learn how to get updated each month on these 21 proven strategies at leaddomination@loreinstitute.com.

For anything you have done well in your life you have probably followed a path that looks like this: First, you were interested in being the best you could be in the subject; second, you were willing to invest the time in getting better; third, you looked for the expertise that could help you prepare, and then you performed what you prepared; finally, you measured the results. Here are the four steps most of us take in anything we do well:

521

1. Prepare

2. Perform

3. Produce

4. Measure your results

I would like to apply these four simple steps to the concept of lead domination.

Prepare

Define what a lead is, locate where your buyers are, and make sure you have diversified your approach. These topics are covered in chapters 1 through 3 of this book.

Perform

After you have prepared, you will perform your prospecting and messaging, which will generate inquiries and leads. These topics are covered in chapters 4 and 5. This performance will lead you to investing and producing revenue.

Produce

Go ahead and invest your money in lead generation. You will do all the necessary steps before you invest in your lead generation. These steps will help produce cost-effective lead generation programs, and this will result in cost-effective sales revenues. Then take the time with the information you have to innovate and execute the new strategies. These topics are covered in chapters 6 through 8.

Measure Your Results

In the end, how well you have done can be measured, and your direction moving forward will be adjusted based on the results of your reviews. These topics are covered in chapters 9 through 12.

These are the four steps from a marketing standpoint. Now let's now look at sales.

Prepare

The main sales techniques to prepare for are developing sales relationships, stating the intent of your presentation, and establishing your all-important discovery process. These topics are covered in chapters 14 through 16. Next, you take what you have practiced and perform.

Perform

After you have prepared, you will perform your product presentation and viewing presentation for your potential owners, which is a critically important part of your sales presentation. These topics are covered in chapters 17 and 18.

Produce

Based on how well you have executed what you prepared for, you will now produce sales revenue by gaining commitments and following up. These topics are covered in chapters 19 and 20.

Measure Your Results

In the end, how well you have done is measured in terms of sales revenue, which provides the raw data for your report cards on how well you are doing with what you prepared for and performed in pure selling with your sales team. This topic is covered in chapter 21.

Below is a visual of what was described above:

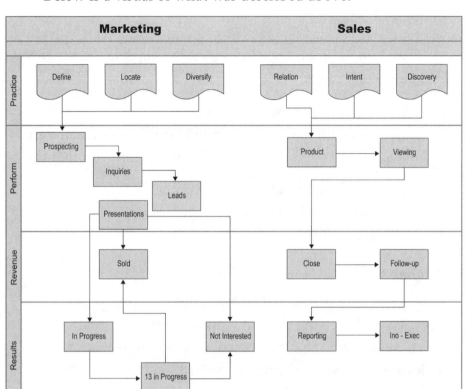

We have established a Marketing Lead Domination Rating (MLDR) and a Sales Lead Domination Rating (SLDR) to help any sales and marketing organization understand how effective it is in terms of lead domination. Figure 1-1 shows an example of our Marketing Lead Domination Rating (MLDR) form, which is what we use to rate companies on their marketing lead lifestyle. Your maximum score on a MLDR is 120. A score of 102 to 120 would represent a lead lifestyle and culture that is moving ahead full speed toward lead domination. A score of 85 to 101 indicates a company that is doing well but has lots of opportunity to improve. Any company with a MLDR score of 84 or below seriously needs to improve its lead management process. I must tell you that I have seen scores, even from big companies, as low as 9 on the MLDR.

There is consensus among numerous sources that sales fails to act on upward of eighty percent of the leads it gets, an astounding fact if it's anywhere near accurate. More than likely, this number is high because many of the "leads" being turned over to sales are not really leads. Still, how sure are you that your sales teams are working all the leads you give them? How sure are you that the leads you give your sales teams are really leads? Do you have a lead management strategy in place to help your marketing and sales teams perform better? These two lead management based company ratings, the MLDR and the SLDR, will help you answer these questions and, most of all, improve whatever you are currently doing.

Marketing Lead Domination Rating

Trait 1	Trait 2	Trait 3	Trait 4	Trait 5	Trait 6	Trait 7	Trait 8	Trait 9	Trait 10	Trait 11	Trait 12
1 5 10	1 5 10	1 5 10	1 5 10	1 5 10	1 5 10	1 5 10	1 5 10	1 5 10	1 5 10	1 5 10	1 5 10
Define	Locate	Diversify	Prospect	Messaging	Assump.	D &R Paper	Approval	Account	Reporting	Direction	Innovation

Figure 1-1

Each category above is rated from one to ten, one meaning you currently do very little in that category and ten meaning you do everything suggested in this book and maybe more. Now that you have read this book, rate your organization in each of these categories and see what your Marketing Lead Domination Rating is. If you would prefer, you can email us at leaddomination@ loreinstitute.com, and we will send you our questionnaire, which will help you rate your marketing lead domination for your company.

This book has one chapter for each category in your MLDR. So as you go through and rate your company in the Marketing Lead Dominating Ratings form, you can use each chapter to review what is expected in that category and compare it to what is currently being done by your company. Let's get your marketing scores up over the 101 level.

Below I will make just a quick statement on each chapter to help you understand the overall direction. Obviously, each chapter you read will take you much deeper into the subject matter.

Define—Have you defined what a lead is? What a lead is not? What an inquiry is? Do you have a full written definition of what your sales and marketing company calls a lead? Is this written definition signed off on by leadership, sales, and marketing? Have you ever checked after the fact to see what percent of the leads you generate met the lead definition? If not, review chapter 1 to improve your MLDR rating.

Locate—Do you know where your buyers are located? It is very hard to prospect for quality leads if you do not know where they are. Strategies for locating buyers are reviewed in depth in chapter 2.

Diversity—Never put all your eggs in one basket, and never put all your marketing into one channel. Learn the power of lead diversification. Chapter 3 provides insurance, if you will, dramatically reducing your financial risk.

Prospecting—Chapter 4 covers what you should do before you spend one single dime prospecting for leads. It's all here, and this information is a "must." The addenda on prospecting will help you understand how very specific programs work.

Messaging—What can you convey in your message to attract the leads you want? What are some of the obstacles that can get in your way and destroy your marketing message and diminish your ability to generate quality leads? Chapter 5 will help you answer these important questions.

Assumptions—This is a key area for any successful marketing program. Your financial marketing assumptions make your marketing program worth pursuing. Chapter 6 will help ensure your assumptions are as accurate and trackable as possible.

Description and Responsibilities Paper—These papers are not used in many of the companies where we have done an MLDR. I must say that these detailed people and process outlines will improve your lead generation dramatically. They provide an opportunity for your team to write down the vital people, responsibilities, processes, and action steps that constitute your marketing financial assumptions. They provide a great way to improve lead effectiveness and are essential if you want to move toward lead domination.

Approval—This is your internal approval process for all of your marketing programs. Most companies do this well, but here we ask you to inform all the different parties who need to approve a marketing program early in the process. That's a sure way to increase your program efficiencies and increase your MLDR.

Accounting—You need to account for the leads you generate. Remember not to spend any lead generation marketing dollars on any program if you cannot account for the leads it generates. You should be able to account for your leads by marketing channel, including cost per lead as well as volume per lead by sales agent. I am surprised at how low the scores have been in many of the companies on the MLDR in this area.

Reporting—This refers to reporting on your lead performance from a marketing standpoint, which is vital to your success. You cannot move toward lead domination without having outstanding performance reports in play. Unfortunately, if you do not have good accounting for your leads, you cannot have good reporting. Without good accounting and reporting, your MLDR scores will not stack up because this affects many other areas in your scoring.

Direction—Performance and Direction reports are very simple to use. When you get your performance reports and review them, what do you do with the information? You should immediately write your performance and direction report. This is a month-end written report that gives your company direction toward the future as far as your marketing by channel is concerned. You must have good accounting and reporting of your leads in order to score high on your MLDR in this category.

Innovation and Execution—How innovative have you been in your marketing programs and processes? How well have you executed against these innovations? Make sure you list the innovations you made for the period being rated and then list the execution levels that you made against that innovation. This rating may be a little subjective, but just make sure you are always looking for ways to innovate and execute in marketing.

As stated before, I believe that lead domination is a journey, not a destination. The important thing is that the journey needs to be moving in a direction that is positive. Take the Marketing Lead Domination Rating (MLDR) test to find out where you are at present. Let us know how you did and if we can help you improve your scores.

Let's move on to the sales side of your enterprise and your Sales Lead Domination Rating (SLDR).

Sales Lead Domination Rating

Trait 13	Trait 14	Trait 15	Trait 16	Trait 17	Trait 18	Trait 19	Trait 20	Trait 21
1 5 10	1 5 10	1 5 10	1 5 10	1 5 10	1 5 10	1 5 10	1 5 10	1 5 10
Execution	Relation	Intent	Discovery	Product	Viewing	Close	Follow-up	Reporting

Figure 1-2

Figure 1-2 shows an example of the Sales Lead Domination Rating (SLDR) form, which is what we use to rate companies on their sales lead lifestyles. Your maximum score on a SLDR is 90. A score of 75 to 90 indicates a lead lifestyle and culture that is moving full speed toward lead domination. A score of 65 to 74 means a company is doing well but has lots of opportunity to improve. Any company with a SLDR score of 64 or below needs serious improvement in this sales area.

Relation—How well does your sales team do in developing sales relationships with its leads? Chapter 14 covers what it really takes to build a great relationship with your clients.

Intent—What is your intent when giving a presentation on your product? I hope it is to sell your product. If that is the case, how do you tell your client up front that this is your intent and have it be a positive part of your presentation?

Discovery—Presentations are *all* about discovering your clients' needs, specifically their essential needs. If you do not score high in this category, it will be almost impossible to reach your full potential. The information in chapter 16 is essential to your SLDR scoring, because if you are low here, you will be low also in many other sales categories. If you aren't discovering essential needs, you won't be making as many sales as you should.

Product—The features, advantages, and benefits of your product need to be tied to the essential needs of your clients. You can score high in this area as long as you are scoring high on discovery.

Viewing—This refers to presenting your physical product. You need to emphasize all the sensory benefits of your product and tie them to essential needs. This strategy really puts the emotion into your product presentation.

Close—Closing or gaining commitments is clearly the report card on all the sales sequences that came before it.

Follow-up—If you are not the best you can be here, your potential is reduced significantly. Chapter 20 shows you how to compete with the best in the world at lead follow-up. If you are not good in this area, the hyenas will be waiting for you.

Reporting—It is very important to review the performance of your sales team members, one-on-one, on a regular basis. Keep in mind that sales agents are the only people who produce revenue from your leads. This process is very important for lead domination.

Innovation and Execution—How innovative have you been in your sales programs and processes? How well did you execute against these innovations? Make sure you list the innovations you made for the period being rated and then list the execution levels you made against the innovations.

I truly hope this book has provided answers to the many questions you probably have had about how to increase your sales and marketing lead production in today's competitive world. Thanks for your interest in this valuable subject and for being a *Lead Domination* customer. Enjoy your journey and your success!

If you have any comments and or questions, feel free to email me at:

leaddomination@loreinstitute.com

Keep up the great work!!

Hope you found great ideas from this book that you can use *today* in your sales and marketing worlds to be more effective with your lead management. Continue to use our 21 proven strategies and you will produce success for yourself and your company. For further advancement please update yourself in lead performance by getting our monthly newsletters.

P.S. Sorry there is no Hyena in the picture; he showed up late for the photo shoot.

Acknowledgments

DARRYL RUND was the one who, when I was twenty years old and working as a meat cutter for Safeway Stores, encouraged me to get my California real estate license as he had. That is how my sales and marketing career began. Without that encouragement, I am sure this book would not have been written. To a great inspirational friend who I will remember and cherish forever.

KENT HARRISON taught me that it's all about the people—that people work for people, not companies. Kent was a master trainer of sales agents and cared deeply about the people who worked with and for him. A lot of what is in the sales side of this book comes from what I learned from Kent over the years. Kent, your sales legacy continues to live on.

About the Author

JAMIE KLEIN has converted leads for companies into over a billion dollars of sales revenue. He is recognized as a sales-and-marketing expert in lead management both from a sales and a marketing standpoint.

He has held senior leadership positions in sales and marketing for many major brands, including Marriott, Four Seasons, and Starwood. He has invested more than thirty years in perfecting his lead management, sales, and marketing practices, including twenty years operating his own highly successful company. Jamie is currently president of The Lore Institute. His company is dedicated to sharing best practices in lead management.

Jamie is a master at developing profitable sales and marketing enterprises through lead management, effectively managing growth, and converting challenges into opportunities. His artistry in lead management has allowed him to craft meaningful new programs to meet the demands of today's changing sales and marketing realities.

As a long-time music enthusiast, Jamie is proficient with a set of drums. His proximity to the ocean allows him to enjoy a variety of ocean-going activities, especially surfing. He improves his mental performance with a vigorous fitness training program. Jamie is a motorcycle aficionado and believes that the definition of motorcycle should read, "Harley Davidson."

He is as energetic about his avocations as he is about his vocation, the world of lead management.

About the Illustrator

BRUCE HIGDON began his cartooning career when a local newspaper bought his editorial cartoon. He was twelve years old at the time and has had the bug ever since.

Bruce graduated from Middle Tennessee State University in 1972 and entered the United States Army. He served in a variety of staff positions around the world.

His many travels also led to cartooning and illustrating numerous army post newspapers, such as *Soldiers, Army Magazine, Stars and Stripes*. Soon, other professional magazines picked up his one-panel strips.

Bruce left active duty in 1980 and began Bruce Higdon Studio in his native Murfreesboro, Tennessee. He continued his editorial and gag cartooning as a daily cartoonist for the *Murfreesboro Press*. His editorials were also picked up by a variety of Tennessee newspapers. Magazines in Canada, Germany, and the US ran the gag cartoons.

The desire to do more illustration led to a three-year stint with the CBS affiliate, WTVF-TV, as a courtroom artist. He illustrated several major murder trials for television and newspapers, as well as federal trials and appeals. Bruce expanded his caricature service to include many major corporate programs.

Today, retired from the US Army as a lieutenant colonel, he lives with his wife, Yong, and two children in Murfreesboro. Bruce continues to freelance his cartoons, caricatures, and illustrations. His work can be seen at *www.punderstatements.com*.

Index

Give the Gift of

Lead Domination

to Your Friends and Colleagues

CHECK YOUR LEADING BOOKSTORE OR ORDER HERE

❏ **YES**, I want _____ copies of *Lead Domination* at $35.00 each hardcover, or $29.00 each softcover, plus $4.95 shipping per book (California residents please add 7.75% sales tax per book). Canadian orders must be accompanied by a postal money order in U.S. funds. Allow 15 days for delivery.

❏ **YES**, I am interested in having Jamie Klein speak or give a seminar to my company, association, school, or organization. Please send information.

My check or money order for $_____ is enclosed.

Please charge my: ❏ Visa   ❏ MasterCard
                   ❏ Discover   ❏ American Express

Name _____

Organization _____

Address _____

City/State/Zip _____

Phone_____ Email _____

Card # _____

Exp. Date_____ Signature _____

Please make your check payable and return to:
Lore Institute Publishing
3824 Vista Blanca • San Clemente, CA 92672

Call your credit card order to: 949-544-1506
Fax: 949-492-3391   **www.loreinstiute.com**